The Importance of Being Honest

Steven Lubet

The Importance of Being Honest

How Lying, Secrecy, and Hypocrisy
Collide with Truth in Law

New York University Press   •   *New York and London*

NEW YORK UNIVERSITY PRESS
New York and London
www.nyupress.org

Library of Congress Cataloging-in-Publication Data
Lubet, Steven.
The importance of being honest : how lying, secrecy, and hypocrisy collide
with truth in law / Steven Lubet.
p.   cm.
Includes bibliographical references and index.
ISBN-13: 978-0-8147-5221-0 (cl : acid-free paper)
ISBN-10: 0-8147-5221-7 (cl : acid-free paper)
1. Legal ethics—United States. 2. Practice of law—United States—Corrupt
practices. 3. Administration of justice—United States. 4. Truthfulness
and falsehood.   I. Title.
KF306.L834 2008
174'.30973—dc22   2007045955

New York University Press books are printed on acid-free paper,
and their binding materials are chosen for strength and durability.

Manufactured in the United States of America

10 9 8 7 6 5 4 3 2 1

To Doris Lubet

Contents

Preface

It happened in the late spring of 1995, on Chicago's predominantly white southwest side. A tough cop, appropriately nicknamed "Bulldog," came up to an African-American grammar school student, shoved him around while spewing a string of racial slurs, and warned the youngster to stay in his own neighborhood. The boy's white friends and teachers tried to intervene, but there was nothing they could to do restrain Bulldog. Perhaps worse, Bulldog's partner — also a white male cop — stood by watching, as though roughing up a black kid was just a routine part of life in the big city.

Fortunately, the student's teachers did not see it that way. They contacted the press, and Bulldog's bullying eventually made headlines — leading to widespread public outrage and calls for the officer to be fired or even prosecuted. No one supports rogue cops, at least not after they've made the evening news, and Bulldog was soon charged with violating the student's civil rights, for which he was placed on federal court supervision (although he was allowed to remain on the police force). That seemed to be a relatively happy ending, and the television and print reporters predictably went on to cover other stories.

It struck me at the time, however, that the problem was much broader than a single confrontation between one hateful officer and one innocent kid. The entire judicial system is put at risk by racist cops because they destroy any sense of trust between minority communities and the police, and that can lead to a breakdown in law enforcement that potentially affects everyone. None of the news coverage had picked up that angle — too abstract, too impersonal, too unemotional — and so I wrote and submitted my first op-ed essay for the *Chicago Tribune*.

> Maybe you think that you won't ever run afoul of Bulldog or that you won't ever need to trust him. Maybe you think that you can live securely in your suburb or high rise, and that Bulldog's boorish conduct can be relegated to the realm of distasteful, but ultimately irrelevant, events.

But that would be wrong. Anyone can be the victim of a crime. Anyone can need the help of the police. Anyone might have to rely on a police officer's veracity, integrity or honor. But when the police are dishonored, as Bulldog and too many others like him have dishonored the Chicago force, that trust just vanishes. And in the absence of trust, the police cannot really protect anyone. Fewer crimes will be reported. Fewer citizens will come to the aid of the police. Fewer witnesses will come forward. Indeed, fewer juries will be satisfied with police evidence and fewer criminals will go to jail.

Never having written for a newspaper before, I was unprepared for the response. I got dozens of phone calls and letters (no e-mail yet in those days) thanking me for writing the column. Invariably, callers would say that they hadn't thought about the broader context of the problem or it's implications for law enforcement. Many people — especially non-lawyers — encouraged me to continue writing about law, especially if I could explain the murkier or less obvious details of the judicial system.

Soon enough, I found myself writing fairly regularly for the *Tribune*, as well as for *Newsday*, the *San Francisco Chronicle*, and several other major newspapers. I recorded a dozen or so commentaries for *National Public Radio*. One of my columns was quoted by Senator Tom Harkin, though without crediting me, in the only evidentiary objection during the entire Clinton impeachment trial (Chief Justice Rehnquist sustained the objection, which might have made me famous if only Harkin had mentioned my name). And it turned out that lawyers, too, are interested in non-technical writing about law. In 2003 I was recruited to write the "Dicta" column for *The American Lawyer*, the idea being — as my then-editor put it — to bring some "Midwestern perspectives" to the magazine.

If there has been one overriding theme in my writing, it is the centrality of honesty (broadly construed) to the integrity of the legal system (also broadly construed). Often, of course, the issues are obvious. Lying witnesses and duplicitous lawyers are dishonest by any standard, and therefore deadly to the administration of justice. On the other hand, the "honesty" question is frequently more subtle. It is easy to see, for example, that Bulldog was a racist and a thug, but he was also a fraud — promising to "serve and protect," when he actually used his badge to smack down anyone who seemed smaller or weaker. And as I tried to point out in that long-ago op-ed, his hypocrisy was ultimately more dangerous than his brutality.

The essays in this book explore the interplay between honesty and candor — or their absence — and the various participants in the legal professions. Sometimes the relationship is direct (as in the case of Oscar Wilde's perjury in his notorious 1896 libel trial), and sometimes it is much more indirect (as in Justice Antonin Scalia's refusal to disqualify himself in the famous 2004 duck hunt case), but I trust that readers will recognize that, even though there is no single definition of honesty, we may fail to achieve it in nearly infinite ways.

Acknowledgments

I am deeply indebted to Dirk Olin and Aric Press, who gave me the opportunity to write for *The American Lawyer,* and to Marcia Lythcott, my long-time editor at the *Chicago Tribune.* I have also benefited over the years from the assistance and input of Jim Foody, Pat Tremmel, Marcia Lehr, Ann Nelson, Jeff Berkson, Don Wycliff, Bob Yovovich, Cynthia Cotts, Jeff Mallow, Kenneth Mallory, and Pegeen Bassett. I am particularly grateful to several coauthors, who have kindly agreed to the adaptation of our mutual work for inclusion in this book: Robert Burns ("The Benevolent Otolaryngolgist"), Tom Hankinson ("Truth in Humor"), and David McGowan ("Confirmation Mud"). I am grateful as well for the generous support of the Spray Trust Fund of the Northwestern University School of Law.

None of this would have been possible without Linda, Sarah, and Natan — they know why.

Introduction

IT IS IMPORTANT to be honest, but that does not mean it is easy. Consider the challenges of simply providing truthful testimony in court. Numerous discrete steps are involved, with opportunities for error at each stage.

- First, a witness needs to have been in a position to observe the relevant events, free from distraction or obstruction.
- In addition, the witness must have been able to observe the entire event, or at least its significant aspects, rather than some unrepresentative part.
- Moreover, the witness must reliably know — not merely assume — that she saw and heard everything of consequence.
- Even then, there is no guarantee that the witness perceived the events accurately — she may have seen things out of context or from an odd angle, or she may have misconstrued certain words and gestures.
- Next, of course, she has to understand everything she perceived, drawing accurate conclusions and avoiding inappropriate suppositions.
- When she finally she gets to court — perhaps months or years later — she has to remember the necessary facts, without gaps or elaboration.
- Even total recall is not enough, however, because she also has to articulate her memories with sufficient clarity and in coherent order.
- Then there is the question of emphasis — our witness must be able to stress the truly important details, without dwelling on trivia or meandering through meaningless details.

But even if our witness somehow manages to succeed in all that, there is no guarantee that the fact-finder will actually understand her. The judge or jury will also have to overcome comparable difficulties of perception, perspective, comprehension, memory, and interpretation. And these may be skewed by extraneous factors (subtle or otherwise) such as bias, preconception, self-interest, self-doubt, self-delusion, fear, caution, sympathy, cynicism, mistrust, attraction, resentment, idealism, conjecture, and more.

Honesty is elusive for all of the players in the legal system — clients, lawyers, judges, teachers — even with the best intentions, because it is inherently difficult to recognize, communicate, and appreciate the truth. Other values, such as confidentiality, autonomy, and fairness, also play a role. Sometimes secrets must be kept and accurate information must be barred. Still, most lawyers do their best to be honest, dealing as much as possible only in truth, within the limits of self-awareness and procedural constraints.

No one pays much attention to honest lawyers, however, for the excellent reason that there is not much to say about them. To paraphrase Leo Tolstoy's famous observation about happy families, all honest lawyers are alike. Or to put it somewhat differently, there is really only one way to be honest — whether we define honesty as truthfulness, candor, integrity, or something else ineffable — which ultimately makes the subject unremarkable, mostly routine if not quite mundane.

Without basic honesty, our entire judicial system — with its structure of rights, autonomy, due process, and the rule of law — would collapse because we could not rely on the good faith of the human beings who administer it. Honesty-deficient lawyers and judges — and, yes, law professors — can do enormous and unpredictable harm to both individuals and institutions because, again paraphrasing Tolstoy, every dishonest lawyer is dishonest in his or her own way.

And it is not only the out-and-out liars who spell trouble. There are nearly innumerable ways, either bold or subtle, in which lawyers can fall short: obfuscation, exaggeration, guile, concealment, misrepresentation, trickery, omission. It is intriguing simply to list these potential departures from pristine honesty, and there are many more, because — let's face it — not all such conduct is prohibited by the legal profession, and sometimes it is even rewarded. In this context, honesty is an elusive aspiration — a platonic ideal — and its negative complement is not so much dishonesty as imperfection.

It is that conundrum, of course, which proves to be endlessly engaging. The legal professions turn out to have a complex and often discomfiting approach to honesty. To be sure, we prize its positive virtues, including disclosure, transparency, and forthrightness. In contrast we condemn such subversive behaviors as lying, cheating, scamming, and fraud. That seems clear enough, but not everything in the world, much less in the courts, can be easily characterized as true or false. Most lawyers operate in the vast distance between those two absolutes, where facts are muddy, motivations are enigmatic, loyalties may be clouded, and duties are frequently vague or contradictory. It is there that we find not only the ever-present temptations to deceit, but also several inescapable impediments to absolute honesty that affect even the most sincere attorneys.

It is a given that faithful lawyers are required to keep clients' confidences and pursue clients' goals. Thus, law practice invariably involves a good deal of selective omission, skillful evasion, and, shall we say, the artful characterization of inconvenient facts. In addition, there are other factors that make it difficult — for lawyers, clients, judges, critics, and everyone else — to recognize or accept the truth. No one is immune to some small measure of hypocrisy, self-delusion, denial, or wishful thinking, all of which diminish our ability to appreciate — and therefore our ability to convey — the utter truth.

The essays in the following pages will explore the strained relationship between honesty and the major participants in the legal system, dividing the discussion into five parts: Clients, Lawyers, Judges, Professors, and a final section on the frequently posited analogy between law practice and medicine. The focus is primarily on poor behavior and questionable practices — not because they are more prevalent or important than elementary decency, but because they are more instructive. In every field, much knowledge is gained from negative examples: pathologists study illnesses to learn more about health; city planners observe traffic jams so that they may eliminate congestion; climatologists measure CO^2 emissions in order to preserve the environment. Thus, we can learn a great deal about improving the legal system by understanding where and how it goes wrong.

Clients

We begin where lawyers always begin, with the perpetually challenging complexities of clients, who, as the Greek philosopher Protagorus would have put it, are the measure of all things. It is not unusual to divide the universe of clients into the two general categories of innocent and guilty (or perhaps blameless or at fault in civil cases, or, more broadly, either decent or unworthy), but that would be inaccurate. From a lawyer's perspective, clients are best described as either reliable or unreliable.

Reliable clients are the best sort because they provide their attorneys with accurate and complete information, thus making possible effective representation. In that sense, reliability stands quite apart from whether a client is right or wrong on the merits. Bad people can be represented quite well, within the bounds of the law, so long as counsel has a realistic understanding of the situation. Good people, alas, hurt only themselves when they keep their lawyers in the dark.

In litigation, some clients simply lie to their lawyers in the misguided hope of selling a phony story to a credulous judge, jury, or adversary. In business transactions, unscrupulous clients entangle unsuspecting lawyers in their slick schemes by getting them to "paper" all manner of crooked deals, fraudulent stock offerings, fictional enterprises, or other imaginative swindles. These baneful characters, though dismayingly difficult to recognize, are bad news for their unfortunate attorneys — lost cases, unpaid fees, professional embarrassment, tort liability, disciplinary proceedings, and sometimes even indictment. Such clients are willfully unreliable, and the only true remedy is to avoid them at all cost.

But a client does not need to be treacherous in order to be unreliable. Because everyone is fallible, especially when it comes to memory and communication, many otherwise respectable clients may convey undependable information. They may do so because they are intimidated, naïve, suspicious, ignorant, arrogant, or merely foolish, and while some of these motives and causations are more excusable than others (it is much easier to forgive fear than bravado), most can be overcome through close questioning and patient explanation of the lawyer's role.

It doesn't always work, but clients tend to become more reliable as their attorneys become more trustworthy.

Lawyers

Every lawyer must constantly contend with the conflicting demands of client loyalty and responsibilities to others, generally putting the client's interests first. Clients may be selfish, inconsiderate, greedy, or mean, but it is nonetheless important to protect their rights and pursue their objectives. It is only a slight overstatement to say that respect for individual autonomy is the defining characteristic of constitutional government and a successful free-market economy, and that lawyers are therefore the stewards of political liberty and social prosperity. Unfortunately, it does not always appear that way.

It is a sad reality that some lawyers abuse their clients' trust or exploit their privileged position in the legal system. They lie or steal or assist in all sorts of nefarious deeds. When caught, they bring disrepute upon themselves and betray their profession. Every bad actor helps create the impression that most lawyers, if perhaps not all, are corrupt connivers dedicated solely to self-enrichment.

That is a hard image to shake because good attorneys do, in fact, doggedly seek to maximize outcomes for their clients, often at considerable cost to others. There are winners and losers in every litigated case, and often in settlements and commercial transactions as well. It is difficult for the public to understand that lawyers provide a widespread social benefit by single-mindedly representing individual interests, especially when the particular individuals are marginalized, unpopular, or disgraced. Unfortunately, many political commentators have seized upon this phenomenon as an excuse to discredit the entire profession, ignoring the diffuse benefits of the adversary system while vilifying the advocates who labor within it.

It is important to be honest about the role of counsel in a free society. Thus, this section of this book will address not only the failings of attorneys themselves, but also the ways in which the legal system has been regrettably, and dangerously, mischaracterized for political purposes.

Judges

Certain judges, needless to say, have their own set of problems with honesty, and I'm not just talking about graft and extortion. Relatively few judges ever take bribes or solicit kickbacks, although judicial miscreants naturally make headlines when they are caught. Fortunately, most lawyers, and litigants, will spend their lifetimes in the courts without ever directly encountering a corrupt judge.

Many more judges, however, fail badly at the task of honest self-appraisal. Entrusted with enormous authority over the rights and fortunes of their fellow citizens (and granted lifetime tenure, in the case of federal judges), they delude themselves into believing that they have special powers of perception and wisdom. Some few judges exhibit the well-known

"God complex," demanding abject obeisance from all who appear before them (and pity the mortal lawyer who offers an affront). Others intermittently demonstrate less serious episodes of "black robe fever," becoming overbearing, short tempered, or arbitrary. And even the best judges have their occasional lapses — ignoring rules of conduct, flouting public expectations, dismissing legitimate concerns — usually because they are unable to recognize in themselves the faults they would censure in others.

These dispositions can be deeply corrosive, verging on the sort of intellectual dishonesty that ultimately tends to undermine the judicial process — "I know it's the right decision, because I'm the one who is making it!" More frequently, the problem amounts only to what we might call "introspection deficit disorder," which is still unpleasant when encountered but not nearly as destructive as absolutism and grandiosity.

It is ironic that so many judges — whose jobs ideally call for reflection, discernment, patience, and, as Chief Justice John Roberts explained at his confirmation hearing, humility — so often fall prey to the vices of egoism, obduracy, arrogance, and (it has to be said) narcissism. Perhaps some preternatural measure of prideful confidence comes in handy, and may even be necessary from time to time, if one is to deliver decisive judgments. In any event, it is no small feat, particularly among the anointed and august, to "see ourselves as others see us." It is therefore understandable, though far from optimal, that judges can be less than searchingly candid when they assess their own behavior or evaluate their own performance.

Academics

Judges and lawyers all began their careers as law students, eager to pursue an onerous course of study and ready for their instructors to initiate them in the intricacies of their chosen profession. At least during the first few semesters, law students look up to their teachers, expecting them to be not only knowledgeable about the black-letter law, but also candid about their own viewpoints and interpretations. A good teacher openly flags his or her opinions and does not try to pass them off as revealed truth. In a world where arguments are evaluated largely on their formal "strength" rather than according to some measure of elemental validity, a diligent law professor can inject a much-needed counterweight of intellectual rigor, and perhaps even objectivity. Many professors are in fact idealists, committed to open-minded inquiry and determined to teach their charges to be thoughtful and tolerant, but the academy also has its fair share (if not more) of cynicism and hypocrisy.

The failings of law professors are often manifested by sharp inconsistencies between what they say and what they do. It is not hard to identify professors who are dedicated to "cutting-edge" research, although increasingly detached from the real world; theoretically broad-minded, but actually narrow and doctrinaire; stern and demanding when it comes to students' assignments, while enjoying the leisure of a minimal teaching load; ostensibly devoted to "neutral principles" that (just coincidentally, mind you) always lead to conveniently partisan results.

Law professors seem to resemble judges in the general nature of their faults — much self-regard and little self-doubt — but there is a significant difference. Judges make meaningful, and sometimes momentous, decisions about people's lives. The impact of teaching and scholarship, with few exceptions, is far less dramatic and much less immediate. After all, what difference does a student's grade make, or the publication of a law review article, compared to a hefty money judgment or a prison sentence? You might therefore expect academics to be rather modest about their enterprise and qualified in their conclusions, but that is not always so. Instead, we find teachers in every field who are dogmatic in their beliefs, rigid in defense of the academic (if not social) status quo, defensive of their perquisites, devoted to hidden agendas, and impatient with outsiders.

Then again, universities have always been a soft target for critics, easily portrayed as the province of absent-minded, fuzzy-thinking, self-indulgent eggheads. Beyond the campus, does anyone even use the word "intellectual" without some slight hint of mockery? Henry Kissenger never really observed that "academic politics are vicious because the issues are so petty," but the caricature is attractive and the imagery is indelible. Every institution can benefit from a little ridicule now and then, but let's be fair. Professors are sincerely committed, by and large, to free expression and the unlimited exchange of ideas. Such lofty ideals are far easier to profess than they are to achieve, so it is foreseeable that we will often stumble.

Medical Practice

There was a time in American life, not so long ago, when lawyers and doctors formed a fairly small and relatively cohesive professional elite — living in the same neighborhoods, belonging to the same clubs and civic organizations, and generally holding each other in good regard. That was before the advent of managed care, the explosion in the sheer number of lawyers, the expansion of state and federal regulatory regimes, the rise of consumer advocacy, the demise of "professional courtesy," the proliferation of tawdry prime-time soap operas, and many similar social and political developments. In the old days, doctors and lawyers believed that they shared, or mutually appreciated, a core set of professional values. Lately, not so much.

Today, doctors and lawyers often seem to be at war. Many physicians complain that they are under assault by a legal system run amok — victimized by ridiculous standards of malpractice liability, penalized by runaway juries, coerced into unfair settlements, and driven to debt by exorbitant insurance premiums. For all of that, and more, they are resentful of judges and angry at lawyers.

In response, lawyers tend to be, frankly, jealous. Doctors, for all their travails, have managed to maintain great public respect. They are widely admired for their altruism, dedication, education, competence, and (despite the occasional scandal) integrity. Lawyers, on the other hand, have become the objects of derision and the subjects of low humor. Even lawyers tell lawyer jokes, whose punch lines inevitably play on some variation of deceit, cupidity, or richly deserved popular scorn.

When doctors are idealized as saintly healers, while attorneys are stereotyped as ethically challenged con artists, it is predictable that many lawyers and lawyer-commentators will look to physicians as models for a better practice paradigm. Perhaps the legal profession could redeem itself — maybe even regain some public trust — if only lawyers behaved more like doctors.

As attractive and hopeful as it may be, the analogy between law practice and medicine is plainly inaccurate. Lawyers proceed from an ethic of autonomy and are required to advocate a client's self-determined goals (so long as they are evidently lawful). Physicians, on the other hand, proceed from an ethic of care (sometimes called benevolence or even paternalism), in which they may administer or withhold treatments according to considerations that may go beyond a patient's immediate requests.

It is that very dissimilarity, however, that makes it useful to compare the practices of law and medicine, with each as a foil for the other. This is particularly the case concerning such honesty-freighted issues as candor, disclosure, and confidentiality, where the norms of attorneys and physicians call for sharply different approaches. Indeed, the comparison of the two professions — single-minded champions of individual rights versus tempered guardians of public health — can help explain just why lawyers do what they do. Surprisingly, lawyers' ethics (the formal rules, that is, if not the daily instantiations) may sometimes provide important lessons for physicians, especially when it comes to practical matters such as conflicts of interest and informed consent.

PART I

Clients

Introduction

THIS SECTION BEGINS with the story of a famous client who did not trust his lawyer, much to his later regret. "Sex, Lies, and Depositions" addresses Bill Clinton's disastrous decision to lie under oath, and explains how his attorney could have saved the president from embarrassment, impeachment, and near ruin — if only the big guy had been candid with counsel.

In contrast, some clients place too much weight on their lawyers' shoulders, attempting to evade responsibilities for their own decisions with the highly questionable claim that "My Lawyer Made Me Do It." Regrettably, some clients go even further, using their lawyers to make outrageous claims, in the hope of intimidating adversaries. That is what happened in the case of "McKinney's Bluff," although the tactic ultimately failed to work.

The next essay presents a situation where no one is lying or blustering, but where the moral truth is still difficult to ascertain. In "Morally Gray," clients on both sides of a lawsuit present sincere and legitimate claims, and there is no easy way to tell which one should win.

"The Truth about Torts" takes the discussion of moral values to a broader level, illustrating virtues of personal injury litigation that have often been obscured and explaining some of the false premises of so-called "tort reform."

The next two essays address the ways that clients may either fail or succeed to explain themselves. "A Missing Witness" explains how Martha Stewart never managed to tell the story of her own innocence, while "Freedom Stories" expands on the power of stories to convey the truth.

Finally, this section ends as it began, with a famous client who lied (about sex) to his lawyer and in court. "The Importance of Being Honest" is the story of Oscar Wilde's self-destructive (and perjurious) testimony in his celebrated defamation suit against the Marquess of Queensberry in 1895.

1

Sex, Lies, and Depositions

ON JANUARY 17, 1998, President Bill Clinton testified at what turned out to be the most significant deposition in the history of the United States. Sworn to tell the truth, he calmly lied about his affair with Monica Lewinsky, falsely stating that he was never alone with her and that he never had sexual relations with her. He would soon repeat his lies on television — "I never had sex with that woman" — and several months later he would attempt to wriggle out of the falsehoods in his videotaped grand jury testimony. But the harm was done. Clinton teetered for nearly a year on the edge of political ruin, becoming only the second president in history to be impeached. Although Clinton never came close to constitutional dispossession, the scandal continued to take its toll. In all likelihood, it cost Al Gore the 2000 presidential election — either because it alienated voters from the Democratic Party, or because the skittish Gore decided not to allow Clinton to campaign with him (or both).

Dozens of books have been written about the Clinton era — by insiders, adversaries, journalists, and even a sitting federal judge. Finally, we got *My Life*, the massive autobiography of Clinton himself, covering the years from his Arkansas boyhood until the inauguration of George W. Bush.

Predictably, much of the buzz was created by Clinton's comments on his affair with Monica Lewinsky ("immoral and foolish . . . my selfish stupidity") and its impact on his family life ("I slept on the couch"). From a professional perspective, however, it is much more interesting to consider Clinton's relationship to one of his lawyers, Robert Bennett, who represented him in the Paula Jones litigation.

Paula Jones sued Clinton for an incident of sexual harassment that allegedly occurred while he was governor of Arkansas. Clinton tells us that he had an early opportunity to head off the case by paying Jones a nominal amount and helping her husband find work in Hollywood. He refused to pay, however, "because I hadn't sexually harassed her." Instead, he hired Bob Bennett to defend him.

Bennett is an exceptionally talented Washington lawyer, highly regarded as a litigator by everyone who knows him. In fact, he eventually succeeded in getting the Jones case dismissed on summary judgment, although not until after the political damage was irreparable. There were other strategies available to Bennett that might have saved Clinton from lying under oath. Unfortunately, Clinton himself evidently foreclosed those options, insisting on a more aggressive approach to the litigation.

And even more significantly, it appears that the president consistently lied to his own lawyer. The details have to be pieced together, but the factual situation seems clear.

As the fateful deposition approached, Clinton had every reason to know that he would be asked about his sexual relationships with female employees, as both governor of Arkansas and president of the United States. As he put it, "The presiding judge, Susan Webber Wright, had given Jones's lawyers broad permission to delve into my private life, allegedly to see if there was a pattern of sexual harassment involving any women who had held or sought state employment when I was governor or federal employment when I was president." An astute attorney himself, Clinton says that he was "certain that the lawyers wanted to force me to acknowledge any kind of involvement with one or more women that they could leak to the press." Moreover, he could not have doubted that Monica Lewinsky's name would come up at the deposition because she had been disclosed on the plaintiff's witness list a month or so earlier.

In advance of the deposition, Clinton had "gone over a series of possible questions with my lawyers," concluding that "I was reasonably well prepared." He did not, however, tell them anything about Lewinsky. Did they ask him about other women? It seems impossible that they did not. Robert Bennett has honorably maintained his silence about his representation of the president, respecting the attorney-client privilege even as everyone else has gone public. But no competent lawyer, let alone the super-capable Bennett, would have failed to ask a client about every person named on the opposing side's witness list. Given the transparency of the plaintiff's tactics — trying to force Clinton to talk about sexual liaisons — we can be all but certain that Bennett put the question directly to his client.

To put it bluntly, Clinton expected to be asked about Lewinsky and he planned to lie, keeping his lawyer in the dark so that he could be sure to get away with it.

True to form, Jones's lawyers used the deposition to pound away at Clinton's relationship with Lewinsky. As Clinton recalls, they asked "how well I knew her, whether we had ever exchanged gifts, whether we had ever talked on the phone, and if I had had 'sexual relations' with her." Silently relying on Judge Wright's somewhat incomplete definition, which arguably excluded unreciprocated oral sex, Clinton "answered no to the 'sexual relations' question."

During a break in the testimony, Clinton discussed Lewinsky with his lawyers, lying to them once more. "My legal team was perplexed," he says, "because Lewinsky's name had shown up on the plaintiff's list of potential witnesses only in early December, and she had been given a subpoena to appear as a witness two weeks later." Of course, they would not have been at all perplexed if Clinton had simply told them the truth about her. Instead, he continued to mislead his lawyers: "I didn't tell them about my relationship with her, but I did say I was unsure of exactly what the curious definition of sexual relations meant."

What are we to make of that assertion? We know, of course, that Clinton did not tell Bennett or the other lawyers about his affair with Lewinsky, which he continued to deny until the following August (after Ken Starr leaked information about the "genetic material" on Monica's now-famous blue dress). But did the president really hint so broadly to his lawyers that a less "curious" definition would lead to a more explicit answer about his sexual relations? Again, we will probably never learn Bennett's version, but it is extremely unlikely that he would have failed to put two and two together. Imagine how the conversation would have gone between lawyer and client (based solely on Clinton's own account):

BENNETT: Mr. President, we are perplexed. Why are they asking you about sexual relations with Monica Lewinsky?

CLINTON: I don't know. But I am unsure what is meant by the curious definition of "sexual relations."

Is it even remotely conceivable that Bennett would have failed to ask a single follow-up question? So we are left with only two plausible scenarios. Either Clinton's memoir is, to put it gently, inaccurate about the hint to Bennett (diverting some of the blame to his lawyer for not figuring out what was going on), or Bennett actually pursued the hint but obtained only more misinformation from his client.

Yes, technically there is a third possibility — namely, that Bill Clinton came clean with Bennett, who then willingly facilitated his client's perjury. In truth, however, that is just about impossible. First, it would have been unethical, and no one has ever suggested that Bennett is anything other than a completely ethical practitioner. Second, we know that Clinton persisted in lying to everyone in sight—his wife, his daughter, his cabinet, his advisors, the American public, and the entire world—so there is no reason to think that he was honest with Bennett. And finally, Bennett was surely smart enough to know that Clinton was courting disaster by lying, and he would have taken immediate steps to get his client out of a quickly deepening hole.

Nearly all of Clinton's woes, up to and including his impeachment, are traceable to his perjury in the Jones deposition. Ultimately, there was no proof that he ever induced anyone else to lie, or that he concealed evidence, or that he destroyed gifts from Monica Lewinsky. But there was no doubt (among any but the most credulous) that he flatly lied in his deposition, and was later less than candid about it when he testified before a grand jury. Clinton himself remains in denial. He wasn't lying, he writes; it was merely that he "had not been trying to be helpful to the Jones lawyers." Or, as he testified to the grand jury, "I was determined to walk through the minefield of this deposition without violating the law, and I believe I did."

Well, he was mistaken. Both Independent Counsel Kenneth Starr and the House of Representatives' impeachment managers concluded that Clinton had violated the law—no surprise there, of course, and not exactly an objective assessment. But so too did Judge Susan Webber Wright, who held Clinton in contempt of court for his "willful failure" to testify truthfully. "Simply put," said the judge, "the president's deposition testimony regarding whether he had ever been alone with Ms. Lewinsky was intentionally false and his statements regarding whether he had ever engaged in sexual relations with Ms. Lewinsky likewise were intentionally false." Clinton was also compelled to surrender his Arkansas law license, admitting that he intentionally gave "evasive and misleading answers" that were "prejudicial to the administration of justice."

The greatest irony—or tragedy, or perhaps farce—is that Bennett could have rescued Clinton, if only the president had told him the truth. Adequately forewarned, Robert Bennett surely would have counseled his client to tell the truth and to skip the coy evasion. If the president refused, there were still feasible alternatives. They could have refused to attend the deposition, claiming that the United States Supreme Court erred in ruling that a sitting president is subject to civil legal proceedings. Or they could have refused to answer "inappropriately personal questions," asserting a right to privacy.

Either measure would have been drastic, but still far preferable to lying — and much less dangerous. Judge Wright would obviously have imposed sanctions under the Federal Rules of Civil Procedure, but they would have been trivial compared to the eventual upshot of Clinton's testimony. In fact, even the most severe sanction — entry of a default judgment — would not have been so bad. It would have ended the case completely, resulting only in the payment of some money by Clinton. And probably not very much money at that. Jones would still have had to prove up her damages, which were relatively modest — by her own account she quickly rebuffed Clinton's crude proposition, and she was never fired or demoted. At worst, she would have gotten the full $700,000 demanded in her complaint, which would have been more than offset by the small fortune in legal fees that Clinton would have saved.

Even after defaulting, Clinton could have maintained his public denial of sexual harassment. A default judgment is not an admission of guilt. Clinton could have characterized his withdrawal from the case as a decision to spare the presidency from the intrusive indignity of the lawsuit, announcing that he would rather spend his time running the country than worrying about lawyers and litigation. In the hands of a masterful politician, a default judgment might have been portrayed as the high road — a noble financial sacrifice for the sake of safeguarding the independence of his office.

We can be almost certain that Bennett asked about Clinton's relationships with women, and Monica Lewinsky in particular, but we do not know how sharply he inquired. Should Bennett have probed more deeply, asking sharper questions and refusing to accept Clinton's blanket denials? Should he have realized that the legacy of the Clinton administration was in his hands?

It is always hard to press your client, and it must be impossibly difficult when he is the president of the United States, the most powerful individual in the world. Bennett cannot be faulted for taking Clinton at his word, or even for failing to pick up on a few oblique hints (if indeed they were given). Robert Bennett trusted his client; it is only too bad that Bill Clinton could not bring himself to return the favor.

2

My Lawyer Made Me Do It

SOONER OR LATER, nearly every lawyer has to confront some variant on the dilemma of zealous representation. How do we justify representing clients whose goals are morally questionable or even flatly offensive? The standard answer is that lawyers serve society by facilitating client autonomy, allowing individuals and corporations to make informed decisions about their legal rights. As Samuel Johnson explained nearly 250 years ago, "A lawyer is to do for his client all that his client might fairly do for himself." Thus, corporate counsel (following each new accounting fraud) and public defenders (in almost every case) deliver the same ready reply to a relentlessly familiar question: How can you defend those people? Well, it isn't always easy, but we are just doing our job.

That is why lawyers are convenient foils, resolutely (if not gladly) taking the heat for their clients. It is also why you so often hear corporate officials or political leaders insist that they "cannot comment" on matters that are "under investigation" or "subject to litigation." No one really believes that hooey, but it is semi-respectable because it is so transparent. It may well be prudent to clam up, especially if you have something to hide, but nothing a lawyer recommends can ultimately prevent an individual from discussing pending litigation. So the "no comment" approach is generally recognized as a face-saving ploy, raised to avoid uncomfortable — and too frequently incriminatory — inquiries by invoking the advice of counsel.

Acknowledging a lawyer's advice is one thing, and accepting it is another, but both are far different from claiming to be a helpless bystander in your own case. Client autonomy, which lawyers are obligated to respect, creates significant responsibilities that cannot simply be reassigned to counsel. Of course, that doesn't stop clients from trying to shift the blame in sticky situations, but you usually expect that sort of behavior from, say, habitual polluters or sleazy congressmen. Until fairly recently, it was a safe bet that no lawyer ever had to worry about taking a hit for a client like the Catholic Archdiocese of Boston, but that was before the sexual abuse scandals that have rocked the church (and many other denominations) for nearly a decade. Almost without fail, high-stakes cases tend to bring out the worst in people, as they search for just about any useful dodge or trumped-up excuse for their conduct. The Boston situation turned out to be no exception, in a novel and rather surprising way.

The clergy abuse litigation in Boston — with over five hundred individual cases — was particularly extensive, involving numerous priests and allegations of repeated cover-ups. It was also extremely acrimonious on both sides. By 2003, many parishioners were openly questioning the basic decency of the church's legal strategy, going so far as to accuse the defense of inflicting new trauma on the abuse victims. Representatives of the archdiocese responded by blaming it all on their counsel — "Our lawyers made us do it" — as though the church had no control over the tactics employed in its name.

Amid charges of stonewalling and complicity, over fifty priests signed a letter declaring "no confidence" in Cardinal Bernard Law, a measure unprecedented in the Catholic Church in the United States. Law resigned in late 2002, and his temporary successor, Bishop Richard Lennon, immediately promised a new tone of reconciliation and healing. He announced his intention to settle the outstanding litigation and promised to make therapy available to every victim who came forward.

In the meantime, however, the church continued to mount a forceful defense in court, engaging in a level of trench warfare that would have made Johnnie Cochran proud. For example, defense lawyers filed a breathtaking motion to dismiss all five hundred cases on First Amendment grounds, arguing that the civil authorities could not interfere with the "bishop-priest relationship." It was claimed that the constant reassignment of known child molesters was beyond the reach of the law because the supervision of priests was exclusively an ecclesiastical matter.

Predictably, the motion was denied, but not before Bishop Lennon explained that his attorneys had insisted on the hardball tactic because "failure to do this could very well result in the insurance companies walking away from us, saying that we have not exercised all of our avenues of defense."

Sounding more like a caught-in-the-act politician than a clergyman, Bishop Lennon had actually adopted the classic lawyer's excuse. Absolving himself of any moral responsibility for the maneuver — much less the cost and anxiety it imposed on the injured plaintiffs — he invoked the nature of the legal process as justification for an outrageous ploy. Attorneys routinely seek to escape the consequences of their actions by deferring to their clients' instructions, but this was a new twist on an old theme. The bishop washed his hands of his own decision, blaming the insurers and lawyers instead.

Then things got worse. The church's defense team began serving deposition subpoenas on plaintiffs' psychotherapists, including some who had actually been hired by the archdiocese itself to provide treatment to abuse survivors. From a legal perspective, of course, this was not particularly out of the ordinary. The psychotherapist privilege is waived when a plaintiff claims damages for emotional trauma.

From a moral perspective, however, it was a disaster. The church had encouraged victims to come forward and had even set up a special Office of Healing and Assistance to facilitate therapy, as part of Bishop Lennon's announced preference for settlement over litigation. Then the archdiocese turned around and insisted on invading the patient-therapist relationship in a way that many victims regarded as jeopardizing their recovery.

The reaction was furious. A coalition of psychologists and victims' rights activists denounced the depositions as involving the "re-victimization" and "re-abuse" of patients who were "already broken members" of the church's flock. Without disputing the church's legal right to take the depositions, the group complained that the tactic was inconsistent with Lennon's professed commitment to justice and healing. The victims' therapy, they said, would be "permanently harmed by the intrusion of the legal system."

One prominent psychotherapist, who had previously been invited to address the United States Conference of Catholic Bishops, put it even more bluntly: "I think that this is very despicable and deceitful. To say [that] 'the church loves you' and 'we want to help you' and then to invade your treatment is really just wrong. It may be legally okay, but it's wrong."

In response, an archdiocesan spokeswoman declared that the depositions were lawful and necessary: "If the victims choose to sue . . . we feel that we're obligated to defend ourselves."

Maintaining that the archdiocese still supported therapy for survivors, she insisted that the support stood "separate and distinct from the litigation process." And lest there be any mistake, another church official remarked, "It's a very tragic set of circumstances, but when you get to the litigation stage, there are certain things lawyers insist on doing to protect their clients."

Thus, the Boston archdiocese inverted the very premise of the attorney-client relationship, relying on the purported demands of counsel to justify its own moral blundering. Lawyers naturally recommend strategies that enhance the likelihood of success in litigation. To those who see themselves as legal technicians, the human toll is irrelevant so long as the tactic is lawful. The client is simply entitled to zealous representation within the bounds of the law, and the attorney is helpless to refuse.

But that same stricture never applies to the clients themselves. There is no conception of litigation in which a client can decline to be an independent moral actor. In fact, the American Bar Association's Model Rules of Professional Conduct specifically call upon lawyers to "defer to the client" in regard to other "persons who might be adversely affected" by litigation. While any good lawyer would urge the archdiocese to authorize the depositions of victims' therapists, no lawyer could compel it. That is why we call it "advice of counsel."

The basic purpose of taking a therapist's deposition, after all, is to undermine the plaintiff's monetary claim for emotional distress. A good deposition transcript, filled with artfully extracted admissions and potential impeachment, becomes a useful weapon in negotiation or at trial. An early deposition in the midst of settlement talks is an unmistakably aggressive move — especially in the case of a vulnerable plaintiff who has suffered clergy abuse — but aggressive representation is never mandatory, and no lawyer could insist on it over the objection of his or her client.

There is no doubt that the leaders of the Boston archdiocese were entitled to choose their own defense strategy, whether it was compromise and settlement or litigation to the bitter end. As an outsider, I would have to defend their legal right to take either route. But no client has the moral right to raise the flag of reconciliation while instructing counsel to scorch the earth.

3

Morally Gray

IN A MORALLY challenging world, it is often difficult to figure out how to do the right thing. Nonetheless, you would think that reporting obvious child abuse would be one of life's less questionable decisions. Sometimes, however, even that manages to be complicated.

Just ask Shirley Gasper of Fremont, Nebraska. While she was working in a Wal-Mart photo lab, she came across a photograph of an infant crawling around in a pile of marijuana leaves mixed with $50 and $100 bills. Alarmed at what appeared to be an extremely dangerous situation, Gasper contacted the local police and gave them a copy of the print. Her fears were well founded. The authorities located the child, who turned out to be bruised and living in an unquestionably unsafe environment. Criminal charges were filed, and the child was taken into protective custody.

But that was not the end of the story. When Gasper's superiors at Wal-Mart found out about her actions, they responded by firing her. It seems that Wal-Mart had a policy requiring employees to notify store managers before turning photographs over to the police. Because Gasper did not follow the chain of command, she suddenly found herself out of a job.

Gasper hired a lawyer and sued her former employer for wrongful discharge. The case eventually went to trial in federal district court and proceeded to a jury verdict.

Gasper contended that she had had no choice. A child was clearly in danger, and her conscience compelled her to make an immediate report. It was just plain wrong for Wal-Mart to fire her for behaving like an exemplary citizen, she explained to a local newspaper: "The last thing I was expecting in this company was getting fired for trying to save a child."

Wal-Mart, of course, saw it differently. "We share the same concerns ... for the safety of the child," said a company spokesman, "[but] we also respect the confidentiality and privacy of our customers." For that reason, each store has a management team that makes decisions about suspicious photographs. According to Wal-Mart, Gasper was not fired for reporting child abuse, but for failing to allow her supervisors to participate in the decision.

Both arguments make good sense. Gasper was acting on the best of motives, seeking only to protect a vulnerable child. The local police praised her for coming forward. It is impossible not to be sympathetic to her claim that Wal-Mart acted unfairly, placing obedience to rules ahead of responsible citizenship. Good deeds should not be punished.

But there is also an institutional perspective. With hundreds of stores and thousands of employees, Wal-Mart strives to have a uniform policy regarding customer privacy. Although Shirley Gasper made a solid judgment about the photograph in question, another clerk in another situation might someday act more impulsively, calling the police over a completely innocent picture. Different people have different moral standards, after all, and Wal-Mart did not want to turn every photo clerk into an independent investigator or free-lance censor. Indeed, guidelines issued by the International Photo Marketing Association recommend that store managers always make the ultimate decision about whether to call the police.

So what is the right result? Was Wal-Mart recklessly endangering children or cautiously safeguarding privacy? Did the company unreasonably punish a hero or simply enforce a necessary policy?

Some people will say there is nothing more important than protecting children, and that Gasper therefore should have won her case. Others will say that Wal-Mart's rules are sound and enforceable, as they are intended to minimize false or unnecessary abuse reports.

Neither position is clearly superior to the other. A victory for Gasper would have probably fostered broader reporting to the police, perhaps exposing more child abuse, but also jeopardizing innocent people-such as the New Jersey grandmother who was arrested in 2000 when she picked up "baby-in-the-buff" photos that she had taken of her granddaughters. On the other hand, a Wal-Mart victory would discourage reporting, meaning that some crimes might never be discovered.

In truth, there is no single morally correct solution. But life is not a philosophy class, and it is not enough to say that the answer is ambiguous or indeterminate.

Gasper suffered a real-life loss. She was fired from her job, and she was entitled to a resolution of her claim. Wal-Mart likewise needed to know whether its policy was legally supportable.

All of which finally brings us back to the courthouse. Many complain that America is over-lawyered, but the fact is that we need a legal system that can resolve perplexing cases and sort out competing interests by allowing each side its day in court. We end up entrusting tough decisions to the courts not because we are litigation-happy, but because there is no better way to get clear-cut answers to otherwise unresolvable problems.

Ultimately, the role of the legal system is to settle disputes that we cannot settle for ourselves. This function is especially important when both sides have legitimate claims that they are unwilling to compromise.

And the verdict? Shirley Gasper's wrongful termination claim was rejected by the jury. Wal-Mart won. After hearing all of the arguments and listening to all of the evidence, the jury decided that Wal-Mart had the right to insist that employees consult their supervisors when deciding whether to report customers to the police. It is hard to say that the jurors were entirely correct because the impact on Gasper was so harsh. But it is also impossible to say that they were wrong. Acting in a moral gray area, the jury had to make a black-and-white decision.

You might argue with the verdict, and a different jury could sensibly have reached a different result. Juries cannot always deliver eternal truths or transcendent solutions, but they can usually give us workable answers after affording people the right to be heard. When that happens, the process works.

4

McKinney's Bluff

IF FORMER CONGRESSWOMAN Cynthia McKinney (D-Ga.) finally gets tired of politics, she probably shouldn't consider a career in poker. Although she obviously thinks she is skilled in the art of the bluff, she has a lot to learn about the risk of going "all in."

On March 29, 2006, McKinney was involved in a scuffle with a Capitol police officer when she tried to bypass the metal detector at the entrance to a government office building. Rather than apologize for hitting the guard, McKinney launched a caustic campaign to discredit the officer and characterize herself as the victim of police brutality. Her claims were extreme, but of course that was the point. The more aggressive the bluff, the more likely it is to work. Except when it doesn't.

While members of Congress are allowed to bypass the metal detectors, it turned out that McKinney was not wearing her identifying lapel pin at the time. According to one account, the officer repeatedly asked her to stop as she walked around the security station. When she continued walking, the officer tried to stop her, and she struck him at least once. It was soon reported that the Capitol police asked federal prosecutors to issue an arrest warrant for McKinney.

The congresswoman responded by lambasting the officer for failing to recognize her. "This whole incident was instigated," she said at a press conference, "by the inappropriate touching and stopping of me — a female, black congresswoman." McKinney's lawyer announced that she was considering filing a criminal complaint or civil lawsuit alleging racial profiling. "Ms. McKinney is just a victim of being in Congress while black," he said.

At that point the facts weren't fully known, so it was hard to tell whether McKinney had a good case. How many times did the officer call on her to stop? How much force did he use in restraining her? Have white congressmen been routinely allowed to breeze through security without their lapel pins? McKinney would have had to provide at least a few favorable answers in order to support her claims.

On the other hand, even McKinney's lawyers conceded that the congresswoman was not wearing her lapel pin as she blew through the checkpoint. Nor had she denied that she kept going when the officer called on her to stop. Nonetheless, McKinney and her lawyers insisted it was the officer's job to recognize her. "The pin is not the issue," she said at the press conference. "The issue is face recognition."

Many observers pointed out that it would be dangerous to base Capitol Hill security on the assumption that every officer will be instantly able to recognize all 535 members of Congress. Were the police supposed to let someone rush past them without going through the metal detector because she might be a congresswoman? Or was it more reasonable to ask her to stop for a moment so that her identification could be checked? And when she ignored repeated requests, what choice was there but to stop her?

You might have expected McKinney or her lawyer to answer those questions, but that is not how a good bluff works. Bluffing depends on uncertainty. Do the Capitol police really have a history of discrimination? Did the officer use excessive force? Did McKinney have solid evidence to back up her claims? And how much were the Capitol police willing to pay — in the currency of reputation and credibility — to find out?

It's hard not to be impressed by the way McKinney skillfully raised the stakes. It would be uncomfortable enough for federal prosecutors to take on a member of Congress in any circumstances, but they were put on notice that they would be publicly branded racists — and perhaps face a civil rights lawsuit — if they filed charges against McKinney. Under that sort of pressure, no one would have blamed them for backing off.

And that is what makes it a potent bluff. Just ask any poker player. By putting enough chips on the table, you make the game too expensive for the other players. Even if they believe they are holding winning cards, a massive raise can succeed in intimidating them into folding their hands, because they have to wonder whether you've got an ace in the hole.

Unfortunately for McKinney, she forgot that others can play the same game. Rather than back off, the prosecutors made a stunning raise of their own. They "came over the top," as card players say, by announcing that a grand jury would consider felony charges against McKinney.

Now it was the congresswoman's turn to face uncertainty. Did the Capitol police have witnesses? Videotape? How much was she willing to pay to find out?

So McKinney flinched. Speaking on the floor of the House, she apologized for the incident and announced her support for the Capitol police

—without a word about racial profiling or discrimination. She even voted in favor of a resolution criticizing her conduct. She thought she knew when to fold her hand, but it actually came too late. Even though the grand jury declined to indict her, McKinney lost her seat in the 2006 Democratic primary. She had badly overplayed her cards, and the voters had the last word.

5

The Truth about Torts

WOODY GUTHRIE ONCE compared outlaws to lawyers, singing in "The Ballad of Pretty Boy Floyd" that some men "rob you with a six-gun, and some with a fountain pen." It's been almost 70 years since Woody wrote that song, and Americans still don't care much for attorneys — in fact, lawyer bashing has more or less turned into a national obsession. Turn on any talk-radio station and pretty soon you will hear someone fulminating about the legal profession. Callers and hosts all agree that the United States is sinkingly over-counseled and that frivolous cases have driven our society to the brink of moral degradation and financial catastrophe. Newspapers have developed a sub-genre that might be called "stupid tort stories," regaling readers regularly with tawdry tales of perfidious plaintiffs — man sues dog over fleas; baby sues parents over diapers; embezzler sues bank for insufficient funds.

Those stories, however, are usually exaggerated or overdrawn, and they often turn out to be simply false — as in the entertaining but completely apocryphal case of a man who insured a box of imported cigars and then, after smoking them, sued his insurance company for failing to pay his claim for fire loss (in an equally fictional denouement, he was prosecuted for arson). It is easy to take pot shots at lawyers, and no one is in favor of truly frivolous lawsuits. The truth, however, is that there is an extremely positive side to the so-called liability explosion, even though the social value of widespread litigation is always subtle and therefore hard to recognize.

Dumbfounded

Consider a letter once answered by Dear Abby. The writer — calling herself "Dumbfounded in Roxboro, N.C." — complained that her husband had "endured a horrible experience in a department store." While shopping for shoes, Mr. Dumbfounded was stopped by a security guard, escorted to a back room, and made to bare his soles as proof that the loafers on his feet were really his own. He left the store "feeling humiliated" and resentful. "Is this the way customers should expect to be treated?"

Dear Abby replied, "Because the exposure to liability is so great, the vast majority of department stores have stringent guidelines limiting the manner in which a customer can be detained. Suspicion is never sufficient cause to stop a customer for questioning." According to Abby, Dumbfounded's husband was the victim of a "bad stop." Report the incident to the store management immediately, Abby advised.

The irony is that Dear Abby, herself a frequent critic of litigiousness, did not appear to realize, did not seem to consider for a moment, that the fear of liability can turn out to be a good thing. But take a closer look at her advice and you will see that Abby actually endorses the litigation system.

"Because the exposure to liability is so great," she said, department stores must now pay careful attention to the tactics of their security personnel. Hence, Mr. Dumbfounded should not expect to be treated so rudely. And why, Dear Abby failed to ask, is exposure to liability so great? Because lawyers are ready and willing to file damage suits on behalf of innocent people who are wrongly detained. The "because" says it all: Because of litigation, security guards are better behaved; if not for the fear of lawsuits, stores might well be rougher in their treatment of suspected (but blameless) customers.

In other words, the legal system works exactly as it should, providing a valuable deterrent that spares innocent consumers the travail and humiliation of interrogation and arrest. Or as Abby put it, thanks to the lawyer-generated potential for damages, "suspicion is never sufficient cause to stop a customer for questioning." Although he was never formally anyone's client, Mr. Dumbfounded was the indirect beneficiary of thousands of well-placed lawsuits.

Of course, every action has a reaction. Hesitation by security guards also allows a certain amount of successful shoplifting. If retail cops had unfettered leeway to nab shoppers, theft would decline and, presumably, prices would fall. So the same litigation that should have protected Mr. Dumbfounded is also responsible for a theoretical increase in the price of shoes. For some reason, however, Dear Abby didn't make that point. She might have told Mrs. Dumbfounded something like "Yes, that is exactly the way customers should expect to be treated. An occasional false arrest is the price we all pay for preventing crime. Stop whining and thank the guard for being so aggressive. It will save everybody money in the long run."

Dear Abby, however, was quite reasonably concerned far more for the dignity of Dumbfounded than she cared about the ramifications for shoe pricing. Intuitively, she made the same sort of judgment that courts and juries make all the time. Our society is better off when we protect the innocent or the injured, even though some people (including some lawyers) have figured out how to exploit the system. Yes, we could restrict access to the courts and cut down litigation. We could diminish the fear of liability or even eliminate it entirely, simply be creating rules that protect businesses from tort cases. And then a luckless consumer like Mr. Dumbfounded could contemplate the vast social benefit of his uncompensated false arrest, as he spends the night in the Roxboro jail, no doubt wishing that he knew a good lawyer.

Lawyers as Heroes

Dear Abby never acknowledged that contingency-fee lawyers play an important, if usually unseen, role in preventing predicaments like Mr. Dumbfounded's, which after all, was not especially severe. Sometimes, however, consumers suffer injuries that are far more devastating than an embarrassing interrogation, and where causation may be hard to discover or establish. In those cases, such as the Firestone tire fiasco of 2000, trial lawyers often turn out to be the unexpected heroes.

By now, everyone knows about the fatal combination of defective Firestone tires and Ford Explorers. But for a long time after the first news stories of fatal or near-fatal blowouts, corporate officials adamantly refused to admit that there was any danger at all. "These are good tires," a Firestone spokeswoman insisted. Ford advanced its own cover-up, blaming everything on Firestone even though the automaker knew about and ignored the exceptionally high incidence of tire failure on its Explorer and Mountaineer SUVs.

While it is natural to be outraged at the evasive tactics of Ford and Firestone, they should hardly come as a surprise. Stonewalling, after all, is what corporations do when they are faced with potentially massive liability — although they call it "crisis management." There is even a certain logic to the tactic. Accidents, including fatal accidents, are to be expected in the automotive industries. At one level, they are regarded as an accounting problem — or "risk assessment," as they say — requiring only that an adequate reserve fund be set up to handle the anticipated injury claims.

No one expects a company to recall 6.5 million tires on the basis of a scattered handful of accidents. Destructive as they might be to the victims and their families, deadly blowouts are part of doing business to vast enterprises such as Ford and Firestone. Or, as a Ford spokeswoman rationalized, "Every accident involves three factors: the vehicle, the driver, and the environment." So why rush to take responsibility?

But seemingly unrelated incidents may turn out to be tragically linked, perhaps by tires produced in a single factory. In large corporations, however, every incentive operates against the early recognition of such connections. Isolated accidents can be blamed on drivers or road conditions — and individual lawsuits can be quietly settled — but the acknowledgment of a defective product can lead to a corporate calamity. So denial becomes the automatic response.

Meanwhile, the National Highway Traffic Safety Administration was in no position to be quickly proactive. Although the NHTSA received early reports of fatalities due to tread separation in Firestone tires and subsequent rollovers, it was years before the underfunded and overburdened agency launched a comprehensive investigation. While the NHTSA does not intentionally suppress bad news, it faces the Herculean task of assembling and interpreting data from literally tens of thousands of accidents each year. Thus, reports of separate accidents tend be pigeon-holed, at least until a pattern becomes inescapably evident.

So how did the story finally come out, given that Ford and Firestone were in deep denial and the NHTSA was overwhelmed and short-staffed?

The answer is that a group of personal-injury lawyers began filing lawsuits and eventually succeeded in bringing the problem tires to public attention. Of course, they didn't do so out of altruism or public spiritedness, but they did have all the right incentives necessary to blow the whistle on a hazardous situation.

A single automobile fatality is nothing more than a statistic to a corporate troubleshooter or a government bureaucrat. But to a lawyer, it's a case — maybe even a big one. So the lawyer has ample reason to investigate each accident, and to search out causes that might make the potential verdict bigger (or easier to get).

To strengthen their cases, trial lawyers collect, share, and publicize information despite the automakers' best efforts to keep things under wraps. Plaintiffs' lawyers also provide the funding for research groups — such as the Center for Auto Safety and Safety Forum — that first drew the necessary connections and branded the SUV tires defective. Indeed, it was a series of personal-injury lawsuits — beginning in 1996 — that finally spurred the NHSTA to begin its own investigation four years later.

Unlike the caricature of greedy lawyers who cook up non-existent damages, the attorneys in the Firestone cases, working hard on behalf of badly injured clients, sought out and exposed dangerous conditions. Without the work of those trial lawyers, there is no telling how much longer Firestone tires would have remained on the road, causing further rollovers and endangering lives.

It is true, of course, that the lawyers only do it to make a buck. But so what? The desire to make a buck turns out to be an extraordinarily powerful engine for the exposure of harmful products. Just as the profit motive can cause corporations to overlook potential safety hazards, it also inspires trial lawyers to uncover them.

Damage Caps

The "runaway jury" is another favorite fable among tort reformers, who constantly repeat stories of mega-damage demands for trivial or self-inflicted injuries, seldom mentioning that most such suits are quickly dismissed long before they ever reach juries. And even in the notorious "spilled coffee" case — involving a seventy-nine-year-old woman who suffered third degree burns, requiring multiple skin grafts and prolonged hospitalization — the jury's initial $2.7 million award was later reduced to $640,000. Nonetheless, many state legislatures have enacted damage caps — often limiting non-economic damages to $250,000 or $500,00 — and similar measures have regularly been proposed in the United States Congress.

If you want to know what's wrong with damage caps, just look at the case of Linda McDougal. In May 2002, McDougal was diagnosed with breast cancer. A biopsy revealed a malignancy so aggressive that her only hope for survival was a double mastectomy, followed by chemotherapy and radiation. Two days after the surgery, however, McDougal's doctor delivered even more bad news — she didn't have cancer after all. The laboratory had mixed up the tissue samples, giving McDougal another woman's results, and two physicians at the Minnesota hospital had failed to check her name against the test records before scheduling the operation. Her two healthy breasts had been amputated because of a pathologist's mistake.

Under typical tort reform proposals, McDougal's ability to sue for malpractice would be drastically limited, primarily to her so-called "economic losses." In this case, that means she would not have to pay for the needless mastectomies or the egregious lab work, she would be reimbursed for reconstructive surgery, she would receive her lost wages (if any) during recovery, and she would be entitled to a lifetime supply of prosthetic bras. Of course, her greatest losses were non-economic: a lifetime of disfigurement, discomfort, and inescapable anguish. Under malpractice reform plans, such as the one advocated by President Bush in 2004, her compensation for "pain and suffering" would be limited to a several hundred thousand dollars, out of which she would also have to pay her lawyer.

McDougal was forty-six years old in 2002, but what if she had been a younger woman, yet to bear children? In that case, her economic losses would also have included the anticipated cost of infant formula. But the sorrow of being unable to nurse her children would not increase the damage cap at all. Under the chilling logic of tort reform, the sum of a person's life is derived from economic activity — wages and bills — while the devastating loss of happiness and fulfillment is worth practically nothing.

There is no doubt that the tort system in general has many flaws, especially in its approach to medical malpractice. Lawsuits are expensive, time-consuming, and uncertain. They are sometimes baseless, and they always distribute resources badly, with too much money going to attorneys and not enough to victims. Sometimes juries go too far, but it is a myth that they are easily swayed by smooth-talking lawyers. In fact, doctors actually win about seventy percent of malpractice trials, and judges are not shy about reversing or reducing unreasonable jury verdicts.

What's more, damage caps do almost nothing to address the issue of frivolous cases, which are usually small-ticket nuisance suits aimed at extracting quick, cheap settlements. Instead, the caps penalize the most severely injured patients with the strongest claims, since they are the ones most likely to win substantial verdicts at trial. The caps benefit insurance companies, and the relatively few incompetent doctors who put their patients' lives at risk. They shield hospital chains, HMOs, and pharmaceutical companies from considerable liability. But they do not eliminate, or even much reduce, most physicians' fears of unfounded litigation, since the vast majority of those cases are unaffected by the caps.

Linda McDougal's tragedy is not all that unusual. The Institute of Medicine (run by doctors, not lawyers) has reported that "at least 44,000 and perhaps as many as 98,000 Americans die in hospitals each year as a

result of medical errors." The number would be much higher if it als
cluded serious non-fatal injuries.

Frankly, doctors and hospitals sometimes need to be sued. At one
Connecticut hospital, for example, the cardiac unit experienced an appall-
ingly high post-surgical infection rate of more than twenty percent, much
of which was attributed to poor sanitation in the operating room. Corrective measures were taken only after the initiation of litigation, reducing
the infection rate to near zero. While the insurance and medical establish-
ments (just like retailers and automobile manufacturers) hate to admit it,
the threat of liability can provide a powerful incentive to limit risk by improving care. Damage caps reverse that incentive; they limit risk exposure
across the board, without regard to treatment standards. They offer good
doctors almost no protection against frivolous litigation, while crippling
the rights of genuine victims.

So the next time someone complains to you about the "litigation
crisis," take a look at the tires on the nearest SUV or the quality controls
at your local hospital, and ask yourself how much more dangerous they
might be if there were no personal injury lawyers. On the other hand, you
might prefer to put your faith in corporate executives and administrators,
depending on their good intentions to subordinate profits to safety — but
only if you like being dumbfounded.

S

NOW THAT MARTHA Stewart has served her time and returned to the world of business and style, we can reflect on her painful odyssey through the federal courts. Her trial surely had all the elements of an epic: a bold heroine with a tragic flaw, facing a powerful and implacable foe. Rather than accept an ignoble plea bargain, she risked personal destruction by defending her integrity and insisting on a trial. Just as honorably, the prosecutors accepted the challenge of overcoming Stewart's seemingly invincible celebrity, which required them to prove her a liar and a cheat. The relative triviality of the charge — lying about a stock transaction that turned out to be perfectly legal — only added drama to the confrontation. Each side stood on principle; no one flinched. Given the classic nature of the encounter, it may not be entirely surprising that part of the answer may be found in ancient Homeric texts.

Although the facts of the Stewart case were straightforward, prosecutors faced a daunting task. They had to prove that the popular, proper, elegant defendant had lied to the Federal Bureau of Investigation about the sale of a small amount of stock. As a media figure, however, Martha Stewart had built an international business empire by establishing a reputation for dependability. Hundreds of thousands — perhaps millions — of customers knew that they could trust Martha Stewart on matters of good taste and discernment. How, then, might it be possible to prove her a fraud?

In the five-week trial, there would be only one witness who could provide direct evidence that Martha Stewart lied. Douglas Faneuil, a twenty-eight-year-old assistant stockbroker at Merrill Lynch, testified that he alerted Stewart to the impending decline of her stock in ImClone and that she ordered him to sell her holdings on the basis of that tip. Stewart had denied those same facts in two interviews with investigators from the Securities and Exchange Commission, and that contradiction formed the basis of the case against her.

Faneuil, however, had grave credibility problems. His own admitted conduct — tipping off a client based on inside information — was far more serious than anything attributed to Martha Stewart, yet he was testifying under a plea bargain in which he was allowed to plead guilty only to a misdemeanor. Moreover, he had no way of controverting Stewart's defense, that she actually sold the stock pursuant to a prearranged "sell order" with Faneuil's boss, Peter Bacanovic. In a believability contest, the iconic Stewart started with a significant advantage over the callow Faneuil, and the prosecutors knew it.

To win, the prosecution had to confront the central dilemma in all litigation. Communication is basically verbal, but comprehension is essentially visual. A witness must describe an event in words, but jurors make sense of the testimony by reimagining the events in their "mind's eye." It would not be enough merely to tell the jurors that Martha Stewart lied about her conversation with Faneuil. They had to be able to see her talking on the phone with the young man, nodding as he explained the imminent decline in ImClone's share price, giving him the fatal instruction, and then betraying her hard-won persona by brazenly lying to investigators from the SEC. Without visualization, there could be no conviction.

The prosecutors had to re-create Martha Stewart's image, changing her from a perfectionist homemaking maven to a greedy liar, and they had to do it through the secondhand description of events that the jury would never see.

This is a familiar task for trial lawyers. It is also the work of storytellers and poets (as well as novelists, journalists, and historians), who use artful language to create a shared understanding of the past, whether remote or recent.

And this brings us to Homer and the Trojan War. Nearly every image we have from that heroic age — the Greek armies massed on the beach, the towers of Troy, the matchless beauty of Helen, the glint of Achilles' shield — derives from the poetry of Homer, who never saw the events he described. So vivid are Homer's descriptions, in fact, that scholars believe that his blindness is only a legend. But even if he could see, the Trojan War occurred many centuries before his birth, in a land he never visited. Nonetheless, his words still have a strong visual impact after 2,800 years, especially when it came to the carnage of the battle. Take, for instance, this passage describing Achilles killing a nameless Trojan:

> Just as he shot past the matchless runner Achilles
> speared him square in the back where his war-belt clasped,
> straight on through went the point and out the navel,

down on his knees he dropped
screaming shrill as the world went black before him
clutched his bowels to his body, hunched and sank.

The mental image is nearly indelible: we cannot avoid thinking about the fleeing Trojan runner, frantically grabbing at his own intestines as he doubles over and falls to the ground.

There was nothing so gripping or graphic in the Martha Stewart trial, and the prosecutors hardly aspired to Homeric verse, but they did make use of some of the same concepts to build their case. Most significantly, they repeatedly called upon witnesses to describe Stewart's venal side — depicting her as demanding, egotistical, and self-centered — so that the jurors could envision her as exactly the sort of person who would eagerly take advantage of an inside tip and then arrogantly attempt to conceal the deed. They played a tape-recorded interview with Bacanovic in which he described his most important client as "someone who gets irascible" about her portfolio, and they introduced an e-mail in which she threatened to withdraw her account and "give my money to a professional money manager who will watch it when I am too busy."

Most significantly, the prosecutors repeatedly illustrated their case with revealing vignettes, including a description of Martha Stewart and Peter Bacanovic posing for a photograph in pink and blue bathrobes. After that, it would be significantly easier for the jury to imagine that Stewart and Bacanovic had a relationship that went beyond stock-broking — one in which they might conspire to dump stock and cover up the details.

In response, the defense painted a picture of, well, nothing. As Jeffrey Toobin observed in the pages of *The New Yorker*, in the entire five-week trial, the defense offered only about three sentences that stressed Stewart's good deeds and accomplishments. Stewart did not testify in her own behalf, and her lawyer produced only one witness on a relatively minor point. Now, there are many good reasons for keeping a defendant off the stand, and Stewart's attorneys can no doubt provide an excellent explanation of their strategy. The cost of silence, however, can be enormous, leaving the jury with a strong visual impression of guilt, but with no way to envision an "innocence" story.

The best trial lawyers, in their own way, are all blind poets, relying primarily on words to convey the reality of events and situations that neither they nor the jury have ever actually observed. It is ironic that Martha

Stewart, who built a luminous career on her polished image, ended up leaving the jury in the dark.

She might have looked at the first sentence of Homer's *Iliad* for some better advice: Sing, O muse.

7

Freedom Stories

IT WOULD BE nice to think that "freedom means freedom for everybody," as Vice President Dick Cheney so memorably opined in his 2004 debate with Democratic candidate John Edwards. For same-sex couples in the United States, however, the freedom to marry exists only in Massachusetts (with "civil unions" available in several other states). In much of the rest of the country, gay marriage seems as distant as ever. Forty-three states have statutes or constitutional provisions that limit marriage to "a man and a woman," and even in California, Governor Arnold Schwarzenegger vetoed a bill that would have allowed same-sex partners to wed.

Then again, it is always darkest before the dawn. There is actually a very good reason to believe that gay marriage will eventually be legalized in the United States, and not just because that would be the fair, progressive, and humane thing to do. You don't have to agree with Dick Cheney (and me) about the meaning of freedom in order to understand why gay marriage rights are almost certain to expand. You just have to know something about the power of stories.

We like to tell ourselves that people are persuaded by logical arguments based on facts, reasons, and morality. It is much more often the case, however, that people are persuaded by stories. It is all a matter of cognition, as the linguist George Lakoff explains in his book *Don't Think of an Elephant!* Human beings tend to be moved by concrete images rather than abstractions. We typically reach decisions through a process of visualization and empathy — which Lakoff calls "metaphorical thought" — as opposed to purely rational, or even moral, deductions. Stories, in other words, can be truer than true, because they encompass nuances, consequences, and relationships that cannot be fully communicated through logic alone.

Thus, we use stories to make sense of the world, and the more vivid the better. Stories invite us (indeed, they impel us) to expand on our own experiences, to imagine the real-life consequences of individual and social choices, and — most importantly — to see ourselves in new or challenging situations. That is why photographs of starving children in Niger, or first-hand accounts of murder in Darfur, can spur world response in ways that logical appeals cannot. Everyone knows that famine and genocide are bad, but we start to take action when we can visualize the problem and therefore empathize with the victims.

A good example is Harriet Beecher Stowe's novel *Uncle Tom's Cabin*, which marshaled more opposition to slavery than countless abolitionist sermons. Her fictional narrative was so forceful — with unforgettable images of the saintly Little Eva, the desperate Eliza, and the brutal Simon Legree — that Abraham Lincoln is said to have called her "the little lady who made this big war."

There is nothing inherently ideological about storytelling. It is accepted and exploited by advertisers, marketers, lawyers, and politicians of every stripe — though some use it more effectively than others. Nonetheless, the theory of "story power" can be used far more readily in support of gay rights than in opposition. Why? Because it is easy to tell stories about the human cost of anti-gay discrimination. And while it is obviously possible to assert moral claims about the depravity of the "gay lifestyle," it is pretty hard to conceive of a story in which marriage (which is, after all, a form of monogamy) makes things worse.

Here is an example of a powerful story.

My parents were always broad-minded and liberal, even when I was a small child in the early 1950s. Their social circle included people of all racial and religious backgrounds, including intermarried couples, which was very unusual at the time. They were also friends with a same-sex couple, whom I will call Stanley and Nick (my dad worked with Stanley). In those days it was dangerous to be openly gay in Chicago — you could be fired, evicted, or beaten up — so Stanley and Nick were officially "roommates." Their closest friends figured out the true nature of their relationship, although no one ever spoke about it, especially at the office.

Stanley and Nick eventually moved to the East Coast, but they stayed in touch with my parents, exchanging birthday cards and occasional telephone calls.

"Can you believe it?" Stanley would say. "I still have the same roommate after all these years."

"Incredible," my dad would reply, knowing the secret but keeping up appearances. "Give Nick our best."

In the early 1990s, Nick had a serious stroke, requiring extended hospitalization and expensive follow-up care. Stanley's job provided medical insurance, but it did not cover Nick. Although they had lived as spouses for more than forty years, they were unmarried and therefore legally unrelated. As far as the insurance company was concerned, Nick and Stanley might as well have been complete strangers. They had to sell their house to pay the medical bills.

My father died a few years ago, and Stanley provided my mother with as much comfort as he could. Old friends are the best friends in times of sorrow, so they spoke often about their younger days when Stanley and my father worked together. One bittersweet phone call came on the occasion of Stanley's eightieth birthday.

"How are you celebrating?" my mother asked.

"I am going to drink a glass of wine," he said, "and then I am going to visit my partner in the nursing home."

That was the first time in over fifty years that she had ever heard Stanley acknowledge his lover as anything other than a roommate.

This is a persuasive story because it is specific and direct, evoking empathy for the difficulty of two men's lives. They stayed together in sickness and in health — not to mention discrimination and debt — but were never granted the comforts or advantages of legal recognition. Marriage would have made their lives better, while harming no one. End of story.

Now try to come up with a counter-story — not an argument or a set of dire predictions, but a plausible narrative, supported by vivid characterizations and believable details, in which people's lives are made worse by gay marriage. I'll bet that nothing immediately springs to mind.

I recognize that there are widely held moral and religious objections to homosexuality. I understand that gay marriage is distasteful, even frightening, to many Americans who are not necessarily mean-spirited or homophobic. My point is not so much that they are wrong, but rather that their arguments will ultimately fail.

During the 2004 Illinois Senate election, Republican candidate Alan Keyes justified his opposition to gay marriage by calling homosexuals selfish hedonists. The foundation of marriage, he explained, must be more than selfishness, and thus, he reasoned, the wedding of same-sex couples would debase the institution. For the moment, let's put aside Keyes's wobbly logic. His argument still lacks persuasive force because it is merely declarative. Gay marriage is bad and will lead to bad things, he insisted, but he could not provide a narrative, or even an anecdote, to support his claim. Even if he were right in some broad sense, there would still be no way to visualize the supposed ill effects of gay marriage.

On the other hand, the tale of Stanley and Nick thoroughly undermines the image of gay couples as selfish hedonists. There is nothing that seems selfish or hedonistic about their generous and dedicated commitment to each other, which survived terribly hard times.

It can take many years to change public opinion in a democracy, but the process is already under way in the case of gay rights. Antidiscrimination laws can be found everywhere; civil unions and domestic partnerships are now recognized in ways that would have been unthinkable even a decade ago. In large part, I think, storytelling is responsible for this transformation in attitudes, and the trend will surely continue, inconsistently but steadily, until Dick Cheney and I can agree that there really is "freedom for everybody."

8

The Importance of Being Honest

LONG BEFORE BILL Clinton ever lied about sex, another out-sized personality made the same mistake on the witness stand, attempting to fool the court, the public, and his own attorney about his illicit liaisons. In 1895, Oscar Wilde was perhaps the most celebrated literary figure in England. A famed poet, playwright, novelist, and belle lettrist, he led an aesthetic revolution against the stifling proprieties of the Victorian era, championing a new freedom in artistic expression.

Wilde was also a lover of young men. Today we would call him a homosexual or bisexual (he was married, with two sons), although neither term was current in the 1890s. In Wilde's own view, he engaged in the

> . . . great affection of an elder for a younger man as there was between David and Jonathan, such as Plato made the very basis of his philosophy, and such as you find in the sonnets of Michelangelo and Shakespeare. It is that deep, spiritual affection that is as pure as it is perfect.
> . . . It is beautiful, it is fine, it is the noblest form of affection. There is nothing unnatural about it. It is intellectual, and it repeatedly exists between an elder and a younger man, when the elder man has intellect, and the younger man has all the joy, hope and glamour of life before him. That it should be so the world does not understand. The world mocks at it and sometimes puts one in the pillory for it.

Sodomy, however, was illegal and officially despised in nineteenth-century England (although evidently much practiced in the upper-class "public schools"). So Wilde flouted more than aesthetic conventions when he involved himself in poorly concealed affairs with other men, most notably, and disastrously, the young Lord Alfred Douglas, nearly 16 years his junior, whom everyone called Bosie.

Unfortunately for Wilde, Bosie's father was John Sholto Douglas, the Marquess of Queensberry and the author of the Marquess of Queensberry rules for boxing. Queensberry was a bully and a tyrant — so much so that his wife divorced him, a nearly unheard-of event in Victorian England. Enraged at the thought of his son embracing the effete Wilde, he began hounding and threatening the pair, attempting to intimidate them into breaking off their relationship. Eventually, the hostilities brought them into court, where Oscar Wilde's conduct proved even more self-destructive than Bill Clinton's.

To my knowledge, no one has ever before compared Bill Clinton to Oscar Wilde — one a politician and the other an artist — although their similarities are in some ways striking. Both were youthful prodigies, although Clinton has survived well into middle age, as Wilde did not. Both men were Oxford-educated outsiders — an Arkansan in Washington and an Irishman in London — who challenged the established order. Both dominated their eras by force of personality, overshadowing their more pallid contemporaries even as they were denounced as corrupt and decadent by cultural conservatives. As we know, both men heedlessly indulged their large priapic appetites, assuming that they could rely on charm and wit to disentangle themselves when they were inevitably caught in the act. They even look somewhat alike, graceful and leonine in their better moments.

Each man was relentlessly stalked by his own Javert, and, most importantly, each thought he could outfox his adversaries in court, and did not bother to inform his lawyers of his intended deceptions.

At least Bill Clinton had an excuse. As the defendant, he was an involuntary participant in the Paula Jones case, which he considered part of a politically motivated vendetta. His affair with Monica Lewinsky was not even remotely related to Jones's complaint; indeed, Judge Wright later ruled it immaterial. While there is no justification for lying under oath, it is possible to sympathize with Clinton's rationalization that he needed to conceal his infidelity in order to preserve his marriage and protect his family.

Wilde, on the other hand, initially came into court as a plaintiff, bringing a false charge of criminal libel against Queensberry, and knowing that he would have to lie to sustain his case. Wilde's motivation must have seemed compelling to him at the time, but it has baffled historians and biographers for over a century. Only recently has the complete transcript of Wilde's first trial been published. Edited by his grandson Merlin Holland, it allows us to draw a few new insights into Wilde's self-inflicted ruin.

Queensberry's pursuit of Oscar and Bosie eventually became nearly intolerable. He followed them to clubs and restaurants, and even accosted Wilde in his own home with an accusation of sodomy: "You look it and you pose it, which is just as bad." The scarlet Marquess (as Wilde called him) threatened to thrash the poet if he ever again saw him in public with his son. Wilde's reply was utterly in character — witty, provocative, and seemingly calculated to make matters worse: "I do not know what the Marquess of Queensberry rules are, but the Oscar Wilde rule is to shoot on sight."

Things came to a head in February of 1895. Wilde's new play, *The Importance of Being Earnest*, was premiering at the St. James Theater in London's West End. Queensberry planned to disrupt the opening performance by haranguing about Wilde's misdeeds. Fortunately, the theater manager was alerted ahead of time and arranged for a police guard to keep Queensberry (who was accompanied by a pugilist) out of the building. A few days later, on February 18, Queensberry showed up at the Albemarle Club, where Wilde was a member. Angrily scribbling something on his card, Queensberry handed it to the club porter, with an instruction to deliver the message to Wilde. "For Oscar Wilde," it read, "posing somdomite [*sic*]."

This was a challenge that Wilde felt he could not ignore. "Bosie's father has left a card at my club with hideous words on it," Wilde wrote to a friend. "I don't see anything now but a criminal prosecution." He engaged a solicitor, Charles Humphreys, to draw up a charge of criminal libel. A cautious lawyer, Humphreys asked Wilde "on his solemn oath" whether there was any truth to the charge of sodomy. Wilde assured him there was not. "If you are innocent," replied Humphreys, "you should succeed."

With that assurance, Humphreys escorted Wilde to the magistrate's court, where they applied for a warrant for criminal libel, accusing Queensberry of making a "false scandalous malicious and derogatory" statement about Wilde, the "tenor and effect" of which was that "Wilde had committed and was in the habit of committing the abominable crime of buggery with mankind."

Queensberry was arrested the next day, and the case was set for hearing. Queensberry retained as his counsel a rising young barrister named Edward Carson, who had been Wilde's classmate at Trinity College, Dublin. Carson immediately showed that friendship would have no part in the case. He prepared a plea of "justification" on Queensberry's behalf, asserting that the statement was true and, as was then required by British libel law, that it had been made "for the public benefit and interest." To support this claim, Carson stated that "Wilde was a man of letters and a dramatist of prominence and notoriety and a person who exercised considerable influence over young men," and whose published works "were calculated to subvert morality and to encourage unnatural vice."

Wilde was eager to defend his writings against charges of immorality, but Queensberry's plea contained other, far more ominous allegations. Based on the work of a private investigator, Carson charged that Wilde had committed "sodomitical practices for a long time with impunity and without detection," and named ten young men with whom Wilde was said to have engaged in "sodomy and other acts of gross indecency and immorality," complete with dates and locales.

By this time, Humphreys had referred the case to a barrister who would handle the prosecution at trial. Sir Edward Clarke was a "veritable titan at the bar," and a former solicitor general of England. Worried about the extreme specificity of Queensberry's charges, Clarke too made a point of questioning his client: "I can only accept this brief, Mr. Wilde, if you can assure me on your honour as an English gentleman that there is not and never has been any foundation for the charges that are made against you."

Wilde did not trouble to point out that he was, in fact, an Irishman, but he did proceed to declare — quite falsely — that the charges were "absolutely false and groundless."

On the strength of that deception, Clarke accepted the case and proceeded to trial. He would surely have refused, if he had known that Wilde intended to commit perjury. Indeed, the entire case was based on Wilde's lies. No competent lawyer, aware of the truth, would have allowed it to go ahead, which ultimately would have been a blessing to his client. Instead, as Wilde's grandson put it, the case pressed forward with a "sickening inevitability." The doorway to the libel court began a direct path to jail.

Reading the complete transcript of the libel trial, it is impossible to miss Wilde's disdain for his adversaries. Yes, he was witty and clever, fencing with Carson and often getting the better of him. But he clearly misunderstood the power of cross examination, little realizing how his evasions could later be turned against him. Not unlike Bill Clinton, he seemed to think that a charming lie would go unchallenged if only he held to it throughout the examination. And also like Clinton, he seized on small ambiguities and equivocations that would come back to haunt him.

Clinton was fortunate in his enemies. Facing the inept attorneys for Paula Jones, the ham-handed Kenneth Starr, and the blustering impeachment managers, he was able to emerge with his presidency intact. Wilde, on the other hand, was confronted by a truly masterful cross examiner.

Carson cut Wilde to ribbons over the course of two days, shredding his credibility and leaving his reputation in tatters. The heroic efforts of Sir

Edward Clarke could not save his client, or even much forestall the inevitable, as Wilde's own lawsuit soon led him to the Reading Gaol.

Throughout the early part of the cross examination, Carson hammered away at the supposed immorality of Wilde's writings and associations, while Wilde deftly defended the indeterminacy of art:

> CARSON: Listen, sir. Here is one of your "Phrases and Philosophies for the use of the Young": "Wickedness is a myth invented by good people to account for the curious attractiveness of others."
> WILDE: Yes.
> CARSON: Do you think that is true?
> WILDE: I rarely think that anything I write is true.

Carson, however, eventually managed to turn Wilde's wit against him, showing the author's condescension toward ordinary people and, by implication, toward the jury.

> CARSON: I will suggest to you *Dorian Gray*. Is that open to the interpretation of being a sodomitical book?
> WILDE: Only to brutes — only to the illiterate; perhaps I should say brutes and the illiterates.
> CARSON: An illiterate person reading *Dorian Gray* might consider it a sodomitical book?
> WILDE: The views of the Philistine on art could not be counted: they are incalculably stupid. You cannot ask me what misinterpretation of my work the ignorant, the illiterate, the foolish may put on it. It doesn't concern me. . . .
> CARSON: The majority of people would come within your definition of Philistines and illiterate, wouldn't they?
> WILDE: Oh, I have found wonderful exceptions.
> CARSON: But the majority of people, I say. Do you think the majority of people live up to the pose that you are giving us, Mr. Wilde, or are educated up to that?
> WILDE: I am afraid they are not cultivated enough.

The cross examination on literature seemed to end in a draw. Wilde managed to evoke ready laughter, but Carson's cross examination had a deeper purpose that would become apparent only after Wilde had retired from the witness box. In any event, Carson next addressed the relationship between Oscar and Bosie, producing several letters written by Wilde to his younger friend. He fastened first on the salutation:

CARSON: You would think, I suppose, Mr. Wilde, that a man of your age to address a man nearly twenty years younger as "My own boy" would be an improper thing?

WILDE: No, not if I was fond of him. I don't think so.

Then Carson read an incriminating passage from the letter, in support of the claim that Wilde, at least, posed as a sodomite:

CARSON: "Your sonnet is quite lovely. It is a marvel that those red rose-leaf lips of yours should be made no less for music of song than for madness of kissing."

WILDE: Yes.

CARSON: Do you mean to tell me, sir, that that was a natural and proper way to address a young man?

WILDE: I am afraid you are criticizing a poem on the ground —

CARSON: I want to see what you say.

WILDE: Yes, I think it was a beautiful letter. . . . The letter was not written — with the object of writing propriety; it was written with the object of making a beautiful thing.

CARSON: But apart from art?

WILDE: Ah! I cannot do that.

The deflection, clever as it was, did not succeed. Carson continued, showing Wilde — perhaps for the first time in his life — that he would not be allowed the last word:

CARSON: But apart from art?

WILDE: I cannot answer any question apart from art.

CARSON: Suppose a man, now, who was not an artist had written this letter to a handsome young man, as I believe Lord Alfred Douglas is. . . . Would you say that it was a proper and natural kind of letter to write to him?

WILDE: A man who was not an artist could never have written that letter.

CARSON: Why?
WILDE: Because nobody but an artist could write it.

Carson was not finished.

CARSON: Supposing a man had an unholy and immoral love towards a
   boy or a young fellow . . . and he addressed him in the language that
   would perhaps probably be used in a love letter — he might use that
   language?
WILDE: He certainly could not use such language as I used unless he
   was a man of letters and an artist.

Wilde had talked himself into a corner, and Carson neatly led him into admitting that "a man of letters and an artist" would have used precisely such
language to declare "unholy and immoral love."

Having extracted that concession, and though Wilde may yet have been
oblivious to his predicament, Carson moved in for the kill. He launched
into a series of questions about Wilde's liaisons with young men, nam-
ing names and sparing few details. Did you ever have immoral practices
with Wood? Did you ever open his trousers? Put your hand on his person?
Did you ever put your own person between his legs? Did you kiss Edward
Shelley? Did you put your hand on his person? Did you sleep in the same
bed with him all night? Each of you having taken off all your clothes, did
you take his person in your hand in bed? Did you become intimate with a
young man named Conway? Did you put your hands inside his trousers?

And on it went. Wilde admitted knowing the young men, treating
them to expensive meals and giving them gifts, but he denied all of the
sexual improprieties. Carson retorted by pointing out that all of the young
men (save perhaps one) were of a lower class than Wilde: a newspaper
peddler, a valet, a groom, an office boy. Why would a man of Wilde's distinction — in class-encrusted Victorian England — spend so much time in
the company of his social inferiors, if he was not pursuing immoral and
unnatural affairs?

Wilde replied that he was merely interested in "the pleasure of being
with those who are young, bright, happy, careless and amusing," insisting
that he did not "care twopence about people's social positions." He got off
another good line — "I would sooner talk to a young man half an hour
than even be, well, cross-examined in court" — but otherwise his defense

flagged. Having earlier declaimed, at Carson's subtle urging, that ordinary people were illiterate "brutes and Philistines" who could never understand his art, Wilde's claim to flaunt social distinctions rang hollow.

Wilde had fallen into the cross examiner's trap. Concentrating on making clever answers to individual questions, he did not recognize the cumulative impact of the examination, which was to undermine his credibility. As a brilliant wit and conversationalist, Wilde did not mind contradicting himself— "I rarely think that anything I write is true"— for the sake of a laugh. But Carson was keeping score. And more importantly, Carson knew, as Wilde could not, exactly where the cross examination was headed.

And then Wilde made another crucial mistake, just as Bill Clinton would one hundred years later. He made an off-the-cuff answer that could be mercilessly exploited by his adversary. In his grand jury testimony, Clinton famously said, "It depends on what the meaning of the word 'is' is." That would have been a fair enough observation in a law school classroom, but it was deadly in court. It allowed his enemies to brand him as a dissembler and equivocator — indeed, as a purveyor of "Clintonisms."

In Wilde's case the slip was even more devastating, as his remark, though nimble, seemed to admit the very vice he had so vigorously denied. Wilde's downfall began when Carson questioned him about a young servant of Bosie's named Walter Grainger. By this time, Wilde was clearly frustrated over the repeated questions about his sex life with young men. He became snappish and careless.

> CARSON: Were you on familiar terms with Grainger?
> WILDE: What do you mean by "familiar terms"?
> CARSON: I mean to say did you have him to dine with you or anything of that kind?
> WILDE: Never in my life. . . . It is really trying to ask me such a question. No, of course not. He waited on me at table; he did not dine with me.

That was the first opening, and Carson quickly followed up, recalling for the jury Wilde's earlier professions of egalitarianism:

> CARSON: I thought he might have sat down. You drew no distinction.
> . . . You told me yourself—
> WILDE: It is a different thing — if it is people's duty to serve, it is their

duty to serve; if it is their pleasure to dine, it is their pleasure to dine and their privilege.

Satisfied with that inconsistency, Carson proceeded. He soon struck gold.

CARSON: Did you ever kiss him?
WILDE: Oh, no, never in my life; he was a peculiarly plain boy.

Carson could not believe his luck. It was just the opening he had been waiting for, and Wilde still had no clue.

CARSON: He was what?
WILDE: I said I thought him unfortunately — his appearance was so very unfortunately — very ugly — I mean — I pitied him for it.
CARSON: Very ugly?
WILDE: Yes.
CARSON: Do you say that in support of your statement that you never kissed him?
WILDE: No, I don't; it is like asking me if I kissed a doorpost; it is childish.
CARSON: Didn't you give me as the reason that you never kissed him that he was too ugly?
WILDE: No.
CARSON: Why did you mention his ugliness?
WILDE: For that reason. If you asked me if I had ever kissed a doorpost, I should say, "No! Ridiculous! I shouldn't like to kiss a doorpost." Am I to be cross-examined on why I shouldn't like to kiss a doorpost? The questions are grotesque.

Wilde was digging himself in ever deeper. If kissing an ugly boy was like kissing a doorpost, then the implication for a handsome boy was obvious. And Carson would not let go of Wilde's emphasis on ugliness.

CARSON: Why did you mention the boy's ugliness?
WILDE: I mentioned it perhaps because you sting me by an insolent question. . . . You make me irritable.
CARSON: Did you say the boy was ugly, because I stung you by an insolent question?

WILDE: Pardon me, you sting me, insult me and try to unnerve me in every way. At times one says things flippantly when one should speak more seriously, I admit that, I admit it — I cannot help it. That is what you are doing to me.

Queensberry must have chuckled to see Wilde on the ropes, completely disoriented and unable to defend himself. And Carson would have been justified in bragging that he was the true artist, at least in the courtroom. He took advantage of Wilde's false note, and played him like a violin.

By the time Carson addressed the jury, there was little doubt how the case would end. Indeed, Clarke interrupted Carson before he had even finished his opening, offering to withdraw the libel case upon a stipulation that Queensberry had established his defense with regard to "posing" as a sodomite. But Carson would not relinquish his advantage. He insisted on a finding of not guilty with regard to the entire plea of justification, without limitation. Clarke had no choice but to agree.

That was the end of the libel case, but not the end of Wilde's trials. By that evening he would find himself arrested on the charge of gross indecencies — based upon the evidence that Queensberry had gathered in his own defense. After one jury failed to reach a verdict, another convicted Wilde of the crime, leading the judge to remark that Wilde's offense was "the worst I have ever tried." Wilde received the maximum sentence, two years at hard labor, and emerged from prison a broken man. He died in Paris in 1900, at age forty-six.

Refracted through a century of social progress, the image of Wilde today is that of a martyr in the cause of sexual liberation, which in many ways he was. In our far more tolerant age, we can understand and sympathize with Wilde's dilemma. Only the law could restrain Queensberry, his tormentor, but the law offered no protection to men of "unnatural habits." To sustain his case, therefore, Wilde himself (through counsel) had to denounce sodomy as the "gravest of all offences" while lying through his teeth about the facts of his own life.

But there is another side to the case that should evoke less sympathy. Wilde was, after all, the complainant in a criminal case. Criminal libel was a serious matter in 1895, carrying a possible sentence of two years' imprisonment. Wilde was quite willing to send Queensberry to jail, and to perjure himself in the process. John Mortimer, author of the *Rumpole* series, calls the conviction of Wilde "a shameful day for British justice," as indeed it was. He might also have observed that the incarceration of Queensberry would have been a comparable injustice.

Oscar Wilde learned his lesson the hardest way possible, as Bill Clinton might have if he had not enjoyed such good fortune and broad support. You can lie to the public and you can lie to the court, but you are far better off telling the truth to your lawyer.

PART II

Lawyers

Introduction

LYING OFTEN STARTS small and may seem harmless, but it can easily spiral out of control. That is the cautionary lesson in "False Flats" which relates the dissembling downfall of one of Wall Street's rising stars.

Each of the next five essays explores variations on the theme of honesty. "Who Deserves the Truth?" asks whether some people are not entitled to honest information (the answer is surprising), while "When Honesty Is Not Enough" considers whether a client should be entitled to more than "technical honesty" from her lawyer. "Hypocrisy on the Left" tells the story of Lynne Stewart — a radical lawyer imprisoned for providing material assistance to terrorists — who cannot seem to admit, either to herself or her supporters, the seriousness of her misconduct. In sharp contrast, "Requiem for a Faithful Lawyer" is an appreciation of the murdered Michael Lefkow, whose devotion to truth was an inspiration to generations of public-interest lawyers. William Jennings Bryan was also a faithful lawyer, though his humane accomplishments have often been obscured by an unfair literary caricature. "Evolution of Myth" attempts to set his record straight.

Even when lawyers are sincere, there is still the problem of communicating important information to clients, which will often require in-depth understanding of their "Hidden Interests." Likewise, lawyers may find themselves giving counterproductive advice if they rely on common assumptions that turn out to be inaccurate, as "When Conventional Wisdom Goes Wrong."

If advising clients can be filled with pitfalls, then communicating with courts and juries can be downright hazardous. An attorney might rely on witnesses who missed key details or did not truly comprehend everything they think they observed — resulting in "Sensory Deception." Attorneys themselves may be misled into crucial cognition errors that can be neutralized only by understanding "How Lawyers (Ought to) Think." And sometimes persuasion can be most effective and accurate when it takes an unanticipated form, such as "Truth in Humor."

Finally, "Confronting Cougars" explains that lawyers must learn to distinguish between real and exaggerated legal problems. Even though it can be lucrative to bill clients for the latter, they are often merely the product of the lawyer's own insecurity.

9

False Flats

AS A YOUNG lawyer, I often represented clients in juvenile court. The defendants — mostly fourteen or fifteen years old — were charged with crimes ranging from property damage to robbery. The most aggravated cases were transferred to adult court, so there was often an attitude of conspicuous nonchalance among the prosecutors and public defenders about the juvie "mopes" who remained. It just wasn't cool to take these cases too seriously — not by lawyers who were all waiting to be promoted to the big time. I stepped rather naïvely into this world, idealistically expecting to treat my young clients' cases like any others.

One day, I was negotiating with a prosecutor about the date for a forthcoming hearing. He was already annoyed with me for presenting a motion to suppress an identification, something that was rarely pursued in juvenile court. For a reason that I do not recall, he was adamant about scheduling the case for a particular day the next week, but I already had a trial set for that day in a different courtroom across town. It wasn't going to be a long trial, I explained, but it would definitely prevent me from getting to court on time.

"Just get here whenever you can," countered the prosecutor.

"I don't think the judge will like that," I said. "He is usually pretty punctual."

"Don't worry about the judge," replied the prosecutor. "Just tell him you had a flat tire on the way to court."

I was astonished. The prosecutor was actually suggesting that I tell a lie to the court — and tell a patently transparent lie at that. It would be a simple enough matter for the judge, or his bailiff, to figure out that there had been no flat tire, if anyone cared to investigate.

But of course, that was the point. No one was going to investigate because no one would care. Lawyers were late for court all the time, and there was a tacit agreement that any remotely plausible excuse would be accepted by opposing counsel, and by the judge as well. It wasn't regarded as lying so much as face-saving. The judge could maintain a strict appearance

— even as defendants and witnesses waited in frustration for the absent attorney — although still indulging the over-scheduled lawyers who had made juvenile court their lowest priority. It was a game that worked for everyone (except for defendants and witnesses, who didn't seem to count), but I still could not bring myself to play. "Forget it," I said. "We'll just have to pick a date when I can get here on time." Taking that position branded me as even more of an outsider. Imagine, a lawyer who wasn't willing to make excuses? What a dummy!

And yes, I was a dummy. I refused to conform to the rather loose standards of the courthouse, but not because I was fundamentally more honest or truthful than the prosecutors and public defenders. I don't think any of them would have lied about something they considered important. Frankly, I think my reluctance might have been motivated, at least in part, by fear as much as by ethics. As a neophyte, I shuddered at the thought of getting caught in a lie, entertaining dismal visions of losing my license before my career ever really got started. With almost no experience to draw upon, it did not remotely occur to me that fibbing might be considered standard operating procedure.

Over the following years (okay, decades), I have come to realize just how remarkably lax the legal culture can be about certain details, especially when it comes to lawyers' mutual convenience. Even when courts attempt to be strict, lawyers tend to extend "courtesies" to each other, such as waiving notice provisions or forgiving missed deadlines. The occasional litigator who insists on rigorous compliance is considered a hard-ass or worse. This may never be more true than in the case of time extensions, where sham excuses seem par for the course. Too often, lawyers simply do not take deadlines seriously, and they seem unembarrassed about offering bald pretexts and blatant rationalizations when they ask for additional time.

In a modest attempt to test this proposition, I surveyed a group of friends and colleagues, asking for their informal impressions about how often lawyers exaggerate or stretch the truth (or worse) when seeking extensions of time or relief from lapsed deadlines. Estimates ranged from fifty percent to ninety percent of the time (though a couple of people said they had almost never seen it happen). Given that some of my friends are hard-bitten cynics and others are trusting to a fault, it seems rather conservative to suppose that extension-seeking lawyers are less than candid somewhere around twenty percent of the time, which is quite a lot. Equally important is the corollary, that usually no one cares when it happens, including judges.

And that brings us to one incident in the life of a lawyer named John Gellene. In late 1993, Gellene was a highly valued young partner in the prominent New York Law firm Milbank, Tweed, Hadley & McCloy. In one of his major cases, he represented the South Street Fund as a claimant in the George Gillett bankruptcy, which was pending in the United States District Court in Denver. In April 1996, after a long period of inactivity, he received a request for documents from the bankruptcy trustee. As busy lawyers often do, he more or less ignored the request, attending instead to more urgent matters. The trustee succeeded in getting Gellene's attention by filing a Motion to Compel Production, which led to an agreement that Gellene would tender the documents within a few weeks.

Gellene, however, continued to ignore the request, allowing the extended deadline to lapse. Frustrated, the trustee filed a motion for sanctions, requesting that South Street's $19 million claim be disallowed. The bankruptcy court granted the motion, and dismissed South Street's claim on August 2, 1996.

Gellene finally took notice of the situation. He hurriedly gathered the necessary documents, which he had recently obtained from Gary Hindes, corporate secretary of the South Street Fund, and sent the material to the bankruptcy trustee on August 8, 1996. The following day, Gellene submitted a motion to the bankruptcy court, seeking to have South Street's claim reinstated. He could not very well say that he had simply blown off the deadline, although that is probably the basic truth. Instead, he apparently decided to contrive a plausible reason, figuring that the documents had been tendered and the court would be in a forgiving mood. The motion stated:

> The delay in responding to the document requests was the result of the winding up of the South Street Funds and an ongoing dispute between the managing partner of the South Street Funds and the fund's portfolio advisor . . . regarding control of the funds and other matters. This dispute is the result of ongoing litigation between the parties and their principals.

Gellene's representations were partially true. The South Street Funds were indeed winding up, and there was ongoing litigation between the principals. But that had nothing to do with the delay in document production. In fact, Gellene had waited until at least late July before he even informed Hindes of the need for documents, even though the request had been served in April. Hindes was not happy about having to assemble the material on short notice — he was preparing for his own deposition in the wind-up litigation — but he managed to comply promptly with Gellene's request.

In other words, Gellene invented an excuse, trying to make himself look better by invoking events that were beyond his control. It probably never occurred to him that anyone would try to investigate his excuse — which was, after all, more believable than a flat tire — and for a while it seems that he was right. Nevertheless, the bankruptcy judge refused to reinstate South Street's claim, although no one challenged the truthfulness of Gellene's motion.

Of course, the dismissal of South Street's $19 million claim was a disastrous outcome, made worse by the fact that it had been entirely avoidable. But Gellene's fib to the court — invoking a false connection between the contentious wind-up litigation and his failure to produce documents on time — went unnoticed at the time. The content of the motion was wholly unexceptional, the sort of thing that lawyers say all the time. Gellene's statement was superficially credible, which was all that mattered. Most likely, no one even wondered about it, or cared. The questions would all come later.

The following year, Gellene's world started to collapse when John Stark, a relentless attorney for Jackson National Life Insurance, began to suspect that Gellene had filed false documents in the hotly contested Bucyrus-Erie bankruptcy case, which had just been concluded in Milwaukee. Soon enough, Stark discovered that Gellene had concealed his law firm's ongoing relationship to one of Bucyrus's main creditors, in violation of the disclosure requirements of the bankruptcy statute.

On the basis of Gellene's fraud, Jackson National sought disgorgement of Milbank Tweed's hefty fee in the underlying bankruptcy case, ultimately recovering $1.86 million. In a separate fraud lawsuit, Milbank Tweed agreed to pay an enormous settlement, reportedly between $27 million and $50 million.

In the meantime, the matter had been referred to the United States Attorney for possible prosecution. Fee disputes and conflict of interest issues are usually resolved as civil matters, but the Milwaukee United States Attorney's office had recently been taking a particular interest in bankruptcy fraud. Nonetheless, it was not at all certain that Gellene would be prosecuted for failing to disclose his law firm's relationship to a creditor. Absent some further evidence of dishonesty or bad faith, the Assistant United

States Attorneys in charge of the case might well have decided that it was not worth pursuing, or perhaps that it warranted a misdemeanor charge at most. The lead prosecutor, Steven Biskupic, thought that the most salient issue was Gellene's state of mind when he made his false representations to the court. In turn, that required an assessment of Gellene's character. If he was generally a truthful and upright person, he might have gotten the benefit of the doubt. A previous pattern of deception, however, would lead Biskupic to the conclusion that Gellene deserved to be prosecuted.

Unfortunately for Gellene, there was such a pattern — and his phony excuse in the Gillett bankruptcy was part of it. Biskupic's investigation eventually led him to Gary Hindes, the corporate officer who had provided the documents to Gellene in the Gillett case. Hindes told Biskupic the entire story of the discovery fiasco, refuting Gellene's claim that intracorporate litigation had been responsible for the delay in document production. This may not have been exactly a smoking gun, but it did provide the prosecutors with an additional instance in which Gellene had lied to a court (there were a couple of others as well), and that cinched his fate.

The rest is unhappy history. Gellene was indicted on three felony counts of bankruptcy fraud and filing false documents. Throughout the subsequent trial, Biskupic and his colleague, Joseph Wall, made effective use of Gellene's misconduct in the Gillett case. The misleading motion was admitted in evidence, and Gary Hindes testified that Gellene's assertions were untrue, thus reinforcing the prosecution's position that Gellene was "someone who was willing to lie when it suited his purposes." In his final argument to the jury, Wall emphasized Gellene's false representations in the Gillett case, saying that he had "shown a total disregard of his obligations, his ethical obligations as an attorney." Biskupic returned to the same events in his rebuttal argument, concluding that Gellene was a lawyer "who lies about big things and . . . lies about small things."

It was a powerful theme, and it worked. After less than three hours of deliberation, the jury convicted Gellene on all three counts. He was sentenced to fifteen months in prison, along with a $15,000 fine. Needless to say, he was also disbarred.

There is no reason to empathize with John Gellene. His false representations in the Bucyrus case were quite evidently calculated and inexcusable. Nor did he take advantage of several opportunities to correct his false statements. Yes, other lawyers have gotten away with similar misconduct (and probably worse), suffering only fee forfeiture or other civil penalties, but that does not excuse Gellene.

The very lack of empathy, however, may make it difficult for other lawyers to learn from Gellene's ill fate. In retrospect, the bankruptcy disclosure statute was absolutely clear, and there was no justification for Gellene's withholding information about Milbank Tweed's conflict of interest. Thus, it would be especially hard for young lawyers to imagine themselves in Gellene's position. Of course, they would make full disclosure.

For that reason, it is crucial to recall that Gellene's misfortunes began with a series of much smaller misrepresentations — some of them fibs more than lies — of the sort that lawyers often use in seemingly routine circumstances. It is easy to understand the temptation to stretch the truth or cobble facts together when seeking a time extension or relief from a lapsed deadline. Just about everyone does it (unlike repeatedly lying about a conflict of interest), or at least it may often seem that way.

Then again, you never know when someone will decide to check out your tires.

10

Who Deserves the Truth?

PROSECUTING ATTORNEYS PLAY two extremely important social roles. On one hand, they are law enforcement officers, working closely with the police in the investigation, apprehension, and interrogation of criminals. On the other hand, they are legal professionals, working in a system dependent upon due process and fair procedures.

There is usually no dissonance between the two sets of expectations, but sometimes the conflict becomes acute. Public safety requires law enforcement to be relentless and resourceful in pursuit of criminals, but liberty and democracy require that the criminal courts operate fairly and honestly. Prosecutors have to function at the intersection of the two systems, striving to put felons in jail while also respecting their rights. It isn't always easy.

On July 8, 1998, a man from Jefferson County, Colorado, named William "Cody" Neal spoke on a cell phone to a sheriff's department investigator, confessing that he had tortured and murdered three women, and had raped a fourth. After several hours of negotiations, Neal said that he would turn himself in, but only if he could first speak to a defense attorney or a public defender.

Rather than locate a defense lawyer, the sheriff's department turned to Mark Pautler, the chief deputy district attorney, who agreed to impersonate a public defender. The ruse worked. Calling himself "Mark Palmer," Pautler promised Neal access to a telephone and cigarettes, and succeeded in persuading him to surrender. Neal was later convicted and sentenced to death.

His colleagues in the district attorney's office congratulated Pautler on a job well done, but Colorado's Attorney Regulation Counsel saw things very differently. Following an investigation, Pautler was charged with a violation of lawyer disciplinary rules, which prohibit conduct involving "dishonesty, fraud, deceit, or misrepresentation."

Pautler himself was unapologetic, insisting that he had done nothing wrong and, in fact, that he would do it all again. "I am quite comfortable with what I did that night," he testified before a special three-judge disciplinary panel. "I did [it] to save lives and take a killer off the street."

To his dismay, the hearing board ruled (with one dissent) that Pautler had indeed committed professional misconduct. It also placed him on disciplinary probation for a year and required him to take a twenty-hour course in legal ethics.

Colorado law enforcement officers were outraged at the finding, claiming that Pautler's actions "quite possibly averted a massive manhunt that may have driven Neal to flee, harm other victims, or take hostages." But many attorneys took a different view, pointing out that the prosecutor, by posing as a public defender, undermined the very basis of the attorney-client relationship. "The ends justify the means only if the legal system is a living fraud," said one defense lawyer. Another decried "the notion that if the crime is bad enough, government lawyers are entitled to lie."

On appeal to the Colorado Supreme Court, Pautler asked the court to craft an "imminent public harm" exception to the disciplinary rules. The justices unanimously rejected his argument, declining to establish such an exception while observing that nothing in the record "indicated that any specific person's safety was in imminent danger." As to the claim that Pautler had been acting as a "peace officer" rather than an attorney (and was therefore authorized to use deception in the apprehension of a dangerous felon), the court noted bluntly that the "obligations concomitant with a license to practice law trump obligations concomitant with a lawyer's other duties, even apprehending criminals." Holding that Pautler's admittedly "praiseworthy motive" was not a defense, the court affirmed the disciplinary finding, including the sanctions.

Again, Pautler did not give an inch. "I think it is more important to save lives," he told the press. "I think this slavish adherence to the Code even though human lives are going to be lost doesn't make sense . . . I don't know how you can minimize somebody who just killed three women."

Was Mark Pautler right or wrong when he lied to Cody Neal? Was the Colorado Supreme Court correct that "purposeful deception by an attorney licensed in our state is intolerable, even when it is undertaken [while] attempting to secure the surrender of a murder suspect"? Or did the ruling, as Pautler put it, "minimize somebody who just killed three women"?

The answer is that Pautler was wrong . . . but not wrong enough to deserve formal punishment. The judicial system absolutely depends upon lawyers telling the truth. We cannot have reliable determinations of guilt and innocence unless attorneys are bound to refrain from "deceit and misrepresentation."

That principle cannot be limited only to the courtroom. It must apply to negotiation, investigation, and everything else leading up to trial, or else the process itself may be hopelessly corrupted. Thus, it is always wrong for prosecutors to lie to defendants or other witnesses.

But Mark Pautler's lie was told in a unique circumstance. It was not done in the course of the formal legal process, but rather in an attempt to arrest a dangerous criminal. The law often recognizes that exceptional circumstances may call for exceptional measures. Police officers in "hot pursuit" may be excused from obtaining search warrants. And every state recognizes the so-called "necessity defense," which excuses otherwise criminal conduct if undertaken to prevent a greater harm.

When Cody Neal bragged about killing three women, he placed himself outside the law. There was no categorical imperative that required law officers to be honest with him before he was safely in custody. It was only at his arrest, when Neal was transformed from a fugitive to a prisoner, that his right to due process came into play.

The distinction is a fine but important one. Lying to obtain a conviction must be absolutely prohibited. Lying to obtain an arrest — well, that has to be judged case by case. In this instance, Mark Pautler made a decision under enormous pressure, temporarily placing public safety ahead of truthfulness.

Pautler's own counsel put it well, though incompletely, when he explained, "We're not advocating a system that allows lawyers to engage in deceit and misrepresentation. What we're saying is, that there are some times when engaging in deceit is justified when loss of life and limb are at stake."

He should not have stopped there. He should have added that simply gathering evidence or extracting a confession can never be one of the situations that justifies lying. To be viable, the "Pautler principle" must draw an unambiguous line between the functions of apprehending criminals and prosecuting them. As a former criminal defense lawyer and a lifelong civil libertarian, I believe that Mark Pautler made the right choice. If he was wrong, he was wrong for a good reason. Let's call it civil disobedience and hope that he is never placed in that situation again.

11

When Honesty Isn't Enough

MOST DAYS, I am proud to be a lawyer (which is a good thing, since I have devoted my professional life to teaching law students — and, I hope, preparing them to be decent, capable, ethical practitioners). Sometimes, however, the legal profession can be downright embarrassing. No, I am not talking about the ubiquitous lawyer jokes, or the so-called malpractice crisis, or even the constant questions about defending "the guilty." I can handle all of that with good humor, and I can usually explain why most of the criticisms are either misguided or just plain wrong. But there are no good answers to widespread complaints about pocket-stuffing lawyers who seem to wring every possible dollar out of their own clients. Being clever lawyers, they know exactly how to do it legally, without any technical misrepresentations — and that makes it all the more troubling.

With that generality in mind, here is a story is about a woman named Mary Corcoran and her encounter with the legal system. It begins in tragedy and ends in frustration.

On October 11, 1998, Mary's husband, Michael, was struck and killed by a railroad train while working on the Union Pacific track bed in Chicago. Shortly after the accident, Mary was contacted by a representative of the railroad, who wanted her to settle out of court. Negotiating on her own behalf, Mary eventually obtained an offer of slightly more than $1.4 million, at which point she decided to see if an attorney could do better for her.

A friend of Corcoran's introduced her to a lawyer named Joseph Dowd, a solo practitioner in suburban Des Plaines, Illinois, who lists his practice areas as bankruptcy, divorce, and real estate. Dowd spoke to Corcoran about the accident, and told her that she needed a personal injury lawyer. She replied that she was interested in retaining Corboy & Demetrio (one of the top personal injury firms in Chicago) because her father had known Philip Corboy in high school. Apparently impressed by her choice, Dowd arranged a meeting with Thomas Demetrio, and Corcoran eventually signed a contingent fee contract. She agreed to pay the firm

"25 percent of any sum recovered from settlement or judgment," and also consented to a referral fee for Dowd in the amount of "40 percent of the attorneys' fees." Referral fees are permissible in Illinois, under certain circumstances, because they encourage attorneys like Dowd to send complex cases to specialists, rather than attempt to handle them alone.

After nearly two years of litigation, the Corboy & Demetrio lawyers came to the conclusion that they could not improve on Union Pacific's offer — so they recommended that Mary accept the original $1.4 million, which had been held open by the railroad. Because they hadn't been able to get an increased offer, Corboy & Demetrio voluntarily waived any fee.

Not so Joe Dowd. He demanded payment of the referral fee — $140,000 — even though the firm actually handling the litigation had waived its fee. By his own admission, Dowd was not an experienced personal injury lawyer, and he had not actively participated in the litigation on Mary Corcoran's behalf. Nonetheless, he insisted, a contract is a contract, and his cut was right there in black and white. Corboy & Demetrio were free to waive their own fee, but he was (as he testified at his deposition) a "small-town, small-time lawyer just trying to make a living," and he wanted his 140 grand.

Like most states, Illinois has adopted a version of the Model Rules of Professional Conduct, including provisions that cover attorneys' fees. Referral fee agreements have to be in writing, signed by the client, and all attorneys' fees have to be "reasonable." Among the factors listed for determining reasonableness are "the time and labor required" of the lawyer and "the amount involved and the results obtained." Most people, including most lawyers, might suppose that $140,000 is an unreasonable amount for attending several meetings, reading a file, and making some phone calls — which pretty much describes the work Joe Dowd claimed to have done for Mary Corcoran. Incredibly, however, the judge agreed with Dowd. The fee agreement would be enforced as written.

Mary Corcoran appealed, represented by Chicago lawyer Christopher Hurley. The appellate court ruled that Dowd had a contractual right to payment, even though neither he nor Corboy & Demetrio had obtained an increase in the railroad's offer. If Mary wanted a pay-only-for-improvement clause, the court held, she should have asked for one. But that ignored the fact that she was depending on the lawyers to draft the contract and protect her interests, and apparently no one specifically pointed out the absence of such a clause. Still, the Illinois Supreme Court refused to hear the case, so Joe Dowd got his money.

This whole sad affair might be dismissed as an aberrant decision by misguided courts, but it is actually more serious than that. With only a few exceptions, no court system has done a good job at policing attorneys' fees, especially on behalf of unsophisticated clients. In fact, Mary Corcoran was lucky that she found a lawyer to defend her against Dowd's fee petition. Most clients in her position would probably have simply acquiesced, out of either ignorance or powerlessness.

Even more fundamentally, the courts and the bar ought to take a closer look at the concept of contingency fees. Although they are prohibited in most other countries, contingency fees are permitted in the United States on the rationale that they provide broad access to the courts. The lawyers stand to make huge profits, but that is justified on the theory that they run the risk of nonrecovery.

In other words, you would think that a proper contingency fee would have to be, well, contingent on accomplishing something. Nonetheless, no state prohibits lawyers from attaching contingent fees to a client's preexisting offer. A client can actually lose money, therefore, if she consults an attorney to determine whether she has a reasonable offer in hand — which is exactly what happened to Mary Corcoran. The problem could be solved by a simple adjustment in the Rules of Professional Conduct, providing that lawyers may collect contingent fees only on the basis of some tangible benefit achieved for the client. Let's call it the "earned recovery." A few states have considered rules along those lines, but the organized bar opposes the change.

States should also consider capping referral fees at, say, five percent of the "earned recovery," and perhaps an absolute limit of $100,000 as well. That would provide plenty of compensation for the referring lawyer, and a standardized fee would eliminate the possibility of bidding wars for the referral of lucrative cases. Florida already imposes a percentage restriction on referral fees, which would have saved Mary Corcoran over $60,000.

Most of the lawyers in the Corcoran case acted admirably. Corboy & Demetrio did not even ask for a fee once they realized that they could not improve on the original offer. Chris Hurley, the appellate lawyer, covered all of Mary's litigation expenses, though he ended up not getting paid. Even the railroad's lawyer decently kept the $1.4 million offer open for over two years.

Only Joseph P. Dowd pursued self-enrichment, providing plenty of ammunition for lawyer bashers, too many of whom already think that we are all parasites. Dowd did not return my phone calls, so I cannot tell you his side of the story. But I do know that he renewed contact with Mary Corcoran following his appellate court victory — he sued her for additional interest on his fee.

In an earlier day, churlish practitioners were shunned by their colleagues, excluded from professional gatherings even as they continued to practice law. Maybe guys like that are incapable of embarrassment, but a little peer pressure might go a long way. I know that I would cross the street to avoid a lawyer who selfishly exploited a naïve client, even if he never actually lied to her and managed to stay within the rules. Shake hands? Not a chance. Sure, it's impossible to say whether that would make any difference. But as an attorney, I know that the effort alone would make me feel better.

12

Hypocrisy on the Left

IT WOULD HAVE been easy to feel sorry for Lynne Stewart, the New York attorney who was convicted in 2005 of providing material support to terrorists and sentenced two years later to twenty-eight months in a federal penitentiary. After three decades of providing dedicated — and sometimes brilliant — representation to the poor and despised, her career was ruined, and (as she once put it) she had no pension plan. Yes, her crimes were dreadful, but she wasn't the first poor soul to be led astray by the romance of somebody else's revolution. Judging from the outpouring of support she received from former clients, colleagues, and even adversaries, she had obviously done much good in her life.

Given all that, I once set out to write a finely balanced account of the Lynne Stewart case, weighing both the good and bad, and perhaps ultimately applauding Judge John Koeltl's decision to give her a far lighter sentence than the prosecution had requested.

But then I read her own words, which were filled with sanctimony and disdain. Far from apologizing for putting innocent lives at risk, she persisted in justifying her illegal conduct while assailing those who disagree with her radical views on the battle against terrorism. So however much I tried to sympathize with Lynne Stewart — because she is an ailing grandmother, or because she has spent many years as a champion of the friendless and outcast — there was no escaping the fact that her goals and actions had undermined the essential values that attorneys in a democratic society should hold dear.

Let's start with Stewart's pre-sentencing letter to Judge Koeltl, in which she attempted to explain why the court should not send her to prison. At a time when one would expect considerable candor and absolute contrition, Stewart could not keep herself from attacking the motives of the prosecutors, accusing them of taking "unfair advantage of the climate of urgency and hysteria that followed 9/11 and that was re-lived during the trial." In contrast to the evidently perfidious prosecutors (and the apparently gullible jury, still swayed by "hysteria" more than four years after the

9/11 attacks), Stewart characterized herself as "caring," "heartfelt," "misunderstood," or at worst "overly optimistic" and "naïve." Not for a moment did she concede that the government might have had a good reason for isolating her convicted terrorist client, Sheikh Omar Abdul Rahman. Nor did she admit to anything other than a minor — and in her view, entirely understandable — error in judgment by notifying the sheikh's followers that he had withdrawn his support for a "cease fire" in their war against the Egyptian regime.

In other words, Stewart insisted that she was wholly righteous, while the prosecutors were malicious or worse. And that was when she was trying to make a good impression.

After Judge Koeltl delivered his surprisingly lenient twenty-eight-month sentence (the prosecutors had asked for thirty years), Stewart reverted to form. On the street in front of the courthouse, she told her assembled fans that the light sentence was a "great victory against an overreaching government" and bragged that she could do the time "standing on my head." Lest anyone take her contrition (such as it was) too seriously, she declared her intention to someday make herself "back into the lawyer I was."

The cheering crowd knew just what she meant. Throughout her career, Stewart had exemplified a certain style of highly politicized lawyering in which she paid nearly as much attention to her clients' anti-government causes as to their legal rights. In her letter to Judge Koeltl she called this "caring for the whole client," but the reality was hardly so benign. As she explained to death-row inmate Mumia Abu-Jamal (in an interview posted on Stewart's own website), "the real essence of this work [is] to defend people such as yourself in these cases as political people." Representing Sheikh Abdul Rahman "as a political person" apparently meant serving as a bridge to his organization, the Islamic Group, which was well known for launching armed attacks against westerners, Coptic Christians, and Egyptian police.

Abdul Rahman, it should be remembered, was convicted in 1995 of plotting a bombing campaign in New York and conspiring to murder Egyptian President Hosni Mubarak. In 1997 his followers murdered fifty-eight European tourists as part of their campaign to cripple the Egyptian economy and topple the government. Afraid that the sheikh would inspire further violence, the U.S. government placed him in extraordinary prison isolation and prohibited him from communicating with the outside world. Only his lawyers (including Stewart, who had defended him at trial) and their translators were permitted access to the sheikh, and they were required to sign affirmations that they would not use their meetings or correspondence with him to pass messages to third parties.

Stewart broke her promise, using her visits to facilitate communications between the sheikh and the Islamic Group. Most egregiously, in 2000 she issued a press release announcing that Abdul Rahman had withdrawn his support for a cease-fire in Egypt that had been in place since shortly after the tourist murders. She also distracted the prison guards — pretending to be speaking to Abdul Rahman while really just talking gibberish — so that her translator could take down messages from the sheikh and pass them along to his acolytes, including the notorious Ahmed Abdul Sattar, who once composed a fatwa that called for "killing Jews wherever they are found."

Stewart and her defenders make two basic claims. First, that her message-carrying for Abdul Rahman was simply vigorous advocacy on behalf of an unpopular client, and second, that her prosecution was part of a government plan to discourage other lawyers from representing accused terrorists. It is hard to decide which claim is more offensive, but let's take them up in order.

According to Stewart, she had no inkling that "the government could misunderstand and misinterpret my true purpose," which was nothing more worrisome than zealously standing "between the Sheik [sic] and the government." Yet here again, she revealed herself. Explaining why the imprisoned Abdul Rahman required such extraordinary protection, Stewart told Judge Koeltl that she had "watched helplessly as his powerful intellect and fervent faith were replaced by imaginings and paranoia. Eight years of incarceration and three years under the [Special Administrative Measures] were taking their intended toll. I found it unbearable."

Intended toll? *Intended toll!* Yes, that's right. Stewart argued that the sequestration of Abdul Rahman was intended to harm him, and not simply to protect the rest of the world from his plots and plans. There can be little doubt that the sheikh was enduring harsh conditions, but he was, after all, a duly convicted terrorist conspirator, tried in open court and afforded full due process of law. He was the acknowledged leader of a violent organization that had no evident qualms about murdering innocent civilians. The Special Administrative Measures — put in place by the Clinton administration, well before 9/11 or the war in Iraq — may have gone too far, but it was outrageous for Stewart to claim that they had been intended to torment her client.

No matter how unbearable she found the sheikh's situation, and no matter how deeply she sympathized with him, Stewart's conduct went far beyond the acceptable limits of legal representation. It is not the job of a lawyer to facilitate political communication — even when it is not between terrorists. By choosing to become the sheikh's envoy, she stepped outside the role of counsel and assumed the risk of carrying out his unlawful goals.

Stewart attempted to justify her decision by claiming that she was working to "foster diplomatic as well as other legal solutions" for Abdul Rahman, by keeping him visible on the public stage so that he might one day be transferred to an Egyptian prison. By that logic, however, advocacy would have no constraints. Virtually any activity could be tenuously linked to a legal objective, justifying all sorts of complicity in a client's potential crimes. Perhaps reconsideration of the cease fire would have enhanced Abdul Rahman's standing in Egypt — conceivably even encouraging a prison transfer — but only by increasing the likelihood of Islamic Group violence. That's coercion, not representation, and lawyers should play no part in it.

Stewart's position is actually an insult to the many admirable and gutsy lawyers who are currently representing unpopular clients — including accused terrorists and Guantanamo detainees — but who have stayed within the requirements of the law. Have they failed to uphold the Stewart-defined standard of zealous advocacy by declining to carry illegal messages? Are they less worthy because they confine the representation to the courts, without becoming the political alter-egos of their clients?

Inevitably, Stewart's unique ideology of full-throttle advocacy raises the specter of the dread "chilling effect." While she does not exactly scorn lesser lawyers, who do not adopt her full-service model, she is afraid that they may be intimidated by the government into short-changing their clients. Her great fear, she told Judge Koeltl, is that they will have to worry about whether their "zealous advocacy will be misinterpreted" by prosecutors. Or as she put it in a radio interview shortly following her conviction, "the fear to me is not the people who will say, 'No, I won't do those cases,' which may also be an outgrowth, but the people who *will* do the cases, but will now do them with an eye over their shoulder to make sure that they're doing [them] the way the government thinks that the case should be done."

Such arrogance is breathtaking, suggesting that her conviction — for lying and running terrorists' errands — will deter honest defense attorneys from doing their jobs. Does she really think that other lawyers would readily engage in similarly unlawful, or even borderline, conduct, if only they did not have to worry about prosecution?

Thankfully, Stewart is dead wrong. The defense bar understands its obligations, and many lawyers have vigorously represented accused terrorists, detainees, and so-called "enemy combatants" — all the way to the United States Supreme Court — with no lack of ardor or commitment, and often with considerable success. Her own lawyer, the estimable Michael Tigar, certainly showed no diminution of zeal on her behalf. Why should others?

Alas, Stewart will never concede that ordinary lawyers can do the right thing, unafraid of indictment because they are uninvolved in their clients' political movements. In her paradigm, the government is always mendacious, while furious resistance is always pure of heart. She has said repeatedly that she is proud of her representation of Abdul Rahman and would do it again if given a second chance. Honorable lawyers know better. So rather than feel sorry for Lynne Stewart, I suggest that we all feel proud of the rest of defense bar — the lawyers who truly uphold the ideals of advocacy within the bounds of the law.

13

Requiem for a Faithful Lawyer

MY FRIEND MIKE Lefkow was murdered on February 28, 2005. You probably know that already, since the killing made headlines around the world. Mike was married to a federal district court judge, Joan Lefkow, whose own life had been threatened by white supremacist Matthew Hale. In fact, Hale had been convicted of conspiring to murder Judge Lefkow, and he was awaiting sentencing when Mike (and his mother-in-law, Donna Humphrey) were found dead in the basement of the family home. Suspicion immediately focused on Hale and his followers, but it turned out that a different embittered litigant was guilty. A man named Bart Ross killed himself during a traffic stop, leaving a note in his car claiming that he shot Judge Lefkow's husband and mother in revenge for her dismissal of his medical malpractice case. The subsequent police investigation uncovered substantial physical evidence, confirming that Ross committed the crimes.

But no matter who murdered Mike, the loss is immeasurable — not only to his family, but to the entire legal community. Mike Lefkow was one of the rare lawyers who devoted himself almost entirely to the public good. He was tireless and selfless, reflective and compassionate, modest and straightforward, brilliant and quirky — just the way a lawyer should be. In 1971 he argued and won *Townsend v. Swank* in the U.S. Supreme Court, establishing a battery of statutory "welfare rights" for public aid recipients across the country.

About a year later, Mike interviewed me for my first job out of law school, at the Legal Assistance Foundation of Chicago. "Why do you want to work in legal services?" he asked.

"Well, I just want to help poor people," I replied.

"Wrong answer," he said bluntly. "Our job is to put poor people in a position where they can help themselves."

He didn't use the word "empower," which would not come into vogue for decades, but he made the same point. For lawyers, Mike wanted me to understand, self-importance is a seductive illusion, and self-obsession is a dangerous distraction from the work at hand. It is the client's case, not yours. Always remember that our highest goal is not beating an adversary or making a brilliant argument, but rather effecting our clients' autonomy, no matter who they are, by putting them in a position to make their own decisions about their own lives and property. And that holds true whether we represent welfare recipients, middle-class homeowners, or large corporations. Mike realized that legal services attorneys have exactly the same obligations as any other lawyers — to serve their clients, not to "help" them.

Well, I got the job, despite my youthful naïveté, and Mike's vision of client-centered lawyering has stayed with me ever since.

One thing that Mike did not mention — during our interview or in the following years when we worked together — was his religious faith. I knew that Mike was a believer, but I was actually a bit surprised to read about the full extent of his involvement in the Episcopal Church, at both the parish and diocesan levels. He was a vestry member, an usher, and a member of the stewardship committee at St. Luke's Church in Evanston. He also served as secretary on the Chicago Standing Committee, a six-person advisory council to the bishop. Christianity was obviously central to the way he lived, but he did not feel compelled to talk about it.

Of course, that contradicts the stereotype of liberal hostility to religion. If you get your information from talk radio and Fox News, you would think that conservatives are overwhelmingly devout churchgoers, committed to the establishment of "moral values," while liberals are skeptics at best, atheists at worst, determined to banish faith from the public square.

Mike Lefkow's life demonstrates the foolishness of that caricature. He was a liberal through and through, devoted to civil liberties, workers' rights, reproductive choice, separation of church and state, and all the other values that make the blue states blue. But he was also a devout Christian, taking his children to Sunday school every week and singing in the choir. For Mike, there was no contradiction between liberalism and Christianity. In fact, they complemented each other in his worldview. I suppose you could call it faith and good works.

Why have so many people come to believe that liberalism and religion don't mix? Part of the reason is surely the drumbeat from the right, pounding home the hot-button message that tax cuts, capital punishment, and Social Security privatization are essential to maintaining "Christian family values" and combating "secular progressives" and their "homosexual agenda."

But part of the problem is attributable to liberals ourselves. We can be guilty, I must admit, of a sort of dogmatic rationalism that must often seem intolerant of religious expression. While we may be opposed in principle to government funding for faith-based social services, we should take far more care to express our appreciation for the energy and devotion of the agencies themselves. Why did it take a Republican administration to set up a White House liaison for faith-based initiatives? Democrats could have engaged in the same outreach during the Clinton years, offering access, expertise, encouragement, and support, if not direct tax dollars. Indeed, there is no reason that Evangelicals shouldn't be tree huggers-given the Lord's command to exercise stewardship over the earth — and more of them might be if they were made to feel more welcome by science-centric environmentalists.

The U.S. Supreme Court has given us a set of ambiguous decisions regarding the constitutionality of displaying the Ten Commandments in government buildings. Conservatives are usually said to favor such displays, while liberals are opposed. I never had the opportunity to discuss this issue with Mike Lefkow, but I am pretty sure that I know what his position would have been. He did everything he could to live by the Ten Commandments, and he did not need to see them plastered on courthouse walls. But he would have taken that position out of love for the Holy Word, not antipathy or distaste.

I do not share Mike's beliefs, but I respect his faith, and I will always admire him for it. An entire generation of lawyers will deeply miss his wise counsel and deep inspiration, which warned us against prideful self-deception and taught us that "representation" calls for humility and humanity. As we say in my tradition: "May the source of peace bring peace to those who mourn."

14

Evolution of Myth

THE CELEBRATED SCOPES "monkey trial" is remembered today as a clash of ideological titans — the progressive warrior Clarence Darrow versus the fundamentalist warhorse William Jennings Bryan. As we have all been told, Darrow won the battle, if not the verdict, by humiliating Bryan in the name of modern science. Or at least that's the usual story. But while Tennessee's anti-evolution law was indefensible, other aspects of that long-ago "trial of the century" were much more complex, and Bryan was far from the Bible-thumping caricature of contemporary myth.

On July 10, 1925, hundreds of spectators packed a courthouse in Dayton, Tennessee, to hear the case against substitute biology teacher John Scopes, who was charged with the crime of teaching evolution to his high school class. The trial was carried on Chicago's WGN radio (making it the first trial ever broadcast) and reported by H. L. Mencken, the acerbic columnist for the *Baltimore Sun*, who memorably dubbed it the "monkey trial."

Earlier in 1925, the Tennessee legislature enacted the "Butler Bill," which made it a crime to teach "any theory that denies the story of the Divine creation of man as taught in the Bible, and to teach instead that man has descended from a lower order of animals." In signing the law, Governor Austin Peay expressed his belief that the provision was merely symbolic and would never be "an active statute." For a short while it seemed that he was correct. No school district sought to enforce the law, no teachers were fired, and Tennessee high schools continued to use a widely distributed biology textbook that included a five-page section on Darwinism and evolution.

The American Civil Liberties Union, however, saw the Tennessee statute as a dangerous precedent, and feared that other states and localities might follow suit (and might not be so benign regarding enforcement). Therefore, the ACLU sent a press release to Tennessee newspapers, seeking a volunteer to test the validity of the anti-evolution law.

In Dayton, a group of civic boosters saw the ACLU notice and seized on the idea that a high-publicity trial could help reverse their town's sagging economy. They convinced Scopes, who was also a football coach, to agree to a "friendly prosecution" as quickly as possible (it was rumored that other towns were contemplating their own test cases). Contrary to legend, the popular Scopes was never persecuted or ostracized for the crime of teaching evolution. In fact, he remained friendly with the local prosecutors and school board officials throughout the trial.

Once Scopes was formally charged, news of the impending "monkey trial" spread across the country. Soon, William Jennings Bryan and Clarence Darrow offered their pro bono services, and the stage was set for a memorable confrontation.

Clarence Darrow has been well served by popular history, his virtues fittingly chronicled and his flaws largely forgotten. Darrow was a masterful courtroom advocate and determined champion of the underdog. He was also a famously outspoken agnostic, which led him to volunteer for the Dayton case. Some ACLU leaders feared that Darrow's controversial reputation would damage their cause, but Scopes was adamant about having Darrow on the defense team.

In contrast, Bryan's reputation has suffered greatly, and unfairly, over the years. Three times the Democratic nominee for president of the United States, he served as secretary of state under Woodrow Wilson, a position he nobly resigned to protest what he considered an overly bellicose foreign policy.

To be sure, Bryan was a staunch fundamentalist Christian, deeply committed to the biblical account of creation. But he was hardly an intellectual luddite or parochial blowhard. In fact, Bryan's biblical literalism told him that all humanity was created in God's image, and this tended to make him an egalitarian on issues of race and gender. Given his times, the "Great Commoner" had remarkably little tolerance for crude racism or anti-Semitism, and he was an early supporter of women's suffrage.

Darrow was also a liberal on race matters, but many of his supporters were not. The supercilious Mencken, who had urged Darrow to get involved in the Scopes case, frequently displayed his stereotypical prejudices, freely referring to African Americans as "darkies" in his caustic reports from Dayton.

More seriously, many of the leading scientists of the day applied a callous version of "social Darwinism" to human evolution, positing that some "races" were more advanced than others. Prominent anthropologists earnestly took measurements of cranial capacity, seeking to demonstrate that

Anglo-Saxons were more highly evolved than other races and therefore more "fit" for survival.

The very textbook that John Scopes used in his classes — George Hunter's *A Civic Biology* — declared that humanity could be divided into five races, each occupying an ascending step on the evolutionary ladder. "The highest type of all," it probably goes without saying, was "the Caucasians, represented by the civilized white inhabitants of Europe and America." The same book, which Darrow championed in the name of progress and enlightenment, also advanced a theory of eugenics, the "science" of racial improvement through selective breeding. It argued that the infirm and feeble-minded should be separated by sex, as a means of "preventing intermarriage and the possibilities of perpetuating such a low and degenerate race."

Then there was the fabled showdown between the giants, when Darrow called Bryan to the witness stand as an expert on the Bible. Despite Darrow's best efforts, Bryan mostly maintained his poise, explaining that his fundamentalism did not preclude an understanding that certain biblical passages, such as "ye are the salt of the earth," were illustrative rather than literal. Other verses, such as "the sun stood still," were rendered in nonscientific language that Bryan said "could be understood at that time." Contrary to the famous scene in *Inherit the Wind*, it was Bryan, not Darrow, who pointed out that the days of creation were not "literal 24-hour days," but instead could have extended for millions of years.

The examination did grow heated as both men became increasingly frustrated. Bryan accused Darrow of prejudice against the Bible, and Darrow responded by ridiculing Bryan's "fool religion." It is hard to say who got the better of the exchange. Bryan was clearly thwarted by some of the toughest questions, but Darrow's outspoken contempt for religion is just as embarrassing in retrospect. Eventually the judge had enough. He stopped the examination and struck all of the testimony from the record.

In the end, it did not matter. Realizing that he could not win in Dayton, Darrow asked the jury to find his client guilty, expecting to appeal the verdict all the way to the U.S. Supreme Court. The Tennessee Supreme Court, however, reversed on a technicality, and the case simply died.

What lessons can we draw from the Scopes trial? It was wrong and foolish, of course, for the Tennessee legislature to outlaw the teaching of evolution. Indeed, the effort to squelch science in the name of religion made an indelible impression on the national memory, blotting out the highlights of Bryan's career. For much the same reason, it would be a tragic mistake to require that theories such as "creation science" or "intelligent design" be taught in biology classes. When superimposed on science, religion is discredited.

But that should not prevent us from recognizing that both science and religion contribute to our understanding of the world. Science cannot claim always to be right, and — as in the case of eugenics — it can sometimes lead us down grievous paths when untempered by humility. In the 1920s, Bryan's creationism proved more tolerant than did early anthropology.

Given today's estrangement between liberals and "people of faith," an open-minded reappraisal of the Scopes trial might remind both sides that you do not have to be secular in order to be a humanist.

15

Hidden Interests

A GOOD LAWYER was sued for malpractice. He had put together a joint venture that eventually went bust. The principal investor lost his life savings, and was now crying conflict of interest. Here is what the good lawyer had to say about the claim: There was no conflict of interest between joint venturers because they had the same objectives and mutual goals — namely, to acquire and develop a certain parcel of real estate. Because he saw no conflict of interest, the good lawyer made no disclosures and gave no warnings. Because he believed that he represented "the venture," he obtained no explicit consents from the individual participants.

The lawyer had introduced two clients to each other. One was a real estate developer in search of financing to redevelop a strip mall; the other was an investor in search of new enterprises. It was a classic a "slam-dunk" project, and the two partners-to-be were plainly perfect for each other. After a short round of friendly negotiations, the lawyer helped them forge a joint venture, drafting the agreement and otherwise papering the deal. The developer would take care of appraisals, permanent financing, renovation, and management. The investor would provide a bridge loan and a substantial infusion of working capital. Once the mall was up and running, they would equally share the plentiful profits.

All went well until an essential "anchor tenant" failed to materialize and the whole deal collapsed. At once, the previously cooperative team members were at each other's throats. The developer declared bankruptcy. The investor discovered that he had all sorts of unanswered questions for his lawyer. Why hadn't there been an independent appraisal? Where was the accounting for the so-called development costs? Why was no security pledged for the bridge loan? How committed had the anchor tenant been in the first place? Why hadn't there been an escrow or performance bond? The good lawyer suddenly looked liable.

And, indeed, it turned out that he was liable — ordered by a jury to pay more than $1 million in damages. His error was a common one, though not a mistake that a layperson would expect a lawyer to make. He had forgotten to pay attention to each word in a sentence. Remember his explanation, "There was no conflict between the joint venturers, because they had the same objectives and mutual goals." The good lawyer had overlooked a crucial and most fateful phrase: "of interest."

The key to avoiding malpractice liability is not just to worry about glaring conflicts, but also to pay attention to more subtle "conflicts of interest." Our good lawyer recognized immediately that his co-clients were not in direct conflict. They were, after all, trying to do a deal that promised to enrich everyone. They had a strong mutual desire to see the mall open and prosper. But so what? Clients who were in direct conflict, who were actually hostile or opposed to each other, wouldn't be doing a deal together in the first place. And if, for some odd reason they were doing a deal, they certainly would not go to the same lawyer. It is hard even to imagine the scenario: "You want the mall to succeed, but I want it to fail; let's see if we can get the same lawyer to help us."

No, the true danger lurking in most cases of joint representation is the unrecognized conflict of interest. Though the parties' ultimate goals may be in complete and utter harmony, their underlying interests may still be inconsistent and diverse. So long as their goals are achieved and wealth ensues, everyone will enjoy the happy ending, and no one will sue for malpractice. But once aspirations are thwarted and hopes are dashed, clients may come to realize that their separate interests were not fully safeguarded.

In the case of our good lawyer, for example, the developer was putting up "sweat equity." He had a half-rehabbed mall on his hands, and he desperately needed an interim loan. His costs were sunk; he would lose everything unless he could attract new money. The developer's interest, then, was in pushing the joint venture through as quickly as possible and with few strings attached. The investor, on the other hand, had liquid capital. If he didn't invest in the mall — well, there were plenty of other places where he could park his million and a half bucks. The investor had a strong interest in caution and security.

Given the competing nature of the two interests, it should now be obvious that one lawyer could not zealously protect them both. It would be impossible to propel the deal urgently (which is what the developer needed) while at the same time judiciously slowing it down (to make sure that the investor's concerns were served). Despite the parties' general concurrence, their interests dictated very different approaches to the process.

This is certainly not to say that the good lawyer was absolutely barred from representing both the investor and the developer. Indeed, it is common, and often preferable, for a single lawyer to represent several partners, incorporators, or joint venturers. It is necessary, though, that each of the clients be fully advised of the risks and implications of the multiple representation. And that requires a clear-eyed understanding of all of their underlying interests. Once there has been full disclosure, the clients may or may not elect to proceed with the same counsel, but their consent must be knowing and intelligent. Most important, it must be based on something more than an absence of direct antagonism.

I have quite purposely referred to our malpractice defendant as a good lawyer. In fact, he was a very good lawyer — careful, thorough, competent, and thoughtful about his legal work. He did pro bono cases and was active in the bar. Good lawyers are not immune from malpractice or malpractice lawsuits. Our good lawyer made one devastating, irrevocable mistake. He looked only at whether his clients were in conflict and he forgot about conflicts of interest.

16

When Conventional Wisdom Goes Wrong

BACK IN THE early 1970s some energetic and youthful legal services lawyers filed a creative lawsuit that challenged the procedures for evicting public-housing tenants in Chicago. Relying on the Supreme Court's landmark opinion in *Goldberg v. Kelly*, they argued that public-housing residents were entitled to fair hearings before eviction cases could be brought. The upshot was the creation of so-called tenant boards, which had to approve every eviction (on grounds other than nonpayment of rent) before the city housing agency could even file a forcible detainer action in court. That seemed like a remarkable success for small-d democracy, but the victory soon proved ephemeral. The residents who volunteered to serve on the boards had little tolerance for their neighbors accused of drug use or violence, or even less harmful infractions like making noise or keeping pets. By the time I joined Chicago's Legal Assistance Foundation, in 1973, its lawyers had basically given up on the tenant boards. My supervisor told me not to represent clients at pre-eviction hearings, explaining that no one had ever won.

I suppose the obduracy of the tenant boards might have given me some interesting insights into the jury system — perhaps ordinary citizens are not really more lenient than "the establishment" — but I was young and idealistic, completely invested in the conventional wisdom (well, conventional within my own liberal circles) that we could always put our faith in the judgment of "the people."

And that brings us to the subject of real jury trials in criminal cases. Just about everyone thinks jury trials provide a relative advantage to defendants, and some very high-profile acquittals seem to underscore the point. (Think of O. J. Simpson, Richard Scrushy, the Amadou Diallo case, and Andrea Yates the second time around.) Lawyers and defendants alike have apparently internalized the lesson, overwhelmingly preferring juries to bench trials. Whether they expect common folk to be more incisive or more gullible than judges, more than three-quarters of defendants in federal cases opt for juries when they go to trial.

Surprisingly, however, the conventional wisdom about jury trials may be wrong, just as Chicago's legal services lawyers were wrong about tenant boards. In a study published in the *Washington University Law Quarterly* in 2005, University of Illinois law professor Andrew Leipold observed that federal defendants fare far worse before juries than before judges. Between 1989 and 2002, Leipold found, there was an eighty-four percent conviction rate in federal jury trials but only a fifty-five percent conviction rate in bench trials. The gap actually increased over the period, with jury conviction rates holding steady and bench-trial convictions falling dramatically. What's more, the disparity held true in every part of the country and in every type of case.

Leipold's statistics are impressive and convincing, and his article — "Why Are Federal Judges So Acquittal Prone?" — is far more readable than the typical venture into empirical legal studies. Most importantly, he asks the right questions about his findings: Why is there such a great difference in outcomes between judges and juries? And perhaps even more intriguing, why do defendants and their lawyers consistently choose the fact finder who is more likely to convict?

Exploring the first question, Leipold notes that federal judges have not always been so acquittal-prone. Not very long ago, judges convicted at higher rates than juries, with the current imbalance really taking hold only in 1989. And that timing, Leipold observes, coincides rather neatly with the November 1987 effective date of the mandatory federal sentencing guidelines, which drastically limited judges' traditional discretion in sentencing.

Many federal judges considered the guidelines draconian or worse, requiring them to impose overly severe sentences in case after case. Thus, Leipold conjectures, the increased bench-trial acquittal rate may reflect judges' reactions to the guidelines. "Put more bluntly," he says, "judges may acquit more often because they found it to be the only way to avoid imposing an unjust sentence they know would follow a conviction."

I doubt that any judge would admit to intentionally acquitting a guilty defendant. That would amount to disrespect for the law. Still, the reality of extra-harsh punishment might well serve to focus judicial attention on the burden of proof. It's well recognized that people tend to take weighty decisions more seriously, so it's reasonable to think judges might do the same, deliberately or not. And who knows? Maybe pre-guideline judges were conviction-happy, deferring to prosecutors and throwing doubt to the winds.

In any event, we may eventually have an answer to this question. In 2005, the Supreme Court partially invalidated the guidelines in *United States v. Booker*. Now that judges are freed from the most confining strictures of mandatory sentencing, it is possible that post-Booker bench trials will begin to return more convictions.

But whether or not the current trend continues, we still have to wonder why defense lawyers have spent fifteen years demanding jury trials when it appears that judges would have been nearly three times as likely to acquit their clients. There are two possible explanations: Either defense lawyers are really stupid, or they are very smart.

According to the stupid-lawyer theory, defense attorneys have simply failed to notice that juries are now much tougher than judges. No matter that juries have regularly sent innocent defendants to prison (in Illinois alone, at least eighteen innocent men were sentenced to death after jury convictions), lawyers have remained faithful to an ideal of jury as protector that has long been eroded by the public devotion to law and order.

Alternatively, it might be the (guiltiest) defendants themselves who are stupid, refusing bench trials because they have deluded themselves into believing they can bamboozle a jury of their peers.

On the basis of my experience, however, I tend to favor the smart-lawyer explanation. The disparity between bench and jury convictions might well reflect a successful strategy on the part of defense counsel, who astutely select the best fact-finder for each case. Under this hypothesis, defense lawyers take their best cases to bench trials because they believe that judges will be more adept at recognizing reasonable doubt. In weak cases, however, where the prosecution evidence is strong to overwhelming, they prefer jury trials in the hope that lightning might strike.

A public defender once explained it to me succinctly. "Our job," he said, "is to win bench trials and lose jury trials." That was many years before Leipold's conclusive study, but he accurately predicted the result.

There is another possible explanation for defense lawyers' seemingly counterproductive preference. In a bench trial, you either win or lose. In a jury trial, you can win, lose, or get a do-over in the form of a hung jury. From a defendant's perspective, the latter result is preferable to a conviction but it would not show up in Leipold's statistics. Remember, it takes only one juror with a reasonable doubt to hang a jury. And after a mistrial it is not unusual for the prosecution to tender a better plea bargain, perhaps by dismissing the more serious counts, in which case there would be no retrial. We don't know how often that happens, but the potential for a deadlocked jury (and the attendant post-trial benefits) could certainly influence defense lawyers' choices.

Even when a jury convicts, there is always the possibility that the judge will give the defendant another chance. In 2006, U.S. District Judge Jack Weinstein did just that in the closely watched "Mafia cops" case in Brooklyn. After the jury found two former New York City police officers guilty of murder and conspiracy for their involvement in eight mob assassinations, Weinstein threw out the convictions on statute-of-limitations grounds. Referring to the defendants as "heinous criminals" who had been "found guilty on overwhelming evidence of the most despicable crimes of violence," Weinstein nonetheless released them because he concluded that the "Constitution [and] statutes" required that he do so. It would have been difficult for a jury to acquit on such a "technicality," said one of the defense lawyers. Indeed.

Finally, let's consider the matter of, well, respect for the jury process. While no sane defendant would prefer conviction to acquittal, I suspect that many find it easier to accept conviction after a jury trial. "If I'm going to do time," I've heard it said, "I want a jury to tell me that I'm guilty." Even criminals, it turns out, may have faith in the system.

17

Sensory Deception

AT TWO O'CLOCK every afternoon in Tombstone, Arizona, several hundred people gather for a re-enactment of the storied Gunfight at the O.K. Corral. The crowds are mostly full of the usual tourists: retired couples, families with young children, a few newlyweds on their honeymoons, and a surprising number of leather-clad bikers. Sitting in a metal grandstand, about fifty yards from the actual site of the confrontation, they watch the three Earp brothers — Wyatt, Virgil, and Morgan — along with Doc Holliday shoot it out with the Clantons and McLaurys. Just like it happened on October 26, 1881, or maybe not (more on that later). Historical accuracy doesn't really matter much to tourists, of course. They just want to be entertained by a rousing Wild West show.

I found myself in Tombstone on a typically hot day in May. Like everyone else, I bought a ticket to the performance and headed to the corral. Unlike the other visitors, however, I had a keen professional interest in the sequence of the shootout. For several years I had been working on a book about the little-known legal proceedings that followed gunfight, so I wanted to see exactly how the crucial events would be portrayed.

The legend, of course, is well known. The Earp brothers were stalwart peace officers, determined to bring law and order to the tough frontier streets. The Clantons and McLaurys, on the other hand, were dangerous desperados who threatened the lives of everyone who got in their way. The Earps and Holliday faced down the four outlaws, killing three of them in self defense.

But there is another version of the story, told from the victims' point of view, in which the Earps were little more than badge-wearing thugs who shot down innocent men. In fact, the Earps and Holliday were arrested for murder shortly after the gunfight. Wyatt and Doc spent much of the next month in the Tombstone jail while Judge Wells Spicer heard the evidence that would decide their fate.

All of the witnesses agreed about the beginning of the fight. Ike Clanton had been blustering around Tombstone for a good many hours, openly carrying arms and threatening the Earps' lives (for reasons that have never been made completely clear). Eventually, he met up with his younger brother Billy and Frank and Tom McLaury in a vacant lot near the back entrance to the O.K. Corral. Billy and Frank (and maybe Tom) were carrying six-shooters.

Meanwhile, Virgil Earp, the town marshal, decided to disarm the cowboys. He called on his two brothers, who were deputies, and brought along Doc Holliday for good measure. When the small posse got within five yards of the Clantons and McLaurys, Virgil called out something like, "Boys, throw up your hands. I have come to disarm you."

Virgil and Wyatt testified that they saw Billy Clanton and Frank McLaury grab their revolvers. Reacting to the threat, Wyatt managed to draw his pistol and get off the first shot. "Then the firing became general" from both sides. Thirty shots were fired in less than half a minute, leaving the McLaury brothers and Billy Clanton either dead or dying. Virgil and Morgan Earp were seriously wounded as well, and Doc had been grazed by a bullet. Wyatt was unharmed, and so was Ike Clanton, who had run away when the shooting began.

Prosecution witnesses told a radically different story, agreeing only that Virgil had called on the cowboys to raise their hands. At that point, according to the prosecutors, Tom McLaury threw open his coat and shouted, "I ain't got no arms." Billy Clanton raised his hands and cried, "Don't shoot me, I don't want to fight." But the Earps, according to the prosecutors, were not really interested in making arrests. "You sons of bitches," shouted Wyatt, "you have been looking for a fight and now you can have it." Without hesitating, Doc Holliday pulled out his signature nickle-plated revolver and started shooting, followed quickly by Wyatt and Morgan Earp. The Clantons and McLaurys returned fire, but only after Billy and Frank had already been hit.

So it all came down to a single question: Who drew first? That was the difference between law enforcement and murder. Did the Earps and Doc Holliday gun down terrified men who were frantically trying to surrender? Or did they react professionally to a mortal danger? Were they simply faster and steadier than the Clantons and McLaurys, or did the Earps trick their victims into raising their hands, intending to kill them all the while? There was more to the story, of course. But stripped of every complication, that was what the prosecution was all about — the scant half-moment when Wyatt Earp followed the fleeting movement of Billy Clanton's hand.

With all of this in mind, I took my place in the Tombstone grandstand. The re-enactment was not going to resolve any historical controversies, but I was still eager to see how the actors would play out the gunfight. Would Billy Clanton and Frank McLaury reach for their guns before the shooting started? Or would they raise their hands in submission, only to be shot down in cold blood?

There has never been a better-prepared witness. I carefully selected my seat to have an unobstructed view of the entire tableau. I knew how the men would approach each other, and where they would be standing. I knew whom I had to watch, and whom I could safely ignore. And I knew precisely which words — "Throw up your hands, I have come to disarm you" — would trigger the violence.

So what do you think happened? Did Doc or Frank draw first? Did Billy raise his hands or make a grab for his gun?

Sorry. I don't know either. I must have blinked at the crucial instant, or maybe I was jostled or somehow distracted. Whatever happened, I just cannot say whether the Earps were portrayed as guilty or innocent on the Tombstone stage.

Sure, I could have stuck around another day for the next show. Or, more easily, I could have just asked the actors afterwards. Ultimately, however, I decided that I would actually learn more by staying in the dark — about the Earp case, and about eyewitness testimony in general.

As every lawyer knows, human observation is a poor tool for reconstructing the past. My own experience in the Tombstone audience confirms that even the most careful (and may I say, well-trained) eyewitnesses are unlikely to see everything important. Nor can they necessarily recall and accurately relate those things they do see. Testimony is always influenced, consciously or subliminally, by the witness's vantage point, perspective, expectations, biases, hopes, qualms, and fears. And those are the witnesses who are trying to tell the truth!

All of which should bring us to a renewed appreciation of cross examination. With so many inevitable impediments to accurate testimony, it is absolutely essential to test every witness's testimony in the proverbial crucible. As the late John Henry Wigmore, the great expositor of the common law of evidence, put it, cross examination is the greatest legal engine ever developed for the discovery of truth. Not because witnesses are lying — overwhelmingly they are not — but because it is so damn hard for any eyewitness to get everything right.

I left Tombstone basically satisfied, if not fully enlightened. And as I thought about it, I realized how much the unresolved ambiguity reinforced my admiration for the Earps' attorney, Thomas Fitch. The facts of the case could easily have gone either way, so he had every reason to fear that his clients faced the gallows. Fitch was one of the most talented and well-known lawyers of his era, and it was a fortunate coincidence for the Earps that he happened to be in Tombstone — then a classic boomtown — at the time.

It was Fitch who saved the day, through novel tactics and masterful technique. Invoking an outdated territorial statute, he figured out a way to put Wyatt on the stand without exposing him to cross examination (which was crucially important, because Wyatt probably lied). Fitch baited one of the prosecution's star witnesses into a disastrous exaggeration, and he cut another off at the knees with a prior inconsistent statement. In contrast, the prosecution team was riven by dissention and hobbled by conflicts of interest, which created even more openings for the artful Tom Fitch.

After 125 years, we will never know whether Wyatt Earp or Frank McLaury drew first, just as the most well-intentioned witnesses at the time could not be absolutely certain. We do know that it took a great lawyer to save Wyatt from the hangman's noose. Talk all you want of lawmen and gunfights, but cross examination really won the West.

18

How Lawyers (Ought to) Think

SHORTLY AFTER SEVEN o'clock on the morning of April 16, 2007, campus police at Virginia Tech University received word of a shooting in the West Ambler Johnson dormitory. Arriving at the scene, officers found that a resident advisor named Ryan Christopher Clark had been killed, and a freshman named Emily Jane Hilscher had been fatally wounded. The police immediately "locked down" the dormitory, but neither they not the university administrators took additional steps to secure the campus. Classes were not canceled, no perimeter was set up, and students were not notified of the shooting (or warned to stay home) for almost two hours. Even the lockdown at West Ambler Johnson was apparently lifted within about thirty minutes. Meanwhile, a twenty-three-year-old student named Seung-Hui Cho was reloading his weapons and mailing a chilling video-tape to NBC News. At about 9:30, Cho entered Norris Hall, a large class-room building, armed with two semi-automatic handguns and seventeen magazines of ammunition. He began shooting, murdering thirty-two peo-ple and wounding another twenty-eight, before he committed suicide.

In retrospect, it is easy to see that the campus authorities made an awful mistake. Knowing that a killer was on the loose, they failed to take relatively simple precautions that almost certainly would have limited the carnage. Cho would have found many fewer victims if only Norris Hall hadn't been so full of students and teachers, yet university administrators allowed classes to convene as though nothing had happened in the Am-bler Johnson dorm. Tragically, however, the investigation followed a blind lead, causing the Virginia Tech leadership team to believe that no one else was in immediate danger. In fact, the police initially turned their attention away from campus, tracking down an innocent man, while Cho continued to make his deadly preparations.

Among the first potential witnesses questioned was Hilscher's room-mate, Heather Haugh. She told the police officers that Emily had spent the weekend with her boyfriend, Karl, a student at nearby Radford University who lived in off-campus apartment, and that he presumably had brought her back to the dormitory earlier that morning. Although the police knew nothing else about Karl (whose last name I am omitting for obvious reasons), that immediately made him a "person of interest." Further questioning revealed that Karl was an avid gun owner and had recently taken Emily to a shooting range. That was enough to turn him into the prime, indeed exclusive, suspect. Despite Haugh's insistence that Karl was not a violent person, the police went racing off to find him — they later stopped his car and searched his home for a murder weapon — leaving the campus essentially unguarded and the unfortunate students uninformed.

How could experienced detectives make such a fatal misjudgment? Far from being irresponsible or negligent, they were in fact pursuing established investigative procedures. Sadly but not inexplicably, their training and instincts took them in precisely the wrong direction because they succumbed to a series of well-documented "cognition errors." The relatively new field of cognitive psychology has identified a number of ways in which human beings routinely err in evaluating information, either by relying on "heuristics" (or shorthand approaches to problem-solving) or by indulging certain "biases" (meaning innate decision-making preferences, not racial or other prejudice).

In the Virginia Tech investigation, the first pitfall was an "availability heuristic," or the tendency to believe that a newly observed event falls into a frequently encountered, known category. Whenever a woman is killed, especially a young woman, the first suspect is almost always a boyfriend or husband, and statistics bear out that grim assumption. Thus, police are taught to look for signs of domestic violence whenever there is a female homicide victim. The more domestic violence they've seen, the more likely they are to look for it in each succeeding case, because the image of a jealous or estranged lover becomes increasingly "available." That appears to be exactly what happened at Virginia Tech, as the investigating officers focused their attention on Hilscher's boyfriend. Even though Karl had no history of violence, and Haugh assured them of his "amazing relationship" with Emily, he nonetheless fell into the category that came most easily to mind.

Then the police learned that Karl owned firearms, leading almost inexorably to "confirmation bias." Having already concluded that Karl was the possible killer, his avid gun ownership — although it is not uncommon in rural Virginia — powerfully confirmed their suspicions. There is nothing wrong, of course, about putting two and two together premised on a combination of probabilities and facts. But the deductive leap from gun-owning boyfriend to double murderer turned out to be worse than unfounded. Once they fastened on Karl as the killer, the police evidently ruled out or discounted other, less available possibilities. And knowing that he did not attend Virginia Tech, the investigators disastrously veered away from campus.

The third and most dangerous cognitive error, therefore, was the "search satisfaction" fallacy — the inclination to stop looking for solutions to a problem upon the discovery of a satisfactory, if not ironclad, answer. It was not a mistake for the police to pursue Karl, based on everything they knew at the time. But it was a catastrophe when they assumed that they had identified the killer, and therefore ignored the real gunman who was stalking the campus for additional victims.

None of this is intended to disparage, or even second guess, the Virginia Tech detectives, who are surely heartbroken over the loss of so many lives. The point, rather, is that cognition errors are inherent in human perception, and no one (least of all judges or lawyers) is immune.

Hard-Wiring

There are many other common cognition errors. The "causation fallacy," for example, creates a presumption of a (frequently nonexistent) causal relationship between events, merely because one followed the other, just as "the pattern heuristic" may create imaginary relationships among isolated occurrences. Closely related is the problem of "hindsight bias," which suggests that an event was foreseeable (and therefore preventable) simply because it ultimately occurred. The "representativeness heuristic" may lead to assessments based on generalities, overlooking atypical or inconsistent factors, while "attribution errors" do just the opposite, focusing on a single (usually negative) characteristic to the exclusion of everything else. The "affective error" reflects a natural tendency to overvalue information consistent with our wishes or needs. "Commission bias" results in a preference for action over inaction, and "momentum bias" can prevent us from reevaluating earlier conclusions or otherwise changing our minds.

In practice, cognition errors are difficult to recognize because they are both subtle and inconsistent, potentially leading in many different directions. We might err either because we rely too much on generalities (domestic violence), or alternatively because we zero in on specifics (the boyfriend owned a gun), or both. The unifying factor for all cognition errors is that they are forms of conclusion-jumping, reaching decisions through often helpful but frequently misleading analytical shortcuts.

The prevalence of cognition errors exposes a profound flaw in the standard conception of legal fact-finding, in which judges or jurors receive information in a linear fashion — first one discrete fact, then another and another — withholding judgment until the very end of the evidence. As we saw in the Virginia Tech investigation, the reality is far different. It is impossible to withhold judgment because new information is immediately evaluated and interpreted in light of preexisting knowledge and reference points, and the mind is constantly drawing seemingly logical (but perhaps inaccurate) connections among facts. Without this sort of conclusion-jumping we could not make ready sense of the world, but unfortunately it can also lead us badly astray. In either case, it is hard-wired in our genetic code.

A thought experiment proves the point. Think back to the origins of humanity, when our earliest hominid ancestors first walked upright on the plains of East Africa. Imagine one such individual — we can call her Lucy — who is out on her daily hunt for roots and berries. She spies a lithe and tawny animal in the distance, with a shaggy mane and a long tale. "Hmm," she might say to herself. "That looks very much like the creature that ate my cousin last week." At this point, Lucy's neuro-pathways might take her in either of two directions. Under the traditional, judicial model, she would withhold judgment and investigate further. "Let's not be hasty," she would figure. "I'd better get closer to make sure."

Even if the beast roared and flashed its fangs, the incrementalist proto-human still would try to accumulate more information before taking precipitous action. That approach is obviously an evolutionary dead-end. Investigating a saber-tooth tiger would lead to a speedy demise, and conclusion-reserving hominids would not live long enough to reproduce. Thus, if there ever was such an inherent disposition, the forces of natural selection would surely have eliminated it en route to the development of *Homo sapiens*.

In contrast, conclusion-jumping hominids would have headed for the figurative hills at the first sight of anything that resembled a carnivorous quadruped, thereby increasing their chances of survival and procreation. The knack for quick decision-making would have been passed along from generation to generation, resulting in the heuristic phenomenon that is still observable today.

Life was nasty, brutish, and short in age of *Australopithecus* when our cognitive reactions first evolved, so Lucy and her heirs were naturally disposed to take few chances, avoid over-thinking, and assume the worst. Those preservationist tendencies clearly account for many of the most frequent heuristics — such as commission bias, affective error, and the causation fallacy — all of which would have helped our distant ancestors stay out of trouble most of the time. An occasional false impulse was a relatively small price to pay in exchange for evading the many ever-present life-endangering threats.

Today's world, however, is not as physically dangerous as it was in Lucy's time, nor are our decisions as simple as fight or flight. Thus, certain neuro-heuristics that were once well-adapted to survival have endured in the form cognition errors, especially when contemporary professionals — doctors, detectives, military officers, rescue workers, and of course judges — are called upon to make complex high-stakes decisions in which the most deductively obvious solutions may frequently be wrong.

How Lawyers Think

There is a substantial literature in some professions — medicine, clinical psychology, and social work, for example — addressing the need to recognize and correct for cognition errors. Interestingly, very little has been written on the subject for lawyers, and even less for judges. It is deeply regrettable that judges are not more attuned to potential cognition errors, although it is understandable given that they are subject to extreme confirmation bias. A judge's resolution of disputed facts is self-confirming, seldom disturbed even on appeal, thus providing little occasion for reexamination. Taking cognition bias to the extreme, Justice Antonin Scalia once remarked about death penalty appeals that "I have been on the court for 20 years and I have not seen a case where I thought there was the slightest doubt about the person's innocence." Statistically, that would seem to be nearly impossible; heuristically, it makes perfect sense.

Practicing lawyers face a different challenge. They need to be aware of their own possible cognition errors, which can cause problems interviewing clients, negotiating with other counsel, assessing witnesses, or evaluating evidence. Uniquely among professionals, however, trial lawyers must also consider the potential cognition errors of judges and jurors, in order to counteract the most likely mistakes or, putting it politely, to accommodate them.

The subject is touchy because the trial process inescapably relies on perceptions, usually second-hand perceptions, to determine facts. Thus, lawyers are often accused of manipulation or deception — taking advantage of a jury's biases, prejudices, or naïveté — which of course could include exploiting predictable cognition errors.

Possible instances quickly come to mind, especially in tort litigation. Did a patient take a particular medication and later suffer a heart attack? The causation fallacy will certainly imply a link. Did the same thing happen to many others? The pattern heuristic will tend to tie them together. Can the heart attacks be traced directly to the drug? That would be the attribution error. Should the pharmaceutical manufacturer have anticipated the danger? Yes, certainly, considering hindsight bias.

So what is the truth? Did the hypothetical medication cause heart attacks, or is that just a crafty, error-loaded insinuation? There is no abstract answer, of course, because some real drugs are foreseeably harmful and others are not. That is why we have trials. As to the role of cognition errors, sometimes they can influence a determination and sometimes they can be neutralized or remedied. That is why we have lawyers, judges, rules of evidence, and due process.

For better or worse, it is an advocate's job to draw plausible connections and a judge or jury's job to sort them out. Fortunately, the legal system comprises a number of correctives that can reduce, if not completely eliminate, the impact of cognition errors. Most important among these — indeed, the bedrock — is the requirement that all testimony be truthful. Lawyers are not free, as some critics charge, to spin stories out of dross, conjuring facts and inventing documents virtually at will. Yes, there are some cheats and fabricators, but, stereotypes notwithstanding, the great majority of lawyers are devoted to ethical practice and would never stoop to falsifying evidence.

Even when a lawyer plays fast and loose with either facts or inferences, opposing counsel is there to point out the missing evidence or logical flaws. For every attorney who tries to take advantage of cognition errors, another is ready to rectify false impressions and caution against mistaken conclusions. Because every argument is subject to rebuttal, the adversary system itself minimizes opportunities to exploit fallacies and heuristics.

Judges, too, play a role, weighing the probative value of evidence against the danger of unfair prejudice and its potential to confuse or mislead. Some rules of evidence specifically address certain cognition errors. For example, the attribution fallacy — that is, the inclination to base broad judgments on a single negative trait — is somewhat neutralized by the rule against offering character evidence to prove that a person acted "in conformity therewith on a particular occasion." In similar fashion, the rules on expert testimony limit the admission of "junk science" that is based more on inference and coincidences than sound data and well-researched etiology.

The most significant, and underappreciated, institutional shield against cognition error is the much maligned citizen jury. An individual judge, however well educated and thoughtful, considers cases from only one perspective; there is no ready counterweight when he or she makes a hasty or ill-founded conclusion. A jury, on the other hand, always brings multiple perspectives to bear on every decision. Despite all the stories of confused or misguided or "runaway" juries, the very process of deliberation tends to highlight, and therefore neutralize, any single juror's cognition errors. In a group of six or twelve, it is extremely unlikely that everyone will simultaneously rely on the same heuristics, such as availability fallacies or confirmation errors, because each person begins from a different set of assumptions, preferences, and experiences. While every juror is susceptible to cognition errors, collectively they will be able to catch, correct, and cancel out many of each other's mistakes.

Nonetheless, cognition errors are inevitable, widespread, usually undetected, and too often dangerous. They can cause serious harm in almost every field, potentially costing lives in medicine and law enforcement, and threatening freedom and property in court. Cognition errors are most pernicious because they always seem sensible — in fact, logical and compelling, as they did at Virginia Tech — when they are made. There is no universal solution to the problem, apart from vigilance and scrutiny. Fortunately, lawyers may have the additional advantage of a well-chosen jury — when and where you can still get one.

19

Truth in Humor

A PHYSICIST, A biologist, and a mathematician are sitting in an outdoor café and observing a vacant house. After an hour, two people walk into the house. A little while later, three people walk out.

"There must have been a measurement error," says the physicist.

"They obviously reproduced," says the biologist.

"If another person goes in," says the mathematician, "that house will be empty again."

Because you are reading this book, chances are good that you thought that my joke was pretty funny, though you probably wondered what it had to do with lawyers. It will take a little explaining (which, of course, will ruin the joke), but there is actually a close relationship between certain forms of humor and certain aspects of law practice. In particular, the principles of improvisational comedy can provide important insights for trial lawyers. But first, back to the empty house.

The introductory joke is funny because it appeals to your intellect, or at least to your education. In order to appreciate it, you need to have a grasp of negative numbers, and to recognize how they are used in equations. It works even better if you are accustomed to the company of academics or professionals, and if you understand how they over-intellectualize every experience. Depending on how well you remember your last math class, you might have had to pause for a moment after the punch line, eventually putting the two parts together before recognizing the premise: mathematicians view the world in terms of abstract numbers rather than real people. Thus, the assumption — bizarre to everyone else, but perfectly reasonable to a mathematician — that a house could hold a negative person (more people exited than entered) so that the addition of an actual person would result in an empty house (negative one plus one equals zero). Pretty smart. And if you get it, that means you're smart, which ought to cause you at least a smile of approval.

A joke is a highly stylized form of communication that is intended to arouse a particular response — a grin, a chuckle, a guffaw. In other words, humor is persuasion. A good joke makes you to laugh because it convinces you (sometimes instantaneously, sometimes following reflection) that something is funny. A joke, therefore, is somewhat comparable to a legal argument or cross examination question, each of which is also intended to evoke a specific belief (or disbelief).

To pursue the trial analogy, we can divide humor into two broad categories. One type of humor operates almost reflexively, jerking the laugh reaction, usually in response to someone else's misfortune. Slapstick is the prime example of this sort of humor, but it also comprises a good part of standup comedy, with its emphasis on outrageousness, embarrassing stories, and putdowns. One successful writer has defined this aspect of humor as "truth plus pain." Trial lawyers occasionally trade in similar goods, attempting to create reactions to witnesses ranging from awe to revulsion. But that is the smaller and lesser part of the lawyers' arsenal — useful in the short term but unlikely to bring long-run success.

There is another sort of humor, however, that does not depend merely on the audience's impulsive reactions. Rather, it emphasizes discovery, or even revelation. It is funny because you have to dig for deeper meanings, which of course makes you feel smart. And that makes you laugh. In improvisational theater and sketch comedy, the ideal is to cause you to laugh not in shock, but in delight.

So here's the point: Lawyers can learn a lot from improvisation theory, and it isn't just a matter of thinking on your feet. The key concept in both disciplines is the creation of a new, temporary reality. In improvisation, the cast must draw the audience into sharing the constructed reality of the stage, such that they can actually "see" the objects and characters portrayed, without the use of props or costumes. In trial, the lawyer must draw the jury into sharing the re-constructed reality of past events, such that they "see" what happened, even though they were not present to witness the original actions. Improvisation theorists and teachers have developed principles that guide performers in creating and maintaining a constructed reality in which the audience participates.

In the theater or comedy club, improvisationalists are bounded only by their imaginations. Trial lawyers (I trust it goes without saying) are far more constrained, limited not only by the actual facts of the case, but also by the laws of physics and common sense (both of which may be suspended at will on stage). There is one crucial restraint, however, that is shared by lawyers and improv artists: Both have to be totally honest about the relationships they portray. Although improvisers may make up facts (as lawyers may not, ever), the connections between details and characters, and therefore between the audience and the troupe, must always ring true for the show to succeed. For that reason, the principles of improv — especially the version known as "long form" — can be of great use to lawyers, who must make the same honest connections in trial presentations.

Long-Form Improvisation

Not all improvisation skills will help at trial. Faking foreign accents, rhyming spontaneously, and inventing witty puns all have their place in "short-form" improvisational comedy — but in court, not so much. "Long-form" improvisation, however, relies much more on the relationships among characters, locations, and situations and often consists of a series of scenes that can last anywhere from twenty minutes to an hour. It is less about being clever, and more about presenting realistic interactions between characters. Long-form improvisers trust that much humor will come from honestly portraying their characters' emotional reactions to the improvised situations. Most importantly, and perhaps counterintuitively, *long-form improvisation is not primarily about being funny*.

What? Long form improvisation is not primarily about being funny? How can that be? To be sure, "improvisational theater" has become almost synonymous with "improvisational comedy." And needless to say, long-form improvisation *is* funny — often hilarious, in fact. Nonetheless, it is not *primarily* about being funny.

Chicago's Del Close is usually considered one of the inventors of long-form improvisation. In his seminal book, aptly titled *Truth in Comedy*, Close explains, "To assume that making the audience laugh is the goal of improvisation is . . . just not true. Still, they laugh. It is a side-effect of attempting to achieve something more beautiful, honest, and truthful, something that . . . puts your attention on what is important about being a human in a community."

It may seem odd that the guru of improvisational comedy speaks so glowingly of not trying to be funny. If long-form improvisation is not about being funny, what makes the audience laugh? Del Close had an answer: "Where do the really best laughs come from? Terrific connections made intellectually, or terrific revelations made emotionally."

The concept of "revelation" is discussed in the work of Viola Spolin, who is America's first and most prolific theorist of improvisation. In her book, *Improvisation for the Theater,* Spolin explained that "With intuitive awareness comes certainty," meaning that improvisation succeeds (and coincidentally draws laughs) when the performers and audience understand something with preternatural certainty, beyond their actual senses.

For example, consider the following sequence from a long-form improvisational show at the IO Theater in Chicago.

Early in the show, a character named Gary told his friend that he had dropped an antique vase. Gary was established as an unlucky klutz, but the scene went on from there, having very little to do with the vase. Almost forty minutes later in the show, a seemingly unrelated scene involved several other characters in an apartment. Suddenly, an earthquake started, and the people inside the apartment reacted in near panic. Just then, Gary made an entrance, as if he had been walking past the apartment building. He was carrying something in both hands. The earthquake tripped him up, and he dropped whatever he was holding and cursed. Then he calmly continued across the stage without saying anything else.

In that moment, the audience recognized the character. They realized, even though no performers said anything about it, that they had just witnessed the moment when Gary dropped his antique vase. The entire audience laughed and applauded. Why? Because they recognized for themselves an element of the performers' constructed reality. Through an intellectual connection to the earlier scene, they recognized Gary and figured out what he must have dropped, even though no one in the earthquake scene named him or mentioned a vase. The audience realized that they now understood why he dropped the vase — because of the earthquake. Because the performers allowed the audience to make the connection, the event itself was enough to get a huge reaction. No clever jokes or silliness required. When the audience, by itself, identifies what must have happened with intuitive certainty, the desired effect — in this case gales of laughter — is sure to follow.

Of course, it only works when the audience has become part of the constructed reality. If instead they perceive the performers as pretending or inventing, they will not enjoy the same moment of recognition or revelation. For the same reason, the description could not have been especially funny to read. Improvised scenes are rarely entertaining when someone tells you about them. You have to experience the scene itself, entering the constructed world and sharing its premises, to understand how wonderful and amazing it was to watch that vase fall to the ground.

There is one more thing to learn from this example. Once an audience member has embraced the constructed reality, the events presented on stage will always be filtered through that reality. Imagine if, after the vase broke in the scene discussed above, another character came out and told a story about how Gary's vase broke when a bike collided with him. The audience will experience this story as one of three things: a lie, a joke, or a mistake. They *saw* the vase break, and they *know* — with intuitive certainty — that it was the result of an earthquake, not a bicycle accident. Though improvisers have the substantial power to create whatever reality they want, they are always stuck with whatever they create. Now we can begin to see how the theory of revelation in improvisational theater connects to trials.

Story and Frame

For lawyers, storytelling is not merely an optional technique. In fact, stories at trial are unavoidable, and so is constructed reality. Jurors bring their own frames of reference to the courtroom, and will fit new information into a storyline no matter what the lawyers do. It is a mistake to think that jurors accumulate facts, one after another, in order to arrive at a conclusion. Rather, they begin to imagine a story almost immediately, interpreting subsequent facts to fit into a familiar framework. Effective trial advocacy therefore requires tapping this narrative instinct by suggesting a powerful story at the very outset. If your story rings true to the jurors, and influences their frame of reference, they will interpret the evidence to fit your case.

The jury's frame of reference, then, can be all-important to the outcome of a case. A trial lawyer must be able to address disparate jurors, with their own experiences and frames of reference, and create a story that will impart a single perspective to the entire jury, a narrative framework in which to view the evidence.

If the trial lawyer is successful, the jurors will not feel like they have been convinced or persuaded — rather, they will feel as if something has been *revealed* to them. A persuasive argument may make the jurors say, "Okay," or "You win," but a powerful story makes them say "Of course," or, better yet, "I knew it!" The combination of evidence and storyline forms what Del Close called "terrific connections made intellectually, or terrific revelations made emotionally," which lead the audience to the desired conclusion. In other words, trial lawyers seek the same type of revelation that Del Close and Viola Spolin posit as the goal of improvisation. You might even say that trials are not primarily about persuasion, in the sense that the best lawyers are never overtly trying to be persuasive. Instead, they build their cases on "terrific connections made intellectually, or terrific revelations made emotionally."

Not surprisingly, then, Spolin discusses improvisation in language that might be easily applied to storytelling at trial. "[S]pontaneity . . . creates an explosion that for the moment frees us from handed-down frames of reference." Jurors, like all audiences, are not fresh canvasses on which trial lawyers can paint. They arrive at the courtroom with expectations and "handed-down frames of reference." The principles of improvisation work to untether the audience, at least in part, from the past, while bringing them into a new frame of reference, sometimes called a "group mind."

"Group mind" is the improviser's term for the collective consciousness that the performers and the audience share during an improvisational show. Group mind allows everyone in the theater to simultaneously "see" a dragon, a spaceship, or anything else on the stage, even though there are no props or special effects to make the stage-reality actually visible.

A trial lawyer shares the goal of an improviser: She wants to bring the jury into a group frame of reference that matches her story, her theory of the case. If she is successful, the jury will feel like they have "seen" the events in question at the trial, even though those events were reconstructed through testimony, not actually present in the courtroom.

Discoveries versus Inventions

Improvisers invite their audiences to see what is being created on stage. They draw the audience into a group consciousness, where mimed props and costumes are perceived directly. When everyone, including the performers and the audience, is part of the group consciousness (the same frame of reference), then details that the performers create seem to spring naturally out of the context of the piece, creating "Of course!" moments. "Of course!" moments occur when created details are experienced by the audience as *revelation*, not creation. It seems to everyone that the detail pre-existed its first appearance in the scene, and the performers simply "pointed it out" or "found it."

In this context, improvisers use "details" as an umbrella term for specific scenic elements. A line of dialogue can reveal a detail. For instance, if a performer says, "That's the tallest crane I've ever seen," then the crane is a detail in the scene. Performers' movements can also reveal details. For instance, if one performer makes a kicking motion, and the other performer "catches" an oblong object and tucks it under his arm, then a football is a detail in the scene.

A detail achieves a certain solidity or certainty when more than one performer acknowledges it in the same way. In the football example, both performers treated the object as a football. If the second performer, however, had simply ignored the kicked object, its nature would have been unclear. But if the second performer had screamed, "No! My baby!" then the kicked object would have become something — in this case, *someone* — entirely different. Note that there is tremendous power vested in the second performer, even though the first performer is the one who introduces the detail. Even if the kicker says aloud, "Catch this football I am kicking to you," the second performer still has the power to determine the force or accuracy of the kick (which could sail over her head or dribble on the ground).

When a scene is going well, improvisation teachers often call the details of a scene "discoveries." Interestingly, in the language of improvisational study, the opposite of a "discovery" is an "invention," which is understood as a pejorative. While clever details that come out of nowhere may get a small, surprised laugh from the audience, "inventions" confound the goal of achieving group consciousness because the audience experiences them as being created, rather than revealed. The reaction is not "Of course!" but rather "How clever!"

The bottom line is that a discovery is experienced as revealed, while an invention is experienced as created. Needless to say, trial lawyers want the jury to experience the evidence as revealed. Thus, long-form improvisers and trial lawyers share the same goal of revealing details and connections through a group frame of reference.

The Contract with the Audience

As Mick Napier, another leading improv theorist, once explained, "In our contract with the audience to make more of the truth we have created, we must sustain our visions and creations regardless of how afraid we feel in the moment." It is a performer's (or lawyer's) commitment to a detail that makes the audience perceive it as revealed rather than invented, thereby allowing the audience to increase its own participation in the group mind. A strong point of view, or story frame, helps improvisers just as it helps trial lawyers.

Imagine that an improviser establishes in a scene that he is a professional ballerina. If he is actually a large, clumsy man, the scene might initially strike the audience as an invented joke. But commitment to this detail over the course of the scene could potentially draw the audience into a reality where they in fact perceive him, for the purposes of the show, as a petite ballet dancer. Perhaps, thirty seconds after mentioning his profession, he tells a short anecdote about his role as a sugar plum fairy in last season's *Nutcracker*. He could ask his scene partner to hold his heavy dance bag while he practices an arabesque against the practice rail. If he is happy about something, he could rise on his toes and clap excitedly. In a creative pantomime, he could fluff out his tutu. With these confirming details, his ballerina-hood will be established as part of the constructed reality of the scene. If another performer refers to him as a corporate executive, the audience will experience it as a mistake, a joke, or a lie, because the consistent details have cemented the ballet-dancer character in their minds.

Conversely, imagine that after he establishes himself as a ballerina he begins acting like a plumber, telling his scene partner how to use a wrench while hiking up his sagging trousers. The audience will likely experience this incongruity without a unified frame of reference. Some will see the character as a ballet dancer who acts strangely. Others will see the character as a plumber who makes ballet jokes. Still others will see no character at all, but rather an improviser who is desperately trying to say funny things. If another performer then calls him an airline pilot, the audience may start looking at their watches or heading for the doors.

In a sense, details of a certain type are like a contract with the audience, or a promise. When you provide a detail in a scene, you are promising the audience that they will later discover more details that are consistent with it, and that you will not contradict it. As improviser (and later *Saturday Night Live* performer) Tim Kazurinsky put it, "If you create a dining-room table early in the scene, you can't just walk through the damn thing later on in the scene."

If you do not deliver on your promises, the audience will feel cheated, even if they do not realize it, and will begin to withdraw from the group mind. If another, more consistent version of "reality" is available within the show, the audience is likely to attach to it, and to react to your personal performance from within that perspective. If the show does not have a consistent version of reality, the audience members will usually react negatively to the performance as a whole.

Juries, of course, can also experience initial details as promises to deliver additional, consistent details. Just as a long-form improvisation audience feels cheated when you "drop" an idea, a jury may come to expect a certain type of evidence based on other evidence that has already been presented. If a cross examiner asks the defendant-driver whether he had his brakes checked, she is promising to say something later about the adequacy of his brake maintenance. If he insists that he kept his car in good condition, the lawyer can point out the absence of repair shop records. In that way, every succeeding detail can draw the jurors more deeply into the group frame of reference, helping them "discover" more and more facts favorable to the cross examiner's case.

Juries may not applaud you for fulfilling the promise of presenting consistent details and making emotional and intellectual connections. The reward in trial will come from achieving a group frame of reference, in which the details of your case seem to be revealed instead of invented. The jury, though maintaining proper courtroom decorum, may well be exclaiming "Of course!" to themselves when provided with successive details that support the constructed reality. Better yet, when the opposition presents inconsistent details, the jury will be more likely to experience them as inventions or mistakes. In other words, once the jury shares your group frame of reference, it becomes very hard for the opposition to work against you, because their case will be situated outside the group mind.

When long-form improvisers perform a scene and when trial lawyers present evidence, they have the same objective: to make the people watching say to themselves, "That's so true." In improvisation, the side-effect of that reaction will be laughter and cheers. In trials, when all goes well, the effect will be a favorable verdict.

20

Confronting Cougars

MOST LAWYERS DO not spend a lot of time camping in the wilderness, and probably very few have ever come face-to-face with a cougar. But confronted with that situation, any good lawyer would know in a flash that it is essential to escape without getting eaten. Risk management and goal assessment are among the profession's most indispensable skills. And while there are precious few certainties in either life or law, I think I can say with absolute confidence that nobody ever wants to be devoured by a big cat.

Of course, the scenario seems a bit far-fetched. Do cougars really eat people? If so, who and how often, and what can be done about it? Fortunately, the answers to these and other pressing wildlife concerns are neatly captured in an engaging little book called *Don't Get Eaten: The Dangers of Animals That Charge or Attack*. In ninety-three pithy pages, naturalist and avid outdoorsman Dave Smith explains how to avoid being clawed, chomped, or trampled by bears, buffalo, cougars, coyotes, javalinas (whatever they are), moose, and wolves.

Some of Smith's advice is pretty straightforward — don't try to pet a buffalo or feed a wolf — but some of it is incredibly complex. Concerning cougars, for example, he provides instructions for responding to attacks in five distinct circumstances, each requiring different tactics. There are, it turns out, six things that you need to do if the cougar is watching you from fifty yards away, three other maneuvers if it is "staring intensely," and yet two more if its tail is "twitching." In all, Smith details sixteen different anti-cougar gambits that should presumably be memorized and practiced before you ever venture anywhere near cougar territory (which evidently has lately included the outer suburbs of Los Angeles).

That probably seems like a lot of homework for a simple hike or camping trip, but cougars (also called pumas or mountain lions) are the largest predators in North America, easily able to snap your neck with a single bite at the base of the skull. So they are capable of killing you but, as it turns out, not very likely to do it. Since 1890, there have been fewer than one hundred documented cougar attacks in the United States, with only a handful of fatalities. Yes, the incidences have been increasing, now averaging perhaps five encounters per year, but you are still more likely to be mauled by your neighbor's dog or stung to death by bees (or, indeed, struck by a proverbial bolt of lightning) than you are to be savaged by a cougar.

But even though a mountain lion attack is pretty unlikely (it is about a ten-million-to-one shot, based on figures from the Census Bureau and the National Park Service), you still can understand why an avid naturalist with literary aspirations would want to squeeze a book out of that sort of material. There are probably plenty of intrepid campers who get a kick out of imagining hungry cougars crouching just outside the tent flap. But really? Who in their right mind would devote hours of study in order to prepare for an occurrence that is almost never going to happen?

Lawyers, that's who. A considerable part of lawyering — in both transactional practice and litigation — depends on contingency planning for improbable events. For better or worse, it is a lawyer's job to identify potential "cougars" and figure out how to handle them, if and when they show up.

Every straightforward real estate transaction, for instance, has to have a "risk of loss" provision, in case the property burns down between the contract signing and the closing date. That doesn't happen very often, but it's a cougar when it does. How about drafting a partnership agreement? Well, even best friends can end up at each other's throats once they're in business together, so you'd better include provisions covering involuntary dissolution, mandatory accounting, default, and disposition of assets. Those are cougars, every one of 'em.

You never know where danger lurks, so compulsive preparation is usually the safest course, especially when the client has sufficient resources to pay for it: Track down every last witness; take every conceivable deposition; research the law in each and every jurisdiction; rack your brain for every single thing that could possibly go wrong, and then rack it some more to come up with a "just in case" solution.

A litigation partner at a large Chicago law firm told me that he always personally examines the handwriting on the significant documents in his cases, whether or not there is an allegation of fraud. That may seem pretty aggressive (not to mention time-consuming), but he once noticed that two signatures — one on a letter and the other on a promissory note — seemed virtually identical, down to the last squiggle. Consulting a handwriting expert, he learned that no two signatures are ever exactly alike, unless one has been copied or traced. And sure enough, it turned out that a crucial letter had been forged. That successful bit of cougar-hunting saved his client a couple of million dollars, and he has been diligently comparing signatures ever since.

Then again, sometimes an obsession is only an obsession, as is often the case with the needlessly redundant language that so many lawyers reflexively stick into contracts and other documents. Apparently, it is never quite sufficient to say that an agreement is binding on "all successors in interest." That would seem pretty definitive to a normal reader, who would naturally assume that "all" means "all." But lawyers frequently feel compelled to elaborate, typically adding that the operative term includes but is not limited to all agents, officers, partners, assigns, heirs, devisees, employees, servants, representatives, affiliates, independent contractors, attorneys, insurers, entities, and all other persons, whether natural or corporate.

The morbid fear of latent ambiguity drives otherwise reasonable lawyers to manic repetition, which they foist on their clients (as well as the public) in the name of thoroughness. In order to gain access to a website, for example, I was recently asked to agree to a 182-word release. It included, so help me, twenty-five synonyms for liability and fourteen descriptions of possible claims.

And all I wanted to do was read about some cell phone options.

That sort of excessive verbiage goes far beyond mere cougar-deterrence, which is, after all, intended to guard against a real, if somewhat speculative, threat. The endless piling of phrase on phrase is more like wearing garlic around your neck to fend off vampires. What? You say there are no vampires? Well, then, the garlic must be working. (You can take that approach if you wish, so long as your clients don't mind the aroma and the expense.)

Good lawyers take care to protect their clients from actual dangers, even those that are contingent or remote. But they don't waste time and money on imaginary problems, and they don't allow their insecurities ("Let's see, have I left out any possible synonyms for debt?") to overwhelm their good sense. Over-lawyering imposes real costs on clients, the judicial system, and the public. In its mildest form, the use of dense legalese makes documents impenetrable and contributes to public skepticism about the law. More seriously, too many lawyers pad their bills by performing pointless tasks that serve only to run up the tab, while reassuring trusting clients that the work is absolutely necessary.

At its best, cougar-hunting is enormously useful to clients, allowing them to recognize unforeseen difficulties and plan accordingly. In complex negotiations — whether commercial, financial, governmental, or prenuptial — everyone is best served when the lawyers painstakingly search out all of the alternatives, so that the parties can determine which risks to undertake and which to ignore. Unfortunately, cougar-spotting is often carried to extremes. That's fine if you are writing a book, but it can be a wasteful imposition on unsuspecting clients. Good lawyers are candid about the difference between real and fanciful threats, and that's what makes them worth hiring.

PART III

Judges

Introduction

CHIEF JUSTICE JOHN Roberts began his confirmation hearings by comparing judges to umpires, but there was much more to the analogy than he allowed. Indeed, "Life Imitates Baseball," even in the courts, but not always as simply as Roberts suggested. One unexpected difference between the judicial system and baseball is that sports rules tend to be clearer, especially when it comes to Supreme Court procedures, as is explained in "The Elusive Transparency of Ethics." Least transparent of all is the Court's approach to recusal and disqualification, most famously on display following Justice Antonin Scalia's highly publicized hunting trip with Vice President Dick Cheney. Although Scalia justified, at great length, his decision to participate in Cheney's case against the Sierra Club, he never really got his "Ducks in a Row."

The chief justice has been vocal about his concern over the "crisis" in judicial compensation. It is hard to disagree that judges are entitled to "An Honest Day's Pay," but some of the arguments for a pay raise turn out to be surprisingly weak.

The judicial confirmation process has become increasingly unpleasant in recent years, with plenty of blame to go around. "Confirmation Mud" addresses some of the more egregious behavior on both sides of the political aisle, while "When a Spouse Speaks" laments the way that the Supreme Court itself has been dragged into partisan controversies.

The next four essays all deal with judges' characteristic inability to see the world from any perspective but their own. Call it blithe detachment or self-delusion, but from the lofty heights of the bench it is all too easy to misperceive or disregard a humble litigant's legitimate needs or requests. "Veiled Justice" tells the story of Ginnah Muhammad, whose religious rights were ignored by a polite but intransigent Michigan judge. "Bullying from the Bench" is an equally unsettling story about a Texas judge who behaved as though his courtroom was a schoolyard and he was the toughest kid on the block. In "Thought Control" the Indiana Supreme Court strained to find offense in an aggressive-but-not-profane footnote. Having bludgeoned a poor lawyer for his unintentional insult, the court would not even accept his apology. "Platonic Censures" is less severe but still troubling, as a federal appellate court imposed its idealized — and completely unrealistic — view of lawyering on struggling practitioners.

For some judges, "Stupid Judge Tricks" says it all.

21

Life Imitates Baseball

CHIEF JUSTICE JOHN Roberts knew he would have to address some controversial issues — abortion, gun control, civil rights, and more — during his testimony before the Senate Judiciary Committee in 2005. In a successful effort to head off too many tough questions, he based his confirmation strategy on an extended baseball simile. "Judges are like umpires," he said, objectively calling balls and strikes without becoming part of the game themselves. As we all know, it worked pretty well for him.

Baseball analogies might not be appreciated everywhere, but they are wildly popular here in Chicago, where the Cubs and White Sox annually contend for civic loyalty. Given the hometown teams' legendary lack of success — as of this writing, the Cubs have gone ninety-nine years without winning the World Series, leading diehard fans to rationalize that anyone can have a bad century — many of us are still slightly delirious over the White Sox victory in the 2005 World Series (their only appearance in the fall classic since 1959).

This being Chicago, however, the championship was not without charges of — how should we put it? — official largesse.

Early in the October playoffs, the White Sox did not exactly look like a team of destiny. Although playing at home, they lost to the Los Angeles Angels in the first game of the American League Championship Series, and at one point they were in serious danger of losing the second game as well, which would have nearly crushed their playoff chances. But they managed to win, thanks to a bitterly disputed decision by the home plate umpire.

The defining moment came with two outs in the bottom of the ninth, and the score tied at 1 to 1. While the hometown fans fretted that the game would go into perilous extra innings, A. J. Pierzynski came to bat for the White Sox. Angels catcher Josh Paul crouched behind the plate, and umpire Doug Eddings stood behind him. Pierzynski took two quick strikes, and then he swung and missed at what appeared to be strike three.

Suddenly Pierzynski dashed to first base, claiming that Paul had dropped the ball (which allows the batter to steal first). Miraculously,

Eddings called the batter safe, and the White Sox went on to win the game. That was alert base-running by Pierzynski, but it was the umpire's call that put the play in motion.

Eddings did not merely announce balls and strikes, as Chief Justice Roberts would describe the job. Rather, he made an outcome-determining decision based on his own judgment and a highly controversial application of an arcane rule. Roberts assured the Senate Judiciary Committee that "nobody ever went to a ball game to see the umpire," but Eddings sure managed to make himself the center of attention. His questionable call was subjected to televised replays from every conceivable angle, as viewers across the country watched it again and again. It turns out that the umpire can be a crucial "player" after all.

With that in mind, here are four observations that should be helpful to current and future Supreme Court justices:

First, textualism only gets you so far. It is fashionable in some circles to claim that the Supreme Court should limit its role strictly to carrying out the original intentions of the Framers of the Constitution, as though there is a handy template for applying its sweeping principles — equal protection, due process, freedom of speech — to modern life. But a look at baseball's rules will demonstrate the futility of that approach — and the Major League Baseball rule book is a model of specificity compared to the Constitution.

Rule 6.09(b) allows a batter to steal first base when the "third strike called by the umpire is not caught." So far, so good, but what happens when the umpire's ruling is challenged on the field?

Rule 9.02(c) allows a mid-game appeal to the umpire who made the questionable call, who "may ask another umpire for information before making a final decision." And there's the rub. An umpire may ask for input from his colleagues, but the rules give him no guidance about when, or how, or under what circumstances — much less how much deference he should give to his colleagues.

Should he be more inclined to get help in the late innings of a close game? Or if it is a pivotal play in the league championship series? Or if the rule involved is seldom applied? Indeed, can an umpire query his colleagues about replays on the stadium's Jumbotron? That would be asking for "information," after all.

seball's framers, however, did not provide much interpretive guid-
leir General Instructions to Umpires are maddeningly ambiguous,
mpletely contradictory: "If sure you got the play correctly, do not

be stampeded by players' appeals to 'ask the other man.' If not sure, ask one of your associates. Do not carry this to extremes, be alert, and get your own plays. But remember! The first requisite is to get decisions correctly. If in doubt, don't hesitate to consult your associate."

In other words, the framers expect the umpire to do the right thing, which calls for a level of situational judgment that written rules can never supply. It's not so much that the rulebook is a "living document" as that it has to be applied to real live games.

The next point is that conflicts of interest are not mere technicalities. They can really influence perceptions, even when it comes to matters of justice. It was painfully obvious to Angels fans that their catcher had not dropped the ball. Yes, it did roll around in his glove, but there always seemed to be some leather between the ball and the dirt. White Sox fans, given voice by the home team announcers, saw it differently, convincing themselves that the ball scraped the ground on its way into Paul's glove. But when successive replays raised too many doubts even for them, they just shifted to another rationalization. The Angels deserved to lose because their catcher should have known enough to tag Pierzynski, just in case.

Angels fans howled at the injustice of losing a game on a bad call, but to White Sox fans the outcome was entirely fair and right. The two sides will never see the play the same way, because they are simply too partisan. Everyone with an emotional stake in the outcome — even if it is only cheerleading — is too heavily influenced to be objective. That should tell us something about the need for recusal whenever a judge (or justice) is too closely identified with one side of a case. You might believe you can put your predispositions aside, Your Honor, but how can you tell whether your very perceptions have been skewed?

That brings us to the third lesson. The appearance of impartiality must be scrupulously maintained. Angels fans were furious at Eddings that night, calling him incompetent, blind, and ill-prepared. But no one ever called him biased. There was simply no reason to believe that he cared about who won the game. If he made a mistake, it was an honest one, which makes it tolerable in the long run.

But imagine the outcry if Eddings had recently gone, say, duck-hunting with White Sox owner Jerry Reinsdorf. In that (purely hypothetical, I assure you) scenario, would anyone believe that the ump could be completely dispassionate about the game? He might try any number of familiar-sounding explanations — I was friends with Reinsdorf before he owned the team; I paid for my own airfare; the hunting wasn't even that good — but so what? Angels fans would never get over the appearance of favoritism. And who could blame them?

Finally, procedure really matters. When Eddings flubbed the crucial call, the Angels had nowhere to turn for relief. Only the home plate umpire could reverse himself. Even if the other umpires disagreed, they were helpless to intercede unless Eddings requested their involvement. The super-slow motion television replays eventually demonstrated (even to this White Sox fan) that Eddings was clearly mistaken, but he held his ground, and his discretion was unreviewable.

Unfortunately, our Supreme Court justices have taken the same position regarding their own recusals. Each justice decides disqualification matters alone, without referral to the full court. If a justice makes a mistake, well, that's the ball game.

But baseball rulings, and even recusals, are trivial compared to the more serious procedural issues in the judicial system. Will death row inmates get better access to federal courts? Will wiretapped suspects get any access at all? Questionable judgments might be fine in a game, but they can be deadly in real life.

22

The Elusive Transparency of Ethics

THE SUPREME COURT'S two newest members — Chief Justice John Roberts and Justice Samuel Alito — took the usual, time-honored approach to their confirmation hearings, answering the perfunctory questions while artfully dodging anything substantive.

Unfortunately, some of the most important questions about the court's future were not even asked. I'm not talking about the meaning of federalism or the future of *Roe v. Wade*. Instead, I'm talking about a couple of necessary reforms in the currently oblique way that the court deals with ethics issues, including (1) revamping the way that it handles the disqualification of individual justices, and (2) adopting a full-scale code of conduct.

Under the Supreme Court's current and longstanding practice, recusal decisions — whether self-initiated or prompted by a party's motion — are made exclusively by the justice in question. This means that each justice acts, in effect, as the sole determiner of his or her own impartiality. No other judges in the United States exercise such absolute discretion over their own capacity to sit. In many courts, disqualification motions are referred to an unaffected judge, and in every court — save the Supreme — an aggrieved litigant may appeal or seek some other form of review.

Disqualification of Supreme Court justices does not come up very often, but it can be highly contentious when it does, as in the case involving Justice Antonin Scalia's controversial hunting trip with Vice President Cheney (discussed at length in the next essay). And while Scalia has drawn the most public criticism, this is not a partisan issue. In 2005, Justice Stephen Breyer determined that he could sit in *United States v. Booker*, a case deciding the constitutionality of the federal sentencing guidelines, despite having drafted part of the underlying legislation when he worked as a Senate staffer and then serving on the sentencing commission itself.

In a time of growing public disaffection with the Supreme Court, its authority depends on the perception that its decisions are based on reasoned deliberation, rather than personal idiosyncrasy. The utility of the court's opinions, moreover, depends on the guidance it provides to the lower courts. The Supreme Court's feudal approach to disqualification — each justice decides alone — fails both tests.

Another problem with the Supreme Court's recusal process is that the justices almost never provide their reasons for sitting or stepping aside. In addition to Scalia's opinion in the Cheney case, there have been only a few times over the past forty years when justices have stated the bases for their disqualification decisions, while recusals have averaged roughly one hundred each term. Justice Breyer, for example, did not explain his decision to participate in the Booker case, although it was reported that he had retained a prominent legal ethics professor to advise him on the question.

And consider the puzzling recusal gyrations in *Credit Suisse v. Billing* (2007). Chief Justice Roberts disqualified himself when the case first arrived at the court, as usual without explanation. Certiorari was granted, and the case was set for hearing before the remaining eight justices. Just a week before the oral argument, however, Justice Anthony Kennedy removed himself from the case (despite having already voted to grant the cert petition), announcing without elaboration "that he now realizes that he should have recused himself from participation in this case, and does now recuse himself." That left seven justices, but not for long. A few days later, Chief Justice Roberts undisqualified himself, rejoining the panel — you guessed it! — without explanation.

Not only do the justices decline to explain their recusals, they have never even provided a rationale for not explaining. But then, there really is no good reason to make the process so mysterious. Either the justices have solid grounds for their decisions or they don't, and in either case the public should not be left in the dark. Americans obviously care a great deal about the composition of the Supreme Court — it has been an important issue in most presidential elections since at least 1968 — and that no doubt extends to its occasional short-handed composition in specific cases.

Moreover, there are some lawyers, including friends and former clerks, who have inside information about the bases for justices' disqualifications — for example, the fact Justice Kennedy's son works for Credit Suisse or that Justice Clarence Thomas's son works for Wachovia Securities — that is only sometimes discovered by enterprising reporters. Thus, former clerks are able to predict recusals, when other lawyers cannot — an admittedly small advantage, but practicing lawyers will tell you that every edge counts.

The chief justice of the United States does not exercise much formal power, but he does control the agenda for the justices' case conferences. Chief Justice Roberts could make a significant statement about ethics issues by agreeing to schedule all future recusal motions for consideration by the full court. He could also set an example by issuing explanatory statements about his own recusals (and nonrecusals, and unrecsuals), while encouraging his colleagues to do the same.

Indeed, Roberts and Alito could show even greater leadership by urging the court to adopt a comprehensive code of conduct. There is nothing new about ethical codes for judges. The first Canons of Judicial Ethics were drafted by the American Bar Association in 1924, under the direction of a committee that was chaired by Chief Justice William Howard Taft. The canons, however, were vague and hortatory, providing little guidance on most difficult issues. In 1972, therefore, the ABA revisited the question of judicial ethics, promulgating the Model Code of Judicial Conduct (which has been periodically revised, and is now being updated by an ABA task force).

Today, all fifty states, the District of Columbia, and the lower federal courts (acting through the Judicial Conference of the United States) have adopted codes of conduct for their judges. Only the U.S. Supreme Court continues to operate on the laissez-faire nineteenth-century model. Congress has filled the void in a couple of areas — such as disqualification, financial disclosure, and outside income — but most ethics issues, including some pretty tough ones, are left entirely to each individual justice's conscience.

The Code of Judicial Conduct covers many subjects for which the Supreme Court has no announced standards, ranging from the highly controversial (acceptance of gifts and favors) to the mundane (service on nonjudicial commissions). Other such areas include: ex parte communications and consultations, public comments on pending or impending litigation, charitable and civic activities, ethics principles for court staff, reporting professional misconduct, and political activity.

Judges know what is expected of them in every other jurisdiction, and more importantly, citizens know what they can expect of their judges. In an age that demands governmental transparency, it is eminently reasonable to ask the first chief justice to be appointed in the twenty-first century simply to articulate the formal ethical standards for the court.

The topic of judicial administration seldom evokes much passion. Professional judge watchers are usually concerned far more about the substance of decisions than about the internal operations of the courts, even at the highest level. But in fact, Roberts and Alito, have an opportunity to improve the Supreme Court's own procedures for handling ethics questions, and now would be a good time to begin.

23

Ducks in a Row

AS EVERYONE KNOWS, Supreme Court Justice Antonin Scalia does not pull any punches. He also says what he means and means what he says. Blunt and outspoken, he is notably impatient with sly legalisms or logical gymnastics and has little tolerance for poor reasoning or flabby rationalizations. Sparing neither hapless lawyers nor his fellow justices, he often uses bitter sarcasm to underscore his arguments. Whether you applaud or cringe at his jurisprudence, there is no denying that Scalia's opinions are penetrating and direct, stating his principles and getting right to the point. Unlike many others, Justice Scalia does not trouble to dress up his premises or disguise his views. You might be tempted to say that he sets an admirable standard for transparency in judging, but that is not quite always the case. When his own conduct is questioned, it turns out that Scalia can be just as oblique, or should we say artful, as the lesser judges whom he so often derides.

In early January 2004, Scalia went on a now-famous duck-hunting trip with Vice President Dick Cheney, and seven others, at a private camp in Southern Louisiana. Such companionship between a Supreme Court justice and a politician would not always raise eyebrows in every quarter, but the timing of this particular excursion made it extremely controversial. Only a few weeks earlier, the Supreme Court, with Scalia's participation, had agreed to hear Cheney's appeal in a sensitive lawsuit.

Shortly after his 2000 inauguration, President Bush named Cheney to head the National Energy Policy Development Group, a task force charged with devising a national energy policy. Cheney's group worked in secret, without releasing interim reports or revealing the names of participants at its meetings. Such secret meetings are usually limited to government employees and officials, but it was widely suspected that Cheney's group also included energy company lobbyists and executives whose input on national policy might not be entirely detached from their own self-interest.

Two public interest groups — the Sierra Club and Judicial Watch — had sued for access to Cheney's records, and had succeeded in obtaining a lower court ruling that required the vice president to disclose certain documents. Noting that he could face a contempt-of-court citation if he failed to comply, Cheney asked the United States Supreme Court to take the case for review.

At some point in the midst of this, Cheney and Scalia confirmed their travel plans, and on December 15, 2003, just three weeks before the duck hunt, the Supreme Court voted to accept the case and scheduled it for oral argument.

Questions were almost immediately raised about Scalia's continued participation in the Cheney case, but he just as quickly discounted concerns about any possible impropriety. In a written reply to an inquiry from the *Los Angeles Times*, Scalia said that "social contacts with high-level executive officials (including Cabinet members) have never been thought improper for judges who may have before them cases in which those people are involved in their official capacity, as opposed to their personal capacity. For example, Supreme Court justices are regularly invited to dine at the White House, whether or not a suit seeking to compel or prevent certain presidential action is pending." Making light of the entire situation, he added that the hunting had been rather poor, but reassured the reporter that the ducks "tasted swell." (Later, speaking on a college campus, he brushed off a question from the audience with a sardonic "quack, quack.")

Not everyone thought it was a laughing matter. Although it is extremely unusual for a litigant to request recusal of a Supreme Court justice, the Sierra Club soon filed a formal motion to disqualify Scalia in the Cheney case, on the statutory ground that Scalia's "impartiality might reasonably be questioned" because of his extraordinary vacation with the vice president.

It is customary for Supreme Court justices to make recusal, or nonrecusal, decisions without comment. To his credit, Scalia departed from that practice, denying the motion in a lengthy opinion. In his characteristically mordant style, Scalia skewered the Sierra Club's request as ill-founded, unsupported, and totally without merit. If your only information about the issue came from Scalia's opinion, you might well wonder why he spent so much effort refuting such glaringly baseless arguments. But of course, that is the trouble. Scalia's tour de force (as some called it) displays not a moment's recognition that he is judging himself, much less that he might not be the most objective judge of his own impartiality, and least of all that his unconcealed umbrage actually makes him appear more partisan rather than less.

Despite its forceful certainty, Scalia's opinion is deficient in almost every conceivable way. It is wrong on the facts, wrong on the law, and wrong on procedure. Whether it is disingenuous, arrogant, or merely tone-deaf, it is clearly the work of a judge who has difficulty looking beyond his own self-conception and who is not much interested in the perceptions of anyone else.

The factual problems begin in the very first paragraph, when Scalia points out that Judicial Watch (the other plaintiff in the Cheney case) did not join the disqualification motion "and has publicly stated that it 'does not believe the presently-known facts about the hunting trip satisfy the legal standards requiring recusal.'" But under the applicable federal statute, Scalia was either disqualified or he wasn't, and Judicial Watch's position, even if "publicly stated," was immaterial. By inserting that gratuitous reference right off the bat, Scalia demonstrated that he would not be constrained by the usual standards of relevance or the formal record — Judicial Watch did not join the Sierra Club's motion, but neither did it file pleadings in opposition — in order to make his point. (It evidently did not occur to Scalia that the Judicial Watch statement might in part have been fashioned simply to avoid offending him, anticipating that he would bridle — as indeed he did, at one point calling the motion cruel — at the request for recusal.)

If Scalia gave himself considerable latitude regarding evidence, he did not extend that privilege to others. The judicial disqualification law requires recusal whenever a reasonable observer would doubt a judge or justice's impartiality. Quite understandably, therefore, the Sierra Club recusal motion cited numerous major newspaper editorials (8 of the 10 largest circulation papers in the country, 14 of the top 20, and 20 of the top 30) that had called for Scalia to step aside. This surely constituted at least some evidence that reasonable people questioned Scalia's appearance of impartiality in the Cheney case — many of the newspapers had endorsed Bush and Cheney in the previous election, so their editorials were not politically motivated — but Scalia would pay them no mind.

Instead, he complained that many of the editorials did "not even have the facts right." Scalia proceeded to provide corrections — disclosing for the very first time the precise details of his vacation — but the discrepancies were mostly trivial. The hunting trip had lasted forty-eight hours, rather than "several days"; their mutual host owns a company that services oil rigs, but he is not an "oilman" or "oil industrialist"; Scalia flew only one-way on Cheney's government jet, not round trip; Scalia was accompanied by his son and son-in-law, not his daughter. None of that makes any differ-ence, of course, because the question is whether Scalia's conduct created reasonable doubts, not whether every observer managed to guess correctly the contours of the trip.

The palpable irony is that Scalia himself is responsible for any public misperceptions. Originally, he steadfastly declined to answer questions about the trip (other than to say "quack, quack"), and then rebuked his critics for getting the facts wrong. Worse, he missed the entire point of the disqualification statute, which recognizes that the public's mistrust is a legitimate concern, even if it is somewhat inaccurate, therefore requir-ing recusal whenever impartiality may be questioned. Given the circum-stances of the duck hunt, and Scalia's refusal to provide details, it was not unreasonable for editors to wonder whether he and Cheney had "huddled together" or spent "quality time" in the Louisiana marsh. The protestations in his opinion — that he and Cheney had never been alone together, hunt-ing always from separate blinds — were ultimately circular, faulting news-papers, and by implication the Sierra Club, for "a blast of largely inaccurate and uninformed opinion," as though Scalia had not in the meantime kept the full story to himself.

According to Scalia, it evidently should not have mattered even if he and Cheney had shared the same room. "Washington officials know the rules," he said, "and know that discussing with judges pending cases — their own or someone elses's — is forbidden." By that logic, however, we would not need a disqualification statute, and certainly not one that requires recusal on the basis of reasonable questions. There would be no worries about the appearance of impropriety because, hey, "Washington officials know the rules." And there would be no real reason to prohibit ex parte communications or require financial disclosure forms, given that "Washington officials know the rules." Fortunately, Congress has legislated otherwise with regard to judicial disqualification, recognizing that citizens are entitled to doubt the conduct of public officials and therefore mandat-ing recusal on the basis of apparent partiality.

So much for the facts, selectively emphasized as they were. Scalia's dis-cussion of the law was also slanted sharply in his favor, beginning with his refusal to "resolve any doubts in favor of recusal." Although that approach would seem to be encompassed by the "reasonable question" standard of the federal statute, Scalia concluded that "even one unnecessary recusal im-pairs the functioning of the [Supreme] Court" by creating the possibility of a four-four split. While no one appreciates a tie vote, the fact is that Supreme Court justices recuse themselves all the time, with little evident concern about the risks of a subsequent draw.

For example, there were about one hundred such recusals during the last full term preceding the *Cheney* case (and at least eight hundred in the previous ten years), each of which might conceivably have occasioned a tie vote — or more likely the denial of a writ of certiorari, given that careful justices will ordinarily make the recusal decision in the initial stages of a case, before they can know its consequences. Prior to his *Cheney* opinion, Scalia had recused himself almost two hundred times since joining the court in 1986.

The justices almost never announce their reasons for stepping aside, but a great number of these disqualifications were no doubt caused by financial conflicts. The federal statute is extremely strict, requiring recusal if a justice owns just a single share of stock in a party to a case. Even still, the justices could easily reduce the number of disqualifications simply by moving their assets into mutual funds (which are not subject to the same strict rules). But most do not, presumably because they consider the composition of their portfolios sufficiently important to risk an occasional disqualification. That's fair enough, but it is also fair to point out nearly every single financial disqualification is therefore "unnecessary" in the sense that it could readily be avoided by switching out of private equities and into mutual funds and government bonds. This is not to say that any of the justices are cavalier about disqualification, but the issue just isn't important enough for them to change their investment strategies.

Notwithstanding the frequency of recusals, the dread four-four ties are exceedingly rare. According to a study by two political scientists, such stalemates occurred only eleven times during the period 1986–2003. During the entire post-war era, 1946–2003, there were 599 cases decided by eight-member courts, but only 49 (just over 8%) resulted in four-four deadlocks. Contrary to Scalia's contention, his colleagues obviously do not view the prospect of recusal as a looming disaster, nor are tie votes a serious problem for the Court.

Moving to the substance of the Sierra Club motion, Scalia concedes that his friendship with Cheney might be a basis for disqualification if the vice president's personal finances or freedom were at stake. But he goes on to assert that friendship "has traditionally *not* been a ground for recusal where *official action* is at issue, no matter how important the official action was to the ambitions or the reputation of the Government officer" (emphasis in original). The key word here is "traditionally," because Scalia cites no actual precedent for this assertion, although he repeats it many times.

On the other hand, he takes the Sierra Club sternly to task for failing to cite any cases that address his posited personal interest/official capacity dichotomy, no matter that the distinction does not seem ever to have been made before in a reported opinion (Scalia cites none) and neither is it found in the disqualification statute. Searching for support for his newly articulated rule, Scalia therefore relies upon the decades-old examples of two deceased justices — Byron White and Robert Jackson — each of whom reportedly vacationed with a high government officer who was simultaneously a named, official-capacity defendant in a pending Supreme Court case. Neither justice thereafter recused himself, nor, as far as we know, did any of the parties file a disqualification motion.

Scalia acknowledges and simply rejects the possibility that "times have changed" since the travels of White (1963) and Jackson (1942). But in fact, times have indeed changed in a very specific and extremely relevant way. Although Scalia does not mention it, the federal recusal statute was amended in 1974, significantly tightening the mandatory disqualification rules. Prior to 1974, the standard for recusal was left entirely to each justice's discretion, to be exercised only when "in his opinion" it was improper to sit in the case. In 1974, however, Congress changed the landscape completely, abandoning the subjective test (whether the justice sincerely believes he can be fair) in favor of an objective standard (whether an observer would reasonably doubt the justice's impartiality). Operating under the old law, the vacationing Justices White and Jackson evidently did not doubt their own impartiality, and it would have been pointless, or worse, for anyone to have suggested otherwise.

Scalia was well aware of the amendment to the recusal statute, having discussed it at some length in an earlier opinion. That makes his omission in the Cheney case baffling at best, and it makes his invocation of Justices White and Jackson both irrelevant and misleading.

Ordinarily, you might expect Scalia's fellow justices to alert him to such a glaring flaw in an opinion, but in this case he was flying solo, which exposes a profound defect in the Supreme Court's recusal procedures. When the Sierra Club's disqualification motion was filed, the full court, invoking its "historic practice," immediately referred it to Justice Scalia to decide by himself. In other words, the other eight justices refused to get involved.

This deferential approach to recusals — each justice decides alone — may be entrenched, but that does not make it right. Apart from the nine Supreme Court justices, no other judge in the United States exercises such unreviewable discretion when his or her impartiality is questioned, and there is no good reason for the members of the Supreme Court to reserve such power for themselves. As we have seen in Scalia's *Cheney* opinion, judges — like all human beings — are just plain bad at evaluating their own motives or objectivity, and worse still when it comes to assessing public reactions.

The justices disagree with one another all the time, often quite sharply, in much more momentous matters than individual recusals. That is why we have a nine-member court in the first place. In the case that invalidated homosexual sodomy laws, to take just one example, Scalia himself accused the six-member majority of abandoning neutrality and "taking sides in the culture war." But if six justices' judgment can be so dubious on an issue of constitutional interpretation, why should a single justice's judgment be sacrosanct on the question of his or her own impartiality?

Whether Scalia was right or wrong in the *Cheney* case, the other justices' abstention means that the public was deprived of a definitive ruling about the propriety of vacationing with litigants. Scalia articulated a new bright-line rule, stating that the ordinary disqualification standards do not apply in "official capacity" cases. Many observers may think that was the right result, my criticism notwithstanding, but no one can know whether it is actually the law. It is impossible to assess the precedential weight of Scalia's nonrecusal decision, because there is no way to tell whether the other justices agree or disagree.

Justice Scalia's opinion in the *Cheney* case was broad ranging, stylishly written, and unquestionably sincere. There can be no doubt that he believes passionately in his own ability to be impartial, no matter what anyone else might think. It is also obvious that he does not like to be challenged and that he bitterly resents criticism — at one point denouncing "the baseless allegations of impropriety that have become the staple of Washington reportage" as a threat to the very survival of the judiciary — while failing to recognize that such open resentment may itself reinforce the perception of bias.

24

An Honest Day's Pay

CHIEF JUSTICE JOHN Roberts drew an unusual amount of attention when he devoted his entire 2007 Report on the Federal Judiciary to a single issue — a request for increased judicial salaries. Of course, publicity was his goal. The chief justices' annual reports are not ordinarily big news, and therefore, as Roberts explained, he thought that the unusual focus would increase the chances that the public would take notice. "That is important," he continued, "because the issue has been ignored far too long and has now reached the level of a constitutional crisis that threatens to undermine the strength and independence of the federal judiciary."

That was a strong claim, but it was not unfamiliar. In many previous years, the late Chief Justice William Rehnquist had referred to a "pay crisis" in which the inadequacy of judicial compensation was "the single greatest problem facing the judicial branch." And who would be inclined to argue? The pay for federal district judges is $165,000 (rising to about $175,000 for appellate judges, and slightly over $200,000 for Supreme Court justices), placing their compensation far, far below the impressive income levels for partners at large law firms. As many have noted before, something seems seriously out of whack when even brand new associates can earn more money than the judges for whom they recently clerked.

If there is a single sentiment that unites the bar, it is the truism that federal judges are grievously underpaid. Calls for substantial increases have come regularly from the American Bar Association, law school deans, and various corporate counsel. The American College of Trial Lawyers responded to the Roberts report by proposing an immediate one-hundred percent raise.

And so it came as a great surprise when I went through all of Roberts's and Rehnquist's reports for the past twenty years and discovered that the case for a pay raise turns out to be remarkably thin (with one ironic exception; more on that later). The economic arguments were particularly unconvincing, relying more on dire suppositions than on meaningful figures or facts.

For example, Roberts opined in 2007 that "many judges who must attend to their families and futures have no realistic choice except to retire from judicial service and return to private practice," echoing Rehnquist's 2003 claim that "low salaries might force judges to return to the private sector rather than stay on the bench." While this may at first seem painfully obvious, the reality is that very few federal judges ever take that step. Rehnquist noted that "more than 70 [federal] judges left the bench between 1990 and May 2002." Five years later, the trend was almost unchanged, as Roberts pointed out that thirty-eight judges had resigned over the previous six years. That sounds ominous — or "sobering," as Roberts put it — until you do the math. On average, only about six federal judges have resigned each year, amounting to fewer than one percent of all life-tenured positions (and fewer still if you count "senior status" judges). And although neither chief justice mentioned it, the resignations include those who have retired to the golf course or lecture circuit, not just those who have returned to active practice.

Compared to virtually any other field of endeavor, a one-percent annual resignation rate is extraordinarily low. Attrition is many times higher — by at least an order of magnitude — at law firms, notwithstanding the stratospheric pay scale. Obviously, then, the rewards of public service continue to outweigh the lure of law practice for the overwhelming majority of federal judges. Besides, as every manager knows, a reasonable amount of turnover is good for an institution, encouraging fresh ideas and innovation.

Understandably, Justice Roberts thinks otherwise, contending that pay-related resignations directly threaten "the viability of life tenure," potentially eroding "the strength and independence judges need to uphold the law." Fortunately, the actual danger, if any, is not very great. The wisdom of the Constitution is to guarantee that judges may continue in office without fear of removal by the president or Congress, short of impeachment, thereby protecting them from political interference or retaliation. Judges might decide to resign for any number of reasons, including their financial needs, but no specific judge can be forced off the bench (absent a high crime or misdemeanor). Thus, the benefits of life tenure do not depend upon a model of lifetime service. It is the security of office that protects judicial independence, not the number of years any particular judge chooses to stay on the job.

And frankly, there have always been federal judges who ought to resign, either because they became jaded and disaffected, or because they were never suited to the job in the first place. Chief Justice Roger Taney, for example, served for twenty-eight years (1836–1864), complaining nearly all the while about his low pay. If only he had returned to his lucrative private practice in Maryland, the nation might have been spared the disgrace of his shameful opinion in the *Dred Scott* case, declaring that African Americans, slave or free, "were so far inferior that they had no rights which the white man was bound to respect."

But even if resignations are not currently a serious problem, what about the effect on future appointments? Rehnquist worried that "many of the very best lawyers" will not be "willing to be considered for a position on the federal bench." This argument might have some impact if there had ever been a shortage of applicants for federal judgeships. The fact, however, is that lawyers line up around the block for every vacancy, surely allowing selection from among the very best. There is no absolute guarantee this will always continue, but it was 1976 when Chief Justice Warren Burger first announced that a pay crisis threatened a "brain drain" from the federal judiciary. That bleak prognosis — repeated by successive chief justices at regular intervals, including a warning by Rehnquist in 1988 that "approximately 30 percent" of federal judges "planned to resign before retirement" — has yet to come anywhere near true.

Roberts shores up his argument, however, by pointing to a change in the composition of the federal judiciary. During the Eisenhower administration, he points out, roughly 65% of federal district judges came from the practicing bar, with 35% from the private sector. "Today the numbers are about reversed — roughly 60% from the public sector, less than 40% from private practice." That is a change, true enough, but Roberts does not say why he believes it is for the worse. In any event, it is not obvious how much of the difference is a consequence of pay levels and how much is attributable to changes in the legal profession. In relative terms, there just weren't that many public sector lawyers in the 1950s, compared to the subsequent expansion of prosecutors' and public defenders' offices, federal and state regulatory agencies, and legal services programs. It is admirable, not regrettable, that presidents have apparently chosen to tap that resource for the federal bench. Additionally, more than half the drop in lawyers from private practice, as can be seen on the graph included in Roberts's report, occurred between the Eisenhower and Kennedy/Johnson administrations, so the decrease over the ensuing four decades has actually been rather small. Finally, at least as indicated on Roberts's graph, nearly four out of five of the public sector appointees appear to have come from other "judicial service," presumably state courts and federal administrative courts. That seems to indicate nothing more than an increasing preference for prior judicial experience, which could reasonably be considered a good thing.

Despite more than twenty-five years of grim predictions, it is apparent that market forces have worked pretty well for the federal judiciary. In exchange for accepting their relatively modest salaries, federal judges gain freedom from the endless pressures of hourly billing, business development, client demands, liability exposure, and intra-firm intrigues, and receive the benefits of life tenure and retirement at full pay — not to mention the prestige of high office and the satisfaction of dispensing justice.

Meanwhile, practicing lawyers report extraordinary levels of job dissatisfaction, sometimes bordering on outright despair. Those high salaries come at an equally high cost, exacting their toll in time and stress. It is hardly surprising, therefore, that lawyers are abandoning private practice at a far greater rate than federal judges are leaving the bench. As a purely empirical matter, there is no pressing need, now or in the foreseeable future, to increase judicial salaries in order to attract or retain first-rate judges.

Before I provoke total outrage, let me add that there is one powerful argument in favor of a decent pay hike for judges. Chief Justice Roberts says that Congress has been "grievously unfair" to federal judges, and he is correct. It is not a matter of market competition, but rather a matter of equitable treatment. In 1969, Roberts points out, federal district judges earned twenty percent more than the dean of the Harvard Law School, while today they are paid less than half as much as the Harvard dean. That comparison is somewhat cooked by the selection of the base year — judges received a huge pay raise in 1969; in 1968 they actually earned slightly less than the Harvard dean — but never mind. It still rankles that many law school deans and professors are paid so much more than even Supreme Court justices. As Roberts and I appear to agree, the similarity of their work — thinking deeply and writing about the law — suggests that their pay ought to be somewhere in the same ballpark.

So the best reason for raising judges' pay is "comparable worth," the principle that compensation ought to bear some relationship to a job's intrinsic value, not solely to the competitive job market. To put it bluntly, federal judges are worth at least as much as law professors — and they are worth much more, by any measure of social utility, than most law firm partners — but they are paid far less. That disparity must surely be disheartening, as judges annually watch their compensation shrink in comparison to that of even mediocre specialists in, say, mergers and acquisitions. Even worse, judges virtually have to beg Congress for small cost-of-living increases, while elite practitioners have routinely raised their billing rates to new extremes. Judging is not a commodity, and it is both unreasonable and demoralizing to treat it like one.

Most conservatives, however, idealize "the market" and therefore reject the very idea of comparable worth, as well as the notion that there is any such thing as a job's intrinsic value. Given the ascendancy of free market fundamentalism, in both legislatures and courts, it is understandable that conservative chief justices annually embellish an essentially equitable case with appeals to economic efficiency. Alas, those who live by the market must die by the market, and the contrived economic rationalizations fall apart under close examination. As in any labor negotiation, such transparent brinksmanship ("More money or we'll quit!") merely encourages bluff-calling. No wonder Congress keeps ignoring judges' salary requests.

In December 2002, President George W. Bush urged Congress to "specifically authorize a pay increase for federal judges." That turned out to be another empty gesture, as he never pressed the issue. In any event, if I were a conservative congressman, I'm afraid I would have to vote against a raise, following the general free market labor policy of extracting maximum work for a minimum wage. As a liberal, however, I believe in pay equity — not only for judges, but also for minorities, women, disabled people, and others. So I would enthusiastically support a very generous salary hike for judges — even the Republicans among them — hoping that the lesson might stick.

25

Confirmation Mud

IT IS UNDENIABLE that the confirmation process for federal judges has become increasingly debased in recent years. Republicans will tell you that the descent began with the Robert Bork hearings in 1987 and accelerated when Clarence Thomas was nominated in 1991. Democrats will counter that Thurgood Marshall received pretty shoddy treatment as far back as 1967 (and in fact, Louis Brandeis was not exactly welcomed by the Senate in 1916). But whenever it began, there can be little doubt that the practice of blockading judicial nominations was raised to a fine art during President Bill Clinton's administration, when the Republican-controlled Senate Judiciary Committee used procedural delays to kill numerous appointments, often based on nothing more than a "blue slip" from a single Republican senator.

Sometimes the tactics were not that subtle. In 1999, for example, then-Senator John Ashcroft nastily attacked the appointment Ronnie White, who was the first African-American justice on the Missouri Supreme Court, by slandering him as "pro-criminal" with a "tremendous bent toward criminal activity." That stereotypical soft-on-crime hatchet job wasn't remotely true — White had repeatedly voted to enforce the death penalty — but it successfully defeated his nomination to the Eighth Circuit Court of Appeals.

Following President George W. Bush's inauguration in 2001, Democrats briefly took control of the Senate when Vermont's Jim Jeffords defected from the Republicans. Almost immediately, they began stalling President Bush's judicial nominations. At the time, that must have seemed only fair, given that Republicans had taken the same approach (and worse) during the Clinton administration. But history has a way of getting even, and the escalating confirmation wars ended up hurting Democrats in the long run.

One of the most controversial cases involved Mississippi District Judge Charles Pickering, whom Bush nominated to the Fifth Circuit in 2002. Many civil rights groups opposed Pickering's elevation, citing one particular case in which he had shown exceptional leniency to a young man convicted of burning a cross on the front yard of an interracial couple.

Although a jury had already found the man guilty beyond a reasonable doubt (after his two codefendants took plea bargains), Pickering decided that the mandatory minimum sentence was "draconian," and he began pressuring the prosecutors to retroactively dismiss some of the charges. When the prosecutors refused — pointing out that the sentencing law, though strict, was absolutely clear and that the defendant had rejected a proffered plea deal — Pickering issued an extraordinary order instructing them to personally discuss the case "with the attorney general of the United States." He demanded that the government provide him with a list of sentences in other cross-burning cases for comparison. And when he didn't get an answer, he made an ethically improper telephone call to a Justice Department official in Washington. Moreover, in his previous eleven years on the bench, Pickering had never published any other opinion decrying excessive sentencing. According to the Almanac of the Federal Judiciary, he was best known for increasing recommended sentences rather than lowering them.

The criticisms of Pickering were harsh but fair, firmly based on his well-documented efforts to circumvent a federal statute — conduct that President Bush might otherwise have branded "judicial activism" — on behalf of a convicted cross-burner. But Republicans, who had considerable confidence in Pickering's character, were outraged (including the wife of Supreme Court Justice Clarence Thomas, as discussed in the next essay). When Democrats on the Senate Judiciary Committee defeated the nomination, President Bush nonetheless used a recess appointment to place Pickering on the appellate bench, leaving emotions to smolder.

After Republicans recaptured the Senate in the 2002 midterm election, they believed their confirmation problems were over. For the first time since 1994, the Senate was controlled by the president's party, so it appeared that Bush would be able to appoint just about anyone he wanted. Democrats, however, had other ideas, including the unprecedented filibuster of unacceptable appellate court nominees. Again, the tactic seemed reasonable, perhaps even obligatory, at the time. Bush's nominees increasingly came from the far Right, and the filibuster was the only way to defeat the most extreme among them. Eventually, Democrats blocked ten nominees, bragging that the successful filibusters would demonstrate that they also could derail any non-moderate Supreme Court appointment.

It was one thing to defeat an appointment when the Democrats held

the majority; that's the legislative process in action. But every filibuster —
in which a minority of only forty senators can prevent a nomination from
even reaching a vote — had to be supported by much more powerful criticisms of the targeted judge, going well beyond a bad decision in a single
case. That put a premium on "opposition research," of the sort previously
reserved for wide-open political campaigns. Things were almost certainly
going to get ugly, as indeed they did when Bush nominated Texas Supreme
Court Justice Priscilla Owen to the Fifth Circuit Court of Appeals. There
were plenty of good reasons to oppose the Owen nomination on the merits. She had been called the most conservative member of the most conservative state supreme court in the nation. She was so far to the right that she
had dissented eighty-seven times from her court, which was composed entirely of Republicans, finding her colleagues either too soft on abortion or
too tough on corporations. One majority opinion — remember, they were
all Texas Republicans! — referred to an Owen dissent as "nothing more
than inflammatory rhetoric [that] merits no response." Another Republican justice called Owen's position in an abortion case "an unconscionable
act of judicial activism." And that was not just any Republican speaking. It
was Alberto Gonzales, who would later become Bush's White House counsel and then attorney general.

But some of Owen's opponents were not content to challenge her record. They also attacked her as "unethical," primarily because she had accepted campaign contributions from Enron and Halliburton, but did not
disqualify herself when those companies had cases before her court. One
liberal activist called her "Judge Enron," saying that she "illustrates the hold
that Enron established over the [Texas] courts."

Owen did not deserve that insulting sobriquet. Texas is one of ten
states in which supreme court justices are chosen in full-throttle partisan
elections. That makes their elections contentious and costly, with candidates raising and spending millions of dollars. Owen's campaign contributions were entirely lawful in Texas (they came from PACs and individuals,
including Ken Lay, but not directly from the corporations themselves) and
were similar to those received by every other justice and most other candidates. As in most states (the sole exception seems to be Florida), the Texas
Code of Judicial Conduct does not require judges to disqualify themselves
in cases involving campaign contributors.

Judicial elections are a bad idea everywhere, and Texas's are worse
than most, but the Texas constitution created that state's system, and
Owen simply played by the rules already in place. Perhaps it was politically

irresistible to tar her with the Enron brush, but it was just plain wrong to make that contrived ethics charge an issue before the Senate — even though it worked for a while.

Eventually, however, the filibusters backfired badly. Senate Democrats came across as petulant obstructionists, leading to more Democratic losses in the 2004 Senate elections, including the defeat of Minority Leader Tom Daschle. Even worse, Republicans were so enraged that they began to reconsider the sanctity of the filibuster rule itself, threatening the "nuclear option" of abolishing the filibuster through a simple majority vote. Repudiating a century-old tradition of comity and cooperation was not just drastic; it would have thrown the Senate into chaos. The Republicans surely would never have contemplated such an extreme measure, but for the Democrats' seeming refusal to respect the prerogatives of the majority.

The filibuster, it turned out, was a scorched-earth technique that could not be employed and re-employed endlessly. Rather than hold it in reserve for the Supreme Court, Democrats squandered it on a series of ultimately insignificant lower court appointments. In the end, they had to settle for a compromise, brokered by the so-called "gang of fourteen," in which Democrats agreed to release Owen's nomination for a floor vote (along with Janice Rogers Brown, nominated to the District of Columbia Circuit, who had also been filibustered) in which Republicans were certain to prevail. More crucially, Democrats also agreed that they would reserve future judicial filibusters for "extraordinary circumstances," as the price for maintaining it, if just barely, in the Senate rules. The nuclear option was averted, but only because the Democrats' use of the judicial filibuster had pretty much bombed.

Undefined as they were, "extraordinary circumstances" were in the eye of the beholder. Thus, potential filibusters were still technically an option in late 2005 when two positions became vacant on the Supreme Court. Push never came to shove over the nomination of John Roberts, Jr., because he was succeeding the equally conservative Chief Justice William Rehnquist. The replacement of Justice Sandra Day O'Connor, however, was another matter, as she represented the court's crucial swing vote.

Almost miraculously, the nomination of Harriet Miers presented Democrats with one last chance to keep a potential centrist on the Supreme Court. Needless to say, they blew it. Despite her well-known gushy admiration for her boss, Bush's White House counsel appeared to be a relative moderate, very much in the mold of O'Connor (that was long before revelations of Miers's highly partisan involvement in the controversial removal from office of eight United States attorneys). Within days, she came under withering fire from the extreme Right. Much of the assault was unkind, to say the least, and included snarky attacks on her background and education. But rather than cut Miers any slack, most Democrats were happy to watch the intra-Republican bloodbath, hoping that it would further weaken the politically wounded Bush. Miers's fate was sealed when it became clear that key Democratic senators, including Patrick Leahy and Charles Schumer, would not vote for her in the Judiciary Committee.

That brought us Samuel Alito, a nominee who, though modest and affable, was a literal avatar of right-wing jurisprudence. Given an opportunity to make a substantive case against Alito during his confirmation hearings, many Democrats wasted valuable time on specious charges of bigotry and unethical conduct.

The ethics allegations against Alito centered on a 2002 case that was decided when he was on the Third Circuit Court of Appeals. Since at least 1990, Alito had been heavily invested in mutual funds managed by Vanguard, holding somewhere between $400,000 and $1 million in multiple Vanguard funds. Nonetheless, he participated in a case in which a Massachusetts woman was suing Vanguard, joining a unanimous decision in the company's favor. About a year later, however, the plaintiff learned of Alito's investments and complained that he should have been recused.

Alito did not agree, but he still removed himself. "I do not believe that I am required to disqualify myself," he wrote to his court's chief judge; "however, it has always been my personal practice to recuse in any case in which any possible question might arise." The case was then reassigned, and a new panel of judges reaffirmed the original decision.

The judicial disqualification statute turns out to be pretty tricky when it comes to mutual funds. Without parsing the intricate details, it is sufficient to say that Alito was barred from hearing the appeal only if his investment in the individual Vanguard funds amounted to an ownership share in the management company. It was not immediately clear whether that is the case, however, at least from an examination of Vanguard's website and promotional materials.

But even taking the worst-case scenario and assuming that Alito got it wrong—initially sitting in the Vanguard case when he should have disqualified himself—he still showed admirable sensitivity when presented with the plaintiff's complaint. He did not dig in his heels and insist that his judgment was unquestionable. He did not engage in self-righteous self-justification (as a certain prominent jurist, the subject of "Ducks in a Row," has been known to do). Instead, he voluntarily stepped back and allowed the matter to be reconsidered by other judges against whom no claim of partiality could be made.

You do not need to be a fan of Alito's judicial philosophy — and I am definitely not — to recognize that he did the right thing when it mattered. Judges make mistakes all the time, on matters great and small. That is why we have appellate courts, and that is why there are nine justices on the Supreme Court. The truly important question is not whether the judge made an error, but how he responded when it was pointed out to him. Nonetheless, suggestions of misconduct in the Vanguard case were insinuated throughout Alito's confirmation hearings, distracting from more serious issues and sullying his reputation for no good reason. There was never much chance that Democrats could stop Alito solely on the basis of his ideology; that may explain but does not justify the last-ditch effort to find some dirt. But desperation shots (especially cheap ones) belong on the basketball court, not in the Senate Judiciary Committee.

Sometimes turnabout is fair play, but not when it comes to character assassination. Too often in the course of confirmation proceedings, senators from both sides of the aisle have strained to dig up minor events from the nominee's past, creating feeble but harmful intimations of unethical conduct. Partisan mud-slinging can sometimes increase the chances of defeating a particular nominee, but it is always unfair and counterproductive. If past is prologue, there appears to me no end in sight.

26

A Spouse Speaks

IN MARCH 2002, Virginia Thomas, the wife of Supreme Court Justice Clarence Thomas, published an op-ed in the *Wall Street Journal* in which she expressed sympathy for Charles Pickering, one of President Bush's then-blockaded nominees to the Fifth Circuit Court of Appeals. Drawing upon her own experience during her husband's stormy confirmation hearings, Thomas urged Judge Pickering not to take the opposition personally. "It helps," she said, "to find your faith and be reminded that you are not called to be popular, but rather to have integrity." But she did not limit herself to commiseration. Instead, Thomas launched into a spirited attack on civil rights groups and "the hard left." Then, leaving no doubt about where she stood, she lambasted Senate Democrats (who then held a slim majority) in highly partisan terms.

Thomas said that "the Democrats on the Senate Judiciary Committee" do not think of Judge Pickering "as human right now." She said that "facts matter little" to Senate Democrats, who opposed Judge Pickering because it bolstered "their fund-raising efforts." She claimed that the Democrats' strategy was to "influence votes, scare off conservatives from being nominated, being defended, or even applying for such positions in public service." These are political thunderbolts of a sort we had never before seen hurled by the spouse of a sitting Supreme Court justice.

Whether one agrees or disagrees with Thomas on the merits, it was surprising to see a Supreme Court spouse make such a pronounced entry into the political fray. Desperate times, of course, call for desperate measures, and Thomas's essay was published on the very morning that the Senate Judiciary Committee was scheduled to vote on the Pickering nomination, which was known to be headed toward defeat in the committee.* Republicans felt that their candidate was being victimized by scorched-earth tactics, and no one was better suited to expose the smear than Virginia

---

* President Bush later elevated Pickering to the appellate court via recess appointment, as discussed in "Confirmation Mud."

Thomas, who had lived through her own confirmation nightmare. Even still, supporters of Pickering and Thomas recognized her involvement as "extraordinary."

So what do we make of the fact that Virginia Thomas so very publicly weighed in on what had become an intensely political controversy?

In the wake of the 2000 Florida election fiasco, it was more important than ever to hold the Supreme Court scrupulously neutral in political disputes, both in fact and appearance. Critics had claimed that the five-vote majority in *Bush v. Gore* was motivated more by political affinity than by constitutional law, sometimes referring to a report that Justice Sandra Day O'Connor reacted with audible dismay when it first appeared that Al Gore would carry Florida and win the presidency.

Defenders, of course, argued that the majority opinion was rigorously correct, unaffected by any motive other than the desire to follow the Constitution.

In either case, it should be obvious that the court's legitimacy depends upon its perceived detachment. The court can be badly damaged if the justices come to be regarded as political players, as occurred in the aftermath of the disputed election of 1876, when the Supreme Court stepped directly into the maelstrom by accepting the appointment of five sitting justices, along with five senators and five congressmen, to the Electoral Commission charged with deciding the outcome of the presidential election. The panel split along strict party lines, with the deciding vote cast by Republican Justice Joseph P. Bradley, thus giving the presidency to Republican Rutherford B. Hayes, who had been soundly defeated in the popular vote.

So controversial was the 1876 decision that Hayes became known as "His Fraudulency," and the court, in the words of constitutional scholar Peter Berkowitz, became tainted with "the appearance of involvement of partisan politics."

More recently, the court suffered when it was disclosed that Justice Abraham Fortas continued to act as a political advisor to President Lyndon Johnson. As a continuing member of Johnson's "kitchen cabinet," Fortas advised the president on a wide range of subjects, from proposed legislation to the Vietnam War, thus calling into question Justice Fortas's participation in a number of cases decided while he served on the Supreme Court.

Other examples abound, but the lesson is the same. The Supreme Court thrives on neutrality and suffers in the shadow of politics. Thus, it is all but axiomatic that the court must do its best to remain painstakingly aloof from political combat.

But to what extent does that axiom apply to spouses?

In one sense, of course, it does not pertain at all. The ethical rules that constrain judges generally do not apply to their spouses. The Code of Judicial Conduct does have a few provisions that touch upon the conduct of family members, but none that impose any direct restraints. In addition, a federal statute requires certain financial disclosures of the assets of judges' spouses, though fewer than are required of the judges themselves.

Needless to say, there has never been an effort, state or federal, to enact a spousal gag rule. Any such attempt would surely be challenged under the First Amendment, and for good reason. Unarguably, Thomas was legally entitled to write whatever she pleased. An exceptionally capable professional, with an important career that is completely independent of her husband's job, she has often had much to say on many issues. It would simply be wrong to require that she, or any spouse, live a life of public silence.

But that does not end the discussion, since the public activities of family members may nonetheless have the effect of compromising the court. Imagine the furor that would have followed if Martin Ginsburg or John O'Connor had actively campaigned for their preferred presidential candidates in the 2000 election. Although the First Amendment surely protects that activity, it would have been a disaster for the court — no doubt prompting demands that Justices Ruth Bader Ginsburg and Sandra Day O'Connor recuse themselves in Bush v. Gore, and perhaps other cases as well.

The Supreme Court is a fragile institution, dependent on its reputation, and often best served by the voluntary circumspection of those connected to it. A decent respect for the court's neutrality, in both reality and appearance, therefore counsels self-restraint. The spouses of most justices seem to recognize this. For example, Justice Ginsburg's husband, a prominent tax attorney, divested himself of perfectly legitimate investments in order to avoid even an appearance of judicial partiality.

Which returns us to Virginia Thomas's appearance on the editorial page of the *Wall Street Journal*.

Unique in the history of Supreme Court spouses, Virginia Thomas has been an active political player during her husband's entire tenure on the court. She initially served on the staff of the House Republican Conference, and she later became a senior policy advisor to Majority Leader Dick

Armey. In 2002, she was the director of Executive Branch Relations for the conservative Heritage Foundation.

In each of those positions, Thomas wisely refrained from open politicking. With her *Wall Street Journal* op-ed, however, she broke another barrier, exploiting her husband's name in what can only be seen as an overt effort to sway public opinion against Democrats and in favor of the Republican administration.

Virginia Thomas showed dreadfully poor judgment in publishing that particular op-ed. It would be a different matter if she had merely written a pro-Pickering essay, or if she had written a piece about the travails of confirmation without resorting to political invective. Instead, she determined to combine the two, capitalizing on Justice Thomas's position in order to score political points.

It is impossible to know whether Virginia Thomas consulted anyone before writing her op-ed. We should assume, to be sure, that Justice Thomas had no part in it. But questions, at least in skeptical quarters, are unavoidable. The fact is that husbands and wives tend to talk with one another about important matters. Is it out of place to wonder whether Thomas, about to take the unprecedented step of going public on a highly contentious political issue, might have asked Justice Thomas whether he had any objection? Might she have mentioned to him that she was planning to publish her resentments in the press? Even without any input from him into the content, that possibility could create the appearance of his tacit approval.

Of course, the supposition could be completely wrong. Justice Thomas might have been more surprised than anyone to see his wife's byline in the *Wall Street Journal*. If so, both Thomases must have been shocked to see the column illustrated by a picture of Justice Thomas himself, presumably inserted by a *Journal* editor (surely unbeknownst to the writer) lest anyone miss the connection.

And if Thomas did not talk it over with her husband, there remains the possibility that she conferred with Republican leaders regarding the plans for her commentary. Certainly she had access to them at the highest level, in her role as White House liaison for the Heritage Foundation. Certainly the timing of the piece, appearing as it did on the morning of the judiciary committee's final vote, suggests some coordination among the writer, the Republican nomination managers, and the editors of the *Wall Street Journal*. In that case, Thomas's bad judgment was their bad judgment as well, and even more so if she had been recruited to the task. It would be the height of strategic cynicism to enlist the prestige of the Supreme Court in aid of a political goal, while claiming to be acting for the good of the judiciary itself.

The greater irony is that Virginia Thomas's own essay attributed nothing but foul motives and duplicity to those who disagreed with her. They were not simply wrong in opposing Judge Pickering; they didn't even think of him "as human." They were "impervious to the truth" as they pursued a political agenda that was "all about abortion and homosexuality." But even as she impugned her opponents, she evidently expected readers to conclude that her own motives were beyond reproach and that she had absolutely no intention of trading on the prominence of her husband's position on the Supreme Court.

At his confirmation hearing, Justice Thomas testified that "it's important for judges not to have . . . baggage." Judges need "to eliminate agendas, to eliminate ideologies," he continued, "because you want to be stripped down like a runner." Unfortunately, the uncompromising political activism of Virginia Thomas may have encumbered Justice Thomas's work on the Supreme Court by threatening the appearance of non-ideological neutrality so vital to the judiciary. Her increasingly open identification with a political party could only have caused doubts about Justice Thomas's ability to maintain the ideal of "stripped down" dispassion.

A federal statute prohibits a Supreme Court Justice from sitting in any case in which his or her spouse has a non-financial "interest that could be substantially affected by the outcome of the proceeding." Until March 14, 2002, no one would have suggested that Virginia Thomas's political affiliations should disqualify Justice Thomas from participating in political cases, even one that determined, say, the presidency of the United States. But after her foray into open partisan warfare, the situation was not so clear.

It is unlikely that we will ever again see a Supreme Court spouse who does not lead an independent life in one realm or another. It would be unacceptable to place formal limits on their activities, but it's not too much to request some prudent discretion. Yes, Supreme Court spouses have the right to advocate whatever they choose. In the future, let us just hope they choose to keep the Supreme Court out of it.

27

Veiled Justice

WHEN GINNAH MUHAMMAD stepped into a Hamtramck, Michigan, courtroom in October 2006, she had no reason to think that her religion would have anything to do with the outcome of her case. As a conservative Muslim, she wore a full veil (or *niqab*) that left only her eyes exposed, but that surely seemed irrelevant to her garden-variety, and decidedly secular, small claims dispute with Enterprise Rent-a-Car. Judge Paul J. Paruk saw things differently, however, eventually dismissing Muhammad's case because she refused to remove her veil.

According to the transcript, Paruk initially sent his court officer to request that Muhammad take off her *niqab* while she was seated in the courtroom. She declined, and approached the bench fully veiled when her case was called. Paruk then politely insisted that she bare her face:

> One of the things that I need to do as I am listening to testimony is I need to see your face and I need to see what's going on and unless you take that off, I can't see your face and I can't tell whether you're telling me the truth or not and I can't see certain things about your demeanor and temperament that I need to see in a court of law.

Muhammad demurred. "I'm a practicing Muslim," she said, "and this is my way of life and I believe in the Holy Koran and God is first in my life." That was not enough for Paruk, who then gave her a choice between removing her veil to testify and having her case dismissed. "I wish to respect my religion," she replied, "and so I will not take off my clothes."

Apparently baffled by her response, Paruk attempted a compromise. "Well, it's not taking off your clothes. All I am trying to do is ask you to take off the part that's covering your face so I can see your face and I can hear you and listen to you when you testify, and then you can put the veil back on."

"Well, Your Honor, with all due respect," said Muhammad, "this is part of my clothes, so I can't remove my clothing when I'm in court."

With that, Paruk ordered the case dismissed, leaving a host of questions unanswered (and not just whether Enterprise had wrongly charged Muhammad $2,750.00 for damage to her rented truck). Was the court's ruling right or wrong? And if the latter, was it the product of anti-Muslim bias, or mere judicial error?

Under the Michigan constitution, a law (or court order) may not be enforced in a way that substantially burdens a person's religious practice, unless it is the least restrictive means of serving a compelling government interest. At first glance, Paruk's ruling might seem to meet that test. After all, judges have to assess witnesses' truthfulness, presumably by scrutinizing their demeanor for signs of evasiveness or deception, and the state certainly has a significant interest in accurate fact finding.

But dismissal of Muhammad's case was far from the least restrictive means of achieving the court's objective. In the first place, it was not obvious that there would be any credibility questions for the court to consider. The issues might have been resolved on the basis of the written contract or other documentary evidence (repair bills, or the lack of them, for example), in which case witness demeanor wouldn't have mattered. Alternatively, Paruk could have allowed Muhammad to proceed, while declining to place full credence in her veiled testimony. Or he could have leveled the playing field by allowing the Enterprise representative to testify with his or her face obscured. He might even have drawn an "adverse inference" from Muhammad's refusal to show her face, which would be comparable to the approach taken in civil cases when a party invokes an evidentiary privilege. Those are all imperfect solutions from Muhammad's perspective, but any one of them would have been preferable to outright dismissal.

Practicalities aside, it is simply wrong to claim that every trial requires face-to-face confrontation. Blind judges (such as Richard Casey of the Southern District of New York and David Tatel of the District of Columbia Circuit) and jurors are hardly unknown, yet they are evidently able to decide cases without looking anybody in the eye. And in some cases there are witnesses whose faces have been disfigured, or paralyzed, or heavily botoxed, but that does not disqualify them from testifying.

In fact, it is largely a myth that judges, or anyone else, can reliably differentiate between honesty and mendacity simply by picking up visual cues. Studies have consistently shown an extremely high error rate in recognizing deception, even among professionals who pride themselves on their ability to weed out deceit. When one set of tests, for example, was given to judges, police officers, trial lawyers, psychotherapists, CIA agents, and customs examiners, no group was able to identify liars at a rate better than fifty percent — which is exactly what they would have achieved through random guessing.

Unfortunately, most people are deluding themselves when they claim to be good judges of character, or that they can spot liars on sight. In most cases, they simply mistake indicators of nervousness (stammering, fidgeting, blinking) for deception, or signs of self-confidence for honesty, often with predictably disastrous results. There is, however, one exception to the rule. Successful professional poker players can, and do, accurately read their opponents' intentions, figuring out when they bluffing, when they are holding winning cards, and exactly what it will take to sucker them into losing bets.

Some of the great poker mavens have revealed their secret techniques for identifying "tells," but they don't provide much support for Judge Paruk. For starters, it is nearly impossible to pick up a reliable tell on the basis of a first impression. Mike Caro, well known as poker's "Mad Genius" and author of the *Book of Poker Tells*, explains that it is crucial "in discovering tells . . . for a player to develop a sense of the baseline behavioral repertoire of one's opponents." That simply can't happen in the compressed time frame of a small claims trial.

Moreover, poker games — unlike trials — provide repeated opportunities to validate one's interpretation of tells. If you suspect that an opponent is inadvertently signaling a bluff, well, all you have to do is call the bet to find out. Over a series of hands, therefore, you can pretty much determine whether your intuition is accurate. Judges' credibility conclusions, however, are self-fulfilling. Suspected liars lose their cases, and that's that. There is seldom, if ever, an equivalent to showing the actual cards.

Judge Paruk is badly mistaken if he thinks that facial expressions hold the key to credibility. In fact, just the opposite is true. As Joe Navarro, a former FBI interrogator who now teaches poker seminars, explains in his book, *Read 'Em and Reap*, the face is actually the most deceptive part of a person's body. "If we couldn't control our facial expressions," he asks, "why would the term 'poker face' have any meaning?" Indeed, says Navarro, "our feet are the most honest part of our body" because they most accurately reveal the instinctive impulse to "freeze, fight or flee" that the evolutionary process has hard-wired in the primal "limbic brain." If you want to know whether someone is angry or worried, look at her feet, not her face. (It is more than ironic that most courtrooms have witness boxes that obscure the judge and jury's view of a witness's feet and legs, but that's a subject for another day.)

And finally, as Navarro also points out, most tells disclose nothing more than a player's level of confidence in his or her hand. In poker, of course, confidence is a reliable proxy for truthfulness — self assurance means good cards while visible doubt suggests a bluff — but that is far from the case at trial, where a witness's lack of confidence is more likely the product of fear or unease, rather than trickery.

It turns out that Judge Paruk had no good reason, let alone a compelling one, to dismiss Muhammad's case, but that does not make him an anti-Muslim bigot. Most judges probably share his belief in the importance of seeing a witness's face, so it would be easy enough to attribute his error to that common misconception. On the other hand, prejudice and ignorance often overlap, and the consequences can be indistinguishable when the victim belongs to a vulnerable minority. For example, consider this colloquy between Paruk and Muhammad:

THE COURT: I mean no disrespect to your religion, but wearing a veil
  I don't think is a religious thing . . . I think it's a custom thing. . . .
  [T]his has come up in my courtroom before, and in my courtroom
  before I have asked practicing Muslims and the practicing Muslims
  have told me that, "No, Judge, what I wear on top of my head is a re-
  ligious thing and what I wear across my face is a non-religious thing.
  It's a custom thing."
MUHAMMAD: Well, that's not correct.
THE COURT: Well, this is what they have told me and so that's the way
  that I am running my courtroom and that's how I have to proceed.

Apparently, it did not occur to Judge Paruk that there might be more than one interpretation of Islam, or that his information might be inaccurate or incomplete, or that in some faiths a "custom thing" might rise to the level of a religious commandment, or that religious customs still might be protected by the "free exercise" clause of the Constitution. In essence, he declared himself a judge of Islamic law — based on hearsay from undisclosed informants, no less — while rejecting Muhammad's explanation of her own beliefs. But in fact, it is well settled under the First Amendment that a judge may not determine the legitimacy of a person's religious practice (as opposed to the sincerity of her belief). In other words, Muhammad had an absolute right to adhere to her own religious views, and the court was required to acknowledge them so long as they were not feigned or a sham.

Thus, Paruk should have realized that he was depriving Muhammad of an important civil right — her day in court — on the basis of her personal religious practice. Regrettably, he was unwilling to reexamine his own preconceptions about the trial process, or even adjust his procedures, in order to accommodate her faith. That amounted to discrimination, and a significant financial loss to Muhammad, even if it was not motivated by animus or ill will. As of this writing, it seems that Paruk has had his own second thoughts. In January 2007 he agreed to reconsider the dismissal of Muhammad's claim against Enterprise, although he refused to say whether he would allow her to testify while wearing her *niqab*. Eventually, though, Muhammad will return to court with her face veiled. That would be a good time for Judge Paruk to realize that Themis, the goddess of justice, wears a blindfold for a reason.

28

Bullying from the Bench

SITTING IN GALVESTON, Texas, federal district Judge Samuel B. Kent never had the slightest use for inept or careless attorneys — and he often let them know it in uniquely colorful terms. During his early days on the bench — he was confirmed in 1990 — Kent's sense of humor was just a local phenomenon. In a 1996, for example, defense counsel in an insurance case moved to transfer venue to Houston "for the convenience of parties and witnesses." Quickly denying the motion, Kent made a point of enlightening the out-of-town lawyer about the realities of life in Texas, explaining that the counsel "is not embarking on a three-week-long trip via covered wagons" when he travels to Galvestion and that "thanks to the efforts of this court's predecessor, Judge Roy Bean, the trip should be free of rustlers, hooligans, and vicious varmints of unsavory kind."

Sometimes, however, things turned nasty and, thanks to the Internet, lawyers all over the country became aware of Kent's penchant for chastising incompetent counsel. Several of his published opinions were also widely circulated and posted, enjoying a long afterlife on various blogs and websites. Here are some choice excerpts from one such Kent opinion, in *Bradshaw v. Unity Marine Corporation*:

> Before proceeding further, the Court notes that this case involves two extremely likable lawyers, who have together delivered some of the most amateurish pleadings ever to cross the hallowed causeway into Galveston, an effort which leads the Court to surmise but one plausible explanation. Both attorneys have obviously entered into a secret pact — complete with hats, handshakes and cryptic words — to draft their pleadings entirely in crayon on the back sides of gravy-stained paper place mats, in the hope that the Court would be so charmed by their child-like efforts that their utter dearth of legal authorities in their briefing would go unnoticed. Whatever actually occurred, the Court is now faced with the daunting task of deciphering their submissions. With Big Chief tablet readied, thick black pencil in hand,

and a devil-may-care laugh in the face of death, life on the razor's edge sense of exhilaration, the Court begins.

After first deriding the defendant's brief, Kent turned his attention to the efforts of the plaintiff's counsel:

> The Court commends Plaintiff for his vastly improved choice of crayon — Brick Red is much easier on the eyes than Goldenrod, and stands out much better amidst the mustard plotched about Plaintiff's briefing. But at the end of the day, even if you put a calico dress on it and call it Florence, a pig is still a pig.

Many lawyers reacted with guffaws, or at least amused chuckles, enjoying Kent's caustic wit. For example, a colleague of mine suggested that we distribute the opinion to our students with a warning that "This is what can happen if you don't study hard in law school." I am told of judges who "got quite a hoot" from it, remarking "this judge is a riot," and "I only wish that I had written it."

Schadenfreude runs deep. It is easy to take guilty pleasure in the misfortune of others, especially when they appear to be as bumbling as the lawyers who drew Judge Kent's wrath. After all, they both apparently filed briefs that were devoid of meaningful authority, while failing to address the central issue before the court. We have all seen the havoc wreaked by poor lawyering, and it is tempting to snicker that the dummies deserved whatever they got.

Let's resist that urge, at least for the time being, while we think a bit about the use and misuse of judicial opinions. In that regard, Kent's comic style turns out to be a symptom, or perhaps an exemplar, of a more general problem for both the judiciary and the legal profession.

Federal judges exercise enormous power over lawyers and their clients. Armed with life tenure and broad discretion, a judge can do great damage to an attorney's reputation and career, while the lawyer has almost no recourse. So when Judge Kent decided to torment the hapless counsel in the *Bradshaw* case — they are identified by name in the published opinion — he was taking aim at people who could not defend themselves. Under prevailing law, they could not even get their case transferred to a new judge. They just had to grin and bear it, in the hope that "His Honor" would not decide to go after them again.

In litigation, the judge is the maximum boss. Everyone else is a supplicant, compelled to engage in ritual demonstrations of obeisance. We stand when the judge enters and leaves the room. Our "pleadings" are "respectfully submitted." Before speaking, we make sure that it "pleases the court." We obey the judge's orders, and we even say "thank you" for adverse rulings. These are the mandatory trappings of respect, but they do not ensure that a judge's actions will always be respectable.

By belittling the lawyers who appear before him, Judge Kent used his authority to humiliate people who — in the courtroom environment — are comparatively powerless. There is a name for that sort of behavior, and it isn't adjudication. It's bullying. It smacks of nothing so much as the biggest boy on the playground picking on the smaller kids who are unable to fight back. Even the "crayon" taunt reveals the judge's own schoolyard perspective, much more than it tells us anything about his unfortunate targets.

This is no defense of the *Bradshaw* attorneys. I assume that their work was thoroughly dismal and that Kent's legal judgments were unfailingly correct. But a federal judge has many decent, reasonable ways of dealing with inadequate lawyers. He can chew them out in court, he can call them into chambers, he can require them to rewrite their briefs, he can impose monetary sanctions. Any one of those steps can be taken with a far greater remedial effect than can be achieved through public shaming. Elementary schools long ago abolished the dunce cap, recognizing that it was both cruel and counterproductive.

Publication of a derogatory opinion, however, is an extraordinary measure. The Judicial Conference of the United States has endorsed a resolution on the limitation of publication, suggesting that it be restricted to "decisions of precedential import." The Fifth Circuit, which encompasses Texas, has adopted a rule providing that "the publication of opinions that merely decide particular cases on the basis of well-settled principles of law imposes needless expense on the public and burdens on the legal profession."

By any standard, Kent's opinion in *Bradshaw* has scant precedential value. The actual issue in the case was is a garden-variety statute of limitations question, which the court answered in a single paragraph while remarking that it could be "readily ascertained." This too was occasion for a barb from the bench: "Take heed and be suitably awed, oh boys and girls — the court was able to state the issue and its resolution in one paragraph . . . despite dozens of pages of gibberish from the parties to the contrary!"

Thus, the only possible purpose for publication was to add to the embarrassment of the attorneys. I have no quarrel with embarrassing lawyers when it is necessary to the outcome of a case — as obviously happens, for example, in decisions regarding frivolous claims, and in habeas corpus petitions based on incompetent representation. But in Bradshaw the comments were entirely gratuitous, not even rising to the level of dicta.

Furthermore, there are severe costs when courts use published opinions for the purpose of humiliation, even when couched in superficially humorous terms. First, we ought to worry about the impact on the parties. While the case was not legally complex, the *Bradshaw* litigation did involve serious personal injuries to a commercial seaman. Kent's decision dismissed an important defendant from the case, causing a definite setback to the plaintiff. Imagine how the crippled Mr. Bradshaw would feel upon reading this passage from the opinion:

> After this remarkably long walk on a short legal pier, having received no useful guidance whatever from either party, the Court has endeavored, primarily based upon its affection for both counsel, but also out of its own sense of morbid curiosity, to resolve what it perceived to be the legal issue presented. Despite the waste of perfectly good crayon seen in both parties' briefing (and the inexplicable odor of wet dog emanating from such) the Court believes it has satisfactorily resolved this matter. Defendant's Motion for summary Judgment is GRANTED.

Put aside the fact that Mr. Bradshaw was injured when climbing from a tugboat to the pier, which Judge Kent chose to use as part of a joke. Until he saw this excerpt, Mr. Bradshaw might have believed that federal judges decided cases out of an obligation to justice, not out of affection for counsel, and certainly not out of morbid curiosity (another bad joke). But when he did see it, Bradshaw would surely have been confused, or more likely appalled, by the court's trivializing reference to the odor of a wet dog. Although you would not know it from reading the opinion, the case was about Bradshaw, not about the judge's relationship to the lawyers — and remember, the plaintiff lost. Upon reading Kent's opinion, could Bradshaw feel that he had received a fair hearing?

Then there is the problem of civility. Many observers, including a good number of federal judges, have bemoaned the decline of civility in the courts. Rambo lawyers, it is said, are too combative, too overbearing, too ready to substitute personal attacks for advocacy. But why should lawyers be polite when the court itself insults and demeans them? If the judge calls my adversary "blithering counsel," adding that his work is "asinine tripe," why should I treat him any differently? If the court engages in that sort of name-calling, why shouldn't I incorporate similar bombast into my own arguments and briefs? What hope is there for civility, when the judge himself coarsens the discourse?

By modeling intemperate behavior, Kent merely invites more of the same from the lawyers in his court and beyond (given the viral notoriety of Kent opinions). As an old Yiddish saying puts it, a fish rots from the head.

We might also be concerned about the quality of justice dispensed in Kent's courtroom. While I have assumed thus far that all of Judge Kent's decisions have been legally correct, there are in fact reasons to doubt his rulings. When the court becomes so contemptuous of lawyers, and so eager to insult them in public, we must wonder whether the resulting judgments are truly free of bias. A judge who becomes so incensed just might possibly be inclined to take it out on the offending counsel (and by extension, on counsel's client).

Of course, there is no way to know for sure. Judges make thousands of discretionary decisions in the course of resolving motions or trying cases. Most of those decisions are not subject to review; many are not even recorded. Does the judge listen closely to the arguments of "blithering" lawyers? Will you get a fair hearing in your next case, if the judge said your brief last smelled like a wet dog? Is the judge open minded, or is he just playing gotcha? Kent, no doubt, believes that he is scrupulously even handed, but we are entitled to question his level of self-awareness, given how little self-consciousness he has shown in several of his opinions.

Finally, we have to consider the morale of the lawyers. I don't mean we should worry about whether their feelings have been hurt. Lawyers are all grown-ups, and most of them are pretty well paid. But we do have to worry about the vigor of the advocacy in Judge Kent's courtroom. Will lawyers pull their punches for fear of incurring his wrath? In one case, Kent blistered a lawyer for seeking a change of venue, rather than moving for transfer to a different division of the court. Admittedly, the mistake was elementary, and counsel compounded it by bringing his motion under the wrong rule, but Judge Kent's reaction was wildly disproportionate. In addition to insulting the lawyer in scathing, if somewhat puzzling, terms — the motion was "patently insipid" and "obnoxiously ancient" — the court determined that the attorney was "disqualified for cause from this action for submitting this asinine tripe."

Imagine that you are a young (or not-so-young) lawyer with a case before Kent. Now imagine that you want to advance a novel claim or make an innovative motion. You know that your chances are slim, but you believe that your position is supported by a "good faith argument for an extension, modification or reversal of existing law."* Judge Kent, however, has a reputation for seeing things in stark black and white. And when he thinks something is "asinine" — well, the roof caves in. This appears to happen with abnormal frequency. A LEXIS search in late 2007 located 13 opinions in which Judge Kent referred to something as "asinine" (often "asinine on its face"), and many others in which he used equally pejorative adjectives, including "ludicrous" (27 times), "ridiculous" (24 times), "absurd" (40 times), and "preposterous" (20 times). In one case he called a lawyer's motion "frighteningly disingenuous, and frankly, moronic." In contrast, a search for all other federal judges, from district courts to the Supreme Court, found only 36 uses of "asinine" since 1990, the year that Kent took the bench.

How much would you be willing to risk in order to bring your inventive motion? Would you be willing to see yourself maligned in a published opinion? Vilified by name in Internet postings across the country? Removed from the case, with the consequent responsibility of explaining the situation to your client?

No matter what the merits of their positions, lawyers will obviously have to tread softly in Judge Kent's courtroom. In a system that is premised on zealous advocacy, that's just a shame.

Samuel B. Kent is not the only martinet on the federal bench. But he has succeeded in becoming one of the best known by virtue of his intentionally outlandish, publicity-seeking opinions. One of the great strengths of our constitutional system is that federal judges are appointed for life — a measure intended to assure the independence of the judiciary. Occasionally, however, a judge, for reasons of large ego or poor judgment, mistakes independence for license and becomes abusive. Unfortunately, there is no good response to that sort of misconduct, which often tends to get worse over time. Lawyers may talk behind the judge's back, but in the courtroom it pretty much has to be "Yes, Your Honor," and "Thank you, Your Honor,"

---

* Such "good faith" claims are permitted under the Rules of Professional Conduct, even if the lawyer realizes they are unlikely to succeed.

lest the client suffer. Other judges are reluctant to criticize a colleague —
that is often understandable, but sometimes it's a serious mistake.

Silence in the face of invective only encourages more of the same. And
laughter at the ill fate of others — even when they are bunglers — just en-
ables further victimization. Judge Kent, and others like him, need to know
that ridicule isn't funny. It's just mean. It isn't judging, it's just showing off.
I agree that slipshod lawyering can be a problem. But in the end, an incompetent lawyer is far less dangerous than a judicial bully.

[Postscript: On September 28, 2007, Judge Kent was formally repri-
manded by the Fifth Circuit Judicial Council for engaging in "sexual harassment" and other "inappropriate behavior toward . . . employees of the
federal judicial system."]

29

Thought Control

EVERY LAWYER KNOWS stories about thin-skinned judges, easily angered by trivial or imaginary affronts. But the Indiana Supreme Court opinion in In re Wilkins took judicial huffiness — or perhaps hubris — to a new extreme.

When Michael Wilkins, an experienced Indiana appellate lawyer, agreed to serve as local counsel for a Michigan insurance company, he had no idea that the case would land him in deep trouble with his state supreme court. And when he submitted his client's brief — written by the company's Michigan lawyers, but reviewed and signed by Wilkins — he never expected that a mildly aggressive footnote would be declared so "scurrilous and intemperate" that it would get him clocked with a thirty-day suspension.

Such harsh discipline would be an extraordinary penalty for even the most boorish advocacy, so you might assume that Wilkins had resorted to personal insults or foul language. But in fact he just tried to present his case forcefully. Seeking discretionary review of an adverse appellate decision, Wilkins filed a petition for transfer (the local equivalent of a writ of certiorari) with the Indiana Supreme Court. He argued in his supporting brief that the appeals court erred badly in ruling against his client, materially misstating the record and ignoring relevant precedents. These claims will sound familiar to anyone who has ever lost a case, and, in fact, the applicable Indiana appellate rule requires comparable allegations as a basis for appeal. But the brief included a fatal footnote that drew the court's ire. Here, in toto, is what it said:

> Indeed, the Opinion is so factually and legally inaccurate that one is left to wonder whether the Court of Appeals was determined to find for the [Appellee], and then said whatever was necessary to reach that conclusion (regardless of whether the facts or the law supported its decision).

That was poor advocacy, to be sure, more likely to annoy than persuade, but it is hardly shocking language among consenting adults. You cannot appeal from a ruling without criticizing it, and Wilkins's brief basically said that the appellate court opinion was so bad as to cause consternation. He was obviously hoping that the overstatement would grab the court's attention, which is not an unheard-of tactic when petitioning for discretionary review.

He got the court's attention all right, but not the way he hoped. The Indiana Supreme Court not only denied the petition; it struck the supporting brief as a "scurrilous and intemperate attack on the integrity" of the lower court. A disciplinary proceeding followed that eventually resulted in Wilkins's suspension (the lead Michigan lawyer was also barred from the Indiana courts).

The three-two majority decided that Wilkins' words violated Indiana Professional Conduct Rule 8.2, which prohibits false statements "concerning the qualifications or integrity of a judge" or judicial panel. To justify this determination, the majority concluded that the offending footnote "suggested unethical motivations" and "deliberately unethical conduct" on the part of the lower court judges by alleging that they "may have been motivated in their decision making by something other than the proper administration of justice." So subversive was the footnote, according to the majority, that it threatened to "weaken and erode the public's confidence in an impartial" judiciary.

That is an astonishing stretch, reading sinister implications into a statement that one dissenting justice more accurately characterized as nothing more than "rhetorical hyperbole incapable of being proved true or false." While the footnote is definitely open to many possible innocent constructions, it certainly falls far short of the malign innuendo somehow perceived by the supreme court's majority. The appeals court might have been "determined to find" for the appellee for reasons having nothing to do with unethical conduct.

Perhaps the footnote implies that the court acted on an intuitive sense of justice, out of inadvertence or inattention, or based on considerations of efficiency. None of these suggestions would impugn the court's integrity, although they might provide grounds for reversal. Indeed, there are entire schools of thought — Legal Realism, Critical Legal Studies — based on the premise that all judging is inevitably outcome-oriented, and another school of thought — Law and Economics — posits that it should be.

Nonetheless, the Indiana Supreme Court fastened on the imputed specter of "unethical conduct"—words that, by the way, never appear in the brief—in order to conclude that the "scurrilous" statement violated a disciplinary rule.

The First Amendment protects not only freedom of speech, but also the right to "petition the government for a redress of grievances," which would surely seem to cover an appeal to a higher court. The right to complain about government officials was a bold idea in the eighteenth century, when European monarchs had no obligation to listen to the grievances of their subjects, but it should not be controversial, much less professionally perilous, today.

In response to Wilkins's First Amendment claims, the Indiana Supreme Court held that the "interest in preserving the public's confidence in the judicial system . . . far outweighed any need for the respondent to air his unsubstantiated concerns." Of course, this completely begs the First Amendment question. Wilkins's concerns can be called "unsubstantiated" only because the majority strained to construe them that way, reinterpreting the footnote as an allegation of unethical conduct rather than garden-variety ineptitude. Thus it was a rigged balancing test in which the lawyer's interests were virtually defined out of existence. Exercising the sole power to decide whether a claim is substantiated—indeed, holding sole power to characterize the claim itself—the majority left little or no real breathing room for free expression.

Worst of all was the majority's approach to the penalty. Wilkins had made several attempts to apologize to both the Court of Appeals and the Indiana Supreme Court, acknowledging that his footnote was "overly-aggressive and inappropriate and should never have made its way into our brief." He repeated his apologies during the disciplinary proceeding.

This was not good enough for the majority, however, because Wilkins continued to maintain that he "believes in the substance of the language contained in the footnote." In other words, it was not sufficient for him to retract the offending statement; he had to purge his mind of the offending thoughts as well. Because he evidently declined to stop thinking that he was right about his case, the majority determined that he had to be disciplined more harshly than his admittedly "outstanding and exemplary" record would have otherwise warranted.

Now, judges may have the authority to control what a lawyer can say in court. But it is a sad, sad day when they seek to constrain his very thoughts.

The demand for abject recantation calls several unpleasant historical parallels to mind, but they are best left unexpressed.

It is ironic to see a lawyer disciplined for such relatively mild language when prominent judges frequently dish it out in much stronger terms. As one dissenting Indiana justice pointed out, U.S. Supreme Court Justice Antonin Scalia is well known for lambasting his colleagues without reserve. He once commented, for example, that an opinion by Justice Sandra Day O'Connor was "irrational" and that her stated views "cannot be taken seriously." In another case he ridiculed Justice John Paul Stevens's "judicial libido" and sarcastically accused his colleague of belonging to the "School of Textual Subversion." Nor are Scalia's barbs reserved for his ideological adversaries. He has accused Chief Justice John Roberts of affecting a "pose of minimalism" while making "meaningless and disingenuous distinctions." Needless to say, Scalia has never been suspended for his caustic words.

Under the widely respected leadership of its chief justice, the Indiana Supreme Court enjoys an outstanding national reputation. The court is generally known for thoughtful innovation, not defensiveness. So it is baffling that the majority, including the chief, found a mere footnote so threatening to judicial dignity. The brief in question could not have been read by more than a dozen or so people. But the judges' disproportionate reaction was reported by both the local press and the *New York Times*, as well as on various websites, probably doing more harm to the court's reputation than any number of rude footnotes.

If anything "weakens and erodes public confidence in the judiciary," it is the perception that judges are imperious, taking umbrage at minor slights and unwilling to tolerate pointed criticism. Courts have the power to compel deference, but they should never fool themselves into mistaking self-importance for dignity.

Perhaps Indiana is an exceptionally decorous place, where formal manners still prevail and deportment is rigidly enforced. Even so, the majority would probably not be thrilled to learn that their opinion echoes a famous quotation from Chicago's late Mayor Richard J. Daley. In a typical overreaction to his adversaries, he once fumed, "They have vilified me, they have crucified me, and, yes, they have even criticized me." The mayor neglected to add, of course, that his critics were well within their constitutional rights.

[Postscript: In a curious coda, the Indiana Supreme Court granted Wilkins a partial rehearing and reduced his penalty from suspension to reprimand, while continuing to hold that the footnote alleged "bias and favoritism" and therefore impugned the integrity of the appellate court. The court made a point of noting that it still rejected Wilkins's First Amendment claim, and that the original opinion (apart from the sanction) remained in full effect.]

30

Platonic Censures

THERE IS SOMETHING about deposition practice that brings out the worst in lawyers. Often the culmination of years of antagonistic litigation, a deposition throws counsel — and frequently their clients — together in a small room where they are unconstrained by the rules of evidence and unsupervised by the judge, whose authority over the process is remote and indirect. Most attorneys behave honorably under the "honor system," but all too often things get out of hand, as lawyers engage in harassment, obstructionism, posturing, and endless bloviation. Actual violence is thankfully rare, but threats and challenges are distressingly common, as immortalized by the famous videotape of Texas lawyer Joe Jamail taunting a witness to "come over here and try it, you dumb son of a bitch."

Most deposition tantrums never come to light, let alone achieve Jamail-like levels of notoriety, but every now and then a nasty dispute becomes the subject of a reported decision. Frequently combining the attributes of both morality tales and soft-core pornography, these cases hold a special fascination for lawyers, especially when they recount the details of a particularly vile squabble. Occasionally, there is even a lesson to be learned, although it is not always the one intended by the court.

Judges, especially when hearing appeals, have a regrettable tendency to premise their rulings on an abstract vision of law practice that is far removed from daily life in the litigation trenches. Platonic ideals — universals are independent of particulars; ideas are more real than things — are fine for philosophers, but they can be dangerous in the hands of courts. The truth is that high principles, no matter how rigorously adduced, must now and then give way to gritty reality. Instead of honestly recognizing their own limitations, however, too many appellate judges put logic (at which they excel) ahead of experience (which they frequently lack), resulting in rules for lawyers that can be nearly impossible to follow.

One such instance is found in *Redwood v. Dobson*, which the Seventh Circuit Court of Appeals described as a "grudge match" between Erik Redwood (a self-styled renaissance man and "Buddhist reverend") and his one-time attorney, Harvey Cato Welch. Spanning more than eight years, the litigation involved angry accusations and counter-charges of incompetent representation, racism, battery, hate crimes, civil conspiracy, and abuse of process, and eventually entangled not only the original adversaries, but also their lawyers, their lawyers' lawyers, and a luckless local prosecutor. Matters came to an ugly boil during the deposition of attorney Marvin Gerstein, who had once represented Welch but had since become a codefendant.

Redwood, the plaintiff, was represented by Charles Danner, who, as the Seventh Circuit noted, "spent the first 30 pages or so of the transcript exploring Gerstein's . . . vehicular violations." Gerstein's lawyer, Roger Webber, instructed him not to answer some of those questions, but Danner continued to pursue equally pointless and irrelevant topics. What happened next, as the Seventh Circuit observed, must be quoted "to be believed."

> DANNER: Mr. Gerstein, have you ever engaged in homosexual conduct?
> WEBBER: I believe it violates Rule 30, and I'm instructing him not to answer the question.
> GERSTEIN: I'm not answering the question.
> DANNER: Mr. Gerstein, are you involved in any type of homosexual clique with any other defendants in this action?
> WEBBER: Same objection. Same instruction.

The deposition continued in a similar vein, with Danner asking intrusive and irrelevant questions, some of which the Seventh Circuit characterized as "unfathomable," and Gerstein becoming increasingly uncooperative. (In a telephone interview, Danner told me that the questions about homosexuality were relevant to his civil conspiracy claim because the local prosecutor's office had show "bias in favor of gays and lesbians.")

In reviewing the mess, the Seventh Circuit called Danner's conduct "shameful" and censured him for conduct unbecoming a member of the bar, adding that repetition of his performance would lead to heavier sanctions, "including suspension or disbarment."

But then — incredibly — the court went on to censure Webber as well, delivering the same warning about possible disbarment. Even though he had been "goaded" by Danner's intolerable behavior, the court held that Webber's representation of his client had been "unprofessional and violated the Federal Rules of Civil Procedure." Rather than instruct Gerstein not to answer the offending questions, Webber should have "called off the deposition and applied for a protective order" from the trial court.

That aspect of the Seventh Circuit's analysis is deeply troubling, creating an unworkable standard for even the most diligent lawyers. Yes, of course, Rule 30(d)(1) states clearly that a lawyer "may instruct a deponent not to answer only when necessary to preserve a privilege, to enforce a limitation directed by the court, or to present a motion [for a protective order]." And yes, Webber's instructions to Gerstein did not fall under any of the provisions of the rule. But surely it is obvious that Webber was simply attempting to protect his client under extremely difficult circumstances, trying to get the deposition finished with the least possible expenditure of time and money.

Imagine the unfair choice that Webber would have faced under the appellate court's approach when Danner asked his first outrageous question: "Mr. Gerstein, have you ever engaged in homosexual conduct?" Webber would have had to direct his client to submit to an invasion of privacy, or else suspend the deposition right then and there. But suspending a deposition is hardly without cost. Webber then would have had to prepare a motion, obtain a court date, appear before the trial judge, and present his argument. Although his objection would no doubt have been sustained, there was no guarantee that he would have been awarded adequate costs. And in any event, he would then have had to go back to the deposition with no assurance that Danner's obnoxious questioning wouldn't resume, in which case Webber would have had to repeat the entire process.

At the time, it must have seemed to be in everyone's best interest — lawyers, parties, trial court — to get everything on the record in one sitting, and to avoid the inefficiency of bouncing back and forth between deposition room and courtroom. Only with the benefit of hindsight does it become apparent that Webber should have blown the whistle much, much sooner.

And therein lies the problem. Working lawyers have to craft pragmatic solutions, usually under extreme time pressure and often on tight budgets. Rules are rules, to be sure, but sometimes there ought to be a little play in the joints, recognizing that the spirit of a rule may be more important than its harsh enforcement. Any lawyer who has ever defended a deposition against an overbearing lout would sympathize with Webber's dilemma, and would understand why running to court wasn't obviously the remedy of first resort.

Unfortunately for Webber, the Seventh Circuit didn't see it that way.

The three formidable judges on the panel — Diane Wood, Ilana Rovner, and Chief Judge Frank Easterbrook, who wrote the unanimous opinion — are as intellectually accomplished as any on the bench, but none of them has significant experience in private practice, much less in a small-town, small-case practice such as Webber's. According to their official biographies, only Wood ever engaged full-time in private practice, and that was a relatively short stint as an associate at a large law firm nearly thirty years ago. Easterbrook's entire pre-judicial career was spent in government and academics. While he was exceptionally successful in both endeavors — arguing numerous cases before the Supreme Court while in the Solicitor General's office and quickly achieving tenure at the University of Chicago — it is quite possible that he has never participated in a deposition (except perhaps as an expert witness during his association with Lexecon, a law-and-economics consulting firm). It is speculation on my part, but it seems likely that none of the three judges ever had sole responsibility for defending a beleaguered individual client, either in trial or at a deposition.

I am not quarreling with Judge Easterbrook's invocation of Rule 30(d) (1), and I'm not suggesting that lawyers should be encouraged to disrupt depositions by instructing witnesses to keep mum. I am suggesting, however, that the court could have cut Webber a little slack.

C'mon, Your Honors, he violated a rule of procedure, not a moral imperative. There was no need to slap Webber with the same punishment (including the threat of disbarment) as was given to Danner, whose conduct was found to be far more egregious. A few words of stern caution would have been sufficient to get the general point across, while still leaving conscientious lawyers some room to maneuver.

But instead of showing flexibility — no harm, no foul — the Seventh Circuit simply laid down the law, censuring both the provocateur and his hapless foil. While that result might seem even-handed, it will inevitably create new headaches for trial judges. In the past, lawyers had a variety of ways of deflecting churlish questions during heated deposition disputes, including an occasional bit of witness-instructing brinksmanship. It wasn't always pretty, and there were regrettable abuses, but the attorneys usually succeeded in resolving matters among themselves, without recourse to the courts. But now it appears that the lesser tactics have been ruled completely out of play, leaving only the nuclear option of terminating the deposition and running to the judge.

Plato famously supposed that our perceptions are no more accurate than shadows on the wall of cave. Whether one accepts or rejects that analogy, it is plain that the Seventh Circuit was able to see only the shadows of shadows in the *Redwood* case, relying on a written record that could not begin the capture the underlying dynamics in the deposition room. Sitting in an environment remote from the messy realities of time pressure, transaction costs, and uncertainty, the appellate judges were misled by their own utopian conception of litigation practice, where lawyers are expected to make perfect choices no matter what the circumstances (and deserve to be punished when they err). Call it naïve insularity or lofty detachment, deliberately self-imposed or unfortunately unavoidable, but there is no other good explanation for why three very smart people would so confidently lay down such an impractical rule in a situation that they did not fully understand.

Alas, the censure of poor Mr. Webber may backfire, as it will likely empower bullies to pursue improper lines of inquiry, knowing that their opponents will either have to answer every question, no matter how foul, or pull up stakes and head to court (which may, in many federal cases, be hundreds or thousands of miles away). The Seventh Circuit believed their pronouncement decision would "defuse . . . the heated feelings" at depositions, but it could well have the reverse effect of making litigation more contentious, potentially turning every deposition into a high-stakes confrontation. Lawyers already spend enough time playing chicken. Now, thanks to the Seventh Circuit's unrealistic demands, they might have to learn a new game — truth or dare.

31

Stupid Judge Tricks

FOR MANY YEARS, there was a folder next to my desk labeled "Stupid Judge Tricks." I would throw case reports and newspaper stories into it as I came across them, eventually using them to update *Judicial Conduct and Ethics* of which I am a coauthor. I emptied the file every summer, having incorporated the important cases and grown tired of the rest.

But now I wish I had saved all of those files. I am starting to think that a survey of "stupid judge tricks" might be helpful to our understanding of a little-discussed subject that could be called "judicial hubris." Fortunately, this thought came to me shortly before I was ready to discard one year's worth of entries, so I had sufficient data to initiate some speculation about the cause of stupid judge tricks.

A "stupid judge trick" is something more than a simple incident of misconduct. It is a judicial or quasi-judicial act that causes you to scratch your head in wonderment and exclaim, "What could that judge have possibly been thinking?" It is an action that blatantly ignores or flouts all of the conventions inherent in the judicial office. Thus, our category excludes such objectionable, but ultimately non-judicial, activities such as drug-dealing, indecent exposure and soliciting, punching a litigant, and ethnic slurs coupled with untruthful denials (all of which are examples from real cases). That behavior is plenty bad, but it could afflict pretty much anyone. So, while these are undeniably "stupid tricks," for present purposes they are insufficiently judge-like. For the obverse reason, we also exclude egregiously bad judicial rulings, such as entering guilty pleas on the records of defendants who pled not guilty, dismissing criminal cases before hearing from the prosecution, and entering judgment without holding trial. These "decisions" may be so fundamentally wrong as to warrant discipline, but they are at least efforts at judging — hence, I hesitate to call them "tricks."

With that in mind, let us begin with some true stories. Nevada Judge Gary Davis regularly borrowed money from court employees and often did not repay the loans, despite written demands for payment. He also directed court employees to provide Spanish translations for customers of his mother's nursery business. And most astonishingly, he conducted a personal business from his chambers, displaying antiques throughout the courthouse and offering them for sale. He used jail trustees to set up the displays, and court employees to drive him on shopping trips in search of antiques. Finally, Davis adopted a practice of instructing defendants to make charitable contributions in lieu of paying fines, directing both the amount to be contributed and the recipient of the funds. In this manner, he diverted a total of over $400,000 from the city treasury to his favored charities.

In Olympia, Washington, Judge Ralph Baldwin likewise misused his chambers, though not for financial gain. While the jury was deliberating in a drunk driving case, Judge Baldwin left the courthouse and returned with a twelve-pack of beer, sharing it with both the prosecutor and defense counsel. Following the jury's verdict of guilty, the judge — still on the bench in his robe, and in the presence of the recently convicted defendant — invited the jurors to join with him in drinking the beer. Stated Baldwin, "I know this is uncommon, and kind of funny following a DUI case. I'll deny it if any of you repeat it." Though two jurors joined the party, the others, evidently more judicious than the judge, declined. By stipulation, Baldwin accepted censure and resigned from the bench.

Nebraska Judge Richard Jones was removed from office after making death threats against one judge and setting off fireworks in another judge's chambers. Jones repeatedly used profanity when referring to other judges, within hearing range of court personnel, lawyers, and bystanders. In particular, he called one female judge a "fucking ass," a "bitch," and a "fucking cunt." He frequently talked about committing acts of violence against her, including turning her head into "pink mist" and putting dynamite in the tailpipe of her car. Jones also signed court forms and orders with names other than his own, including Adolf Hitler, Snow White, and Mickey Mouse, a practice that he attempted to justify in the name of humor.

Sexual harassment by judges is a recurring problem, and the case of Mississippi's Judge Howard "Buster" Spencer is fairly typical. Spencer consistently made improper sexual suggestions to female court staff, once commenting that he was tempted to buy a pair of "small red panties" for a clerk, and on another occasion offering to wash the blue jeans of a female staff person if she would "take them off right [then]." A clerk testified that the judge once came over to her desk carrying a stress ball and asked her if she would "like to squeeze his balls" while he looked down at his crotch and laughed.

In California, Judge Gregory Caskey was publicly admonished for sending the following e-mail to an attorney:

> I am considering summarily rejecting [opposing counsel's] requests. Do you want me to let [opposing counsel] have a hearing on this, or do we cut [opposing counsel] off summarily and run the risk [of] the [Court of Appeals] reversing? . . . I say screw [the other party] and let's cut [opposing counsel] off without a hearing. O.K.? By the way, this message will self-destruct in five seconds.

The recipient of Caskey's message replied as follows: "Your honor, I don't feel comfortable responding ex-parte [sic] on how you should rule on a pending case." By return e-mail, the judge sent a one-word response, stating, "chicken."

Finally, a Louisiana judge, Sharah Harris, made the list by indulging in a sixteen-month-long, extra-marital romantic liaison with a convicted felon, Rodney Jones, whom she had sentenced to prison for armed robbery. To Harris's credit, she did not begin dating the man until after he was released from jail. On the other hand, he remained on parole — and therefore under legal supervision — during the time of their affair. As their relationship came to an end, the parolee went on a "crime spree," committing various felonies such as car theft, burglary, and three armed robberies, which resulted in his return to prison. Apparently, their attachment was quite public, as it became known to the judge's then-husband who reported it to law enforcement authorities. The Louisiana Supreme Court suspended Harris for sixty days without pay, declining to impose a harsher sanction in view of her genuine remorse and the fact that "[her] relationship [with Jones] had significantly diminished by the time Jones initiated his crime spree in 1996."

Why do some judges behave so scandalously? Is there something about the job of judging that encourages outrageous acts? Are there shortcomings in the Code of Judicial Conduct, or is there an absence of judicial education, so that judges do not fully understand what is expected of them? Or are we merely seeing a manifestation of the law of large numbers — put enough judges in enough courtrooms and eventually someone will go off every imaginable deep end?

It is initially tempting to attribute stupid judge tricks to, well, stupidity. A judge would have to be truly slow-witted not to realize that it is wrong to serve alcohol to jurors or peddle antiques in his courtroom. What else would motivate an otherwise rational jurist to risk loss of dignity, esteem, and career over such senseless or fatuous behavior?

But stupidity is too easy an excuse. Most of the conduct involved was extended or repeated, and for that reason it cannot be explained as a momentary lapse in judgment. Ultimately, the defense of stupidity is a rationalization that seeks absolution — saying in effect, "I don't know why I behaved that way. It was really stupid." But that is no answer at all, and it should not satisfy either judges or their critics.

Other possible explanations might be arrogance, hubris, or chutzpah. For reasons of personality or temperament, the judge is simply out of control. Each characterization seems plausible, though difficult to address or rectify other than in specific cases. With many thousands of active judges in the United States, surely some will exhibit at least one of virtually every negative personality trait — including arrogance, egotism, presumptuousness, vanity, pomposity, imprudence, and lewdness. We can be vigilant, of course, watching for such judges and taking action when necessary, but on that basis, a broad solution still eludes us.

When we step back and look at the overall picture, however, perhaps we can comprehend the phenomenon at a more useful level of generality. When I appraise stupid judge tricks in the widest possible perspective, what I see is an over-active sense of entitlement, verging on self-attributed invulnerability. The judges conduct themselves as though they believe they can do no wrong, as though their office confers upon them a license to behave as they please without fear of consequences. A few decades ago we probably would have referred to this as power-tripping, yet the term fits equally well today.

Indeed, we hear echoes of power-tripping in the responses and statements of several of the judges themselves. Judge Baldwin, who served beer to jurors, clearly delighted in violating accepted norms, at one point boasting to his staff, "[I'll] bet you've never met a judge like me before," and, "I don't play by the rules."

When Judge Jones signed court orders as Mickey Mouse, Snow White, and Adolf Hitler, he justified doing so as an exercise that would keep his staff "on their toes." He frequently set bond in bizarre amounts, including a fictitious "zillion pengos," which he equated with setting no bond at all. Jones is also the judge who repeatedly threatened and demeaned his colleagues, set off fireworks in chambers, referred to a judicial colleague with an obscene slang term for the female anatomy, and falsely claimed on several occasions that she had offered him oral sex. To Jones, however, these actions were merely "pranks" of the sort that other judges engaged in as well. He further insisted that his insulting treatment of a female judge was motivated by his own frustration at her refusal to attend to her paperwork.

In such cases, and I am sure in others, the judges apparently believed that their positions entitled them to act with impunity. Cloaked with great authority for a very specific and limited reason — judging cases in furtherance of the public good — these individuals declined to accept conventional limits on their behavior, essentially insisting on extending their power into other realms as well.

Judges necessarily get to order other people around. It's an essential part of their job. They deserve and should receive deference, but only by virtue of their official position, not by reason of some inherent entitlement. Some judges, however, fail or refuse to recognize the essential separation between the office and the person. The legitimate exercise of power in one context is taken as a license to act without restraint in others, and that leads to stupid judge tricks.

Introduction

CAN FULL DISCLOSURE ever go too far? "Baring It All" tells what can happen to law students who have said — or shown — too much.

Education is almost synonymous with testing, but sometimes the tests themselves can be misleading or worse. "False Positive" addresses the problems generally inherent in law school examinations, which emphasize quick recall rather than meaningful analysis. Students who rely on law school test-taking skills may find themselves in serious difficulty once they begin practice. "Truth in Citizenship" exposes a more troubling problem in the Citizenship and Immigration Service's naturalization examination, which seems to advance a hidden political agenda in the guise of testing knowledge about history and civics.

The next three essays discuss the role of candor within educational institutions. "The Best Policy" questions the definition of honesty employed by administrators at a leading public university. "Clinical Commandments" questions the approach to case selection by a law school legal clinic. "Pluto's Plight, and Ours" explains why science curriculums — from the definition of planets to the origin of species — should not be subject to popular votes.

The final two essays — "The Bedouin Horse Trade" and "There Are No Scriveners Here" — address the discipline of Law and Economics and its frequently discontinuous relationship with ordinary reality. An academic hypothesis that seems efficient and logical may still fail completely when it is applied to actual people in ordinary situations. It's not that the theorists are dishonest or disingenuous, but rather that they simply fail to account for human factors such as pride, emotion, history, insecurity, or overconfidence — which makes their theories sincerely wrong.

32

Baring It All

TABLOID JOURNALISM IS sensationalist by nature, so it was hardly surprising when the *New York Daily News* devoted half of its April 10, 2007, front page to the story of Adrianna Dominguez, a Brooklyn Law School student who had appeared nude in an Internet video series called "Naked Happy Girls." To adapt an old editors' adage, a naked young woman on the Internet is not news, but a naked young law student *is news* — or at least that must have been the idea. Of course, there wasn't much to the story beyond the basic facts (she was a third-year student and the treasurer of the Legal Association of Activist Women), and even the *Daily News* needs something more than voyeurism and a clever double entendre — she "shed her briefs" — to justify front page coverage. So the reporter had to dig pretty hard for a plausible human interest angle. Hey, maybe the exposure will ruin the poor girl's career. Could it even keep her from being admitted to the bar?

It was a contrived question, but the newspaper managed to coax a usable response out of the New York Bar's Committee on Character and Fitness. "It may have an effect," speculated an unnamed committee representative. "It's a possibility in the worst-case scenario that the person does not get admitted." That was just the hook the story needed to make it respectable — there's more than prurient interest here, folks! — and it was quickly picked up by the *Wall Street Journal's* on-line edition, followed by various legal-academic blogs, all of which weighed in on the question of character and fitness. Most of the commentators tut-tutted about Dominguez's conspicuously poor judgment, although virtually no one thought the video should prevent her admission to practice. After all, we are long past the time when character and fitness committees served as guardians of Victorian rectitude. Today's committees wisely focus on the likelihood of a candidate's future misconduct, not her immodesty or audacity. And frankly, there just isn't any discernable connection between light-hearted flashing and, say, the potential to lie to judges or steal from clients.

Then again, perhaps there is a more profound principle involved. UCLA Professor Eugene Volokh, a constitutional law scholar and the libertarian ringleader of the widely read Volokh Conspiracy blog, raised the discourse to another level, opining that it would be a "clear First Amendment violation for a state bar to consider this in the character and fitness evaluation." Making "sexually themed videos," he said, is protected by the Constitution, if they do not cross the line into hard-core or child pornography.

First Amendment claims are always attractive, but it was not long before another law student put Volokh's theory to the test. Two days after the awful murders at Virginia Tech, an anonymous post on the despicable Autoadmit website (previously best known for repulsive comments about women and minorities) seemed possibly to threaten a similar shooting at a San Francisco law school. The post was headed "Just decided not to do a murder-suicide copycat at Hastings Law." Hastings' Dean Nell Newton recognized that it was probably a "sick joke," but she obviously had to take it seriously, which meant evacuating the school and canceling classes for the day. The FBI subsequently determined that the poster, who had used the pseudonym Trustafarian, was a first-year law student at the University of California, Berkeley (Boalt Hall). The following week, Boalt's Dean Christopher Edley announced that the law school would seek to expel Trustafarian (although the school did not release his real name), due to "the intrinsic wrongness of the act . . . and the disruption, turmoil and emotional toll" that it caused.

Dean Edley accurately described Trustafarian's post as an "astounding instance of . . . reckless disregard for the welfare of others," but let's assume that it did not actually violate any laws (as of this writing, no charges have been filed). Like it or not, sick jokes are covered by the Constitution, just like erotic videos, so Trustafarian was sure to argue that he could not be disciplined by a state-operated law school (or kept out of the bar, if he ever managed to make it that far) for non-criminal speech. But could he really count on the same broad protection — it's just one more form of free expression — as Adrianna Dominguez? The answer turns out to be pretty complex.

The First Amendment makes no ready distinction between playful nudity and creepy-though-not-quite-threatening rants. In both disciplinary and bar admission proceedings, however, the inquiry is not limited by the familiar "clear and present danger" standard. As many courts have held, the ultimate issue is not the expressive nature of the applicant's speech, but rather its predictive value. In other words, does the aspiring lawyer's questioned behavior raise a strong and reliable inference of future misconduct? If so, admission can be denied. If not, welcome to the bar (but try not to do it again).

The best known encounter between free speech and bar admission is the case of racist and anti-Semitic cult leader Matthew Hale, who was refused admission to the Illinois bar because his "publicly displayed views" were "diametrically opposed" to the legal profession's obligation to equality and nondiscrimination. At the time, I went on record in support of Hale's application, arguing in an op-ed that "racist ideas are ideas nonetheless" and that he should not be penalized for his opinions. Well, it turned out that the bar examiners understood Hale better than I did. His strident expressions of "Aryan" supremacy, even though protected by the First Amendment, did indeed evidence his utter contempt for the law. Following his exclusion from the bar, he was convicted of soliciting the murder of a federal judge, whom he had described as a "probable Jew."

That precedent spells big trouble for Trusafarian, who revealed himself to be distressingly cavalier about people's fears and reactions, and perhaps dangerously unstable. Not exactly a pillar of trust and confidence. On the other hand, it could be a mistake to wield the Hale rule too broadly. Hale had made a career out of virulent racism, leading an organization — the so-called World Church of the Creator, of which he was the self-styled "Pontifex Maximus" — that was committed to subjugation of the "mud people." His repeated pronouncements meant something, and it was impossible to dismiss them as merely rash or ill-considered. Trusafarian, in contrast, apparently made a single appalling and outrageous statement, which he can attempt to characterize as an aberrant incidence of web-induced dementia. As Yogi Berra once cautioned, "It's tough to make predictions, especially about the future," and that insight might conceivably cause either university or bar authorities to give Trustafarian another chance — perhaps following several years of enforced hiatus — although I wouldn't bet on it.

Brooklyn Law School and Boalt Hall are a full continent apart, which also happens to be the metaphoric distance between one student's harmless exhibitionism and another's alarming screed. So no matter what happens to Trustafarian, it is almost certain that the New York bar examiners will eventually decide — if they ever even reach the question — that video nudity has no bearing on fitness to practice law. That won't be quite the last word on the matter, however, because there is one more ethics issue to consider.

Once she is admitted to the bar, would Dominguez ever have to tell her clients about her brush with notoriety? In many jobs, of course, her risqué lark will be completely irrelevant — no law firm client would fret about the naked escapades of an associate assigned to library research or document production. But what if she were to become a public defender? And what if there are some knuckle-draggers in the prosecutor's office who like to brag about ogling her video? That presumably wouldn't upset Dominguez. "I'm not that shy," she told the cameraman, "so it wouldn't bother me if, say, the opposing counsel has seen these pictures of me." Her clients, however, might not be so nonchalant about the possible impact on her advocacy. It is difficult enough for any young defense lawyer to get respect from the prosecution, especially when it comes to plea bargaining, and let's face it, naked pinups are not going to make anyone seem tougher. No one could blame a vulnerable defendant, with his or her liberty at stake, for wanting a lawyer who doesn't draw sniggers, even if the sniggering is puerile and unfair. Uncomfortable as it may be, that suggests a duty of disclosure.

The New York Code of Professional Responsibility provides that crucial decisions belong "exclusively" clients, who must therefore be informed of all "relevant considerations." But what happens when client autonomy collides with an attorney's right to privacy? To be sure, Dominguez herself has starkly waived any possible privacy interest, but it is not hard to imagine other situations where a lawyer's effectiveness may be seemingly (if not actually) compromised through no fault of his or her own — perhaps as the target of an outrageous slander or an unwilling participant in a lurid divorce.

There must be some personal information — about activities, associations, experiences, beliefs — that lawyers are entitled to keep to themselves, even if certain clients might reasonably prefer to know the details. But how and where do you draw the line? That could be the most intriguing question raised by the Dominguez story, but it is far too subtle ever to be addressed on the front page of the *New York Daily News*.

33

False Positive

THIS IS A story about law school exams, so it may cause a few twinges of discomfort or anxiety. Although it is a true story, I have changed a few details for the sake of anonymity.

My friend, whom I'll call Bruce, is a thoughtful and talented fellow who runs an extremely successful program at a private university that brings Chinese officials to the United States to study public administration. Among his many roles, Bruce teaches them administrative law, which has lately caused him some frustration. Planning to give a four-question midterm exam, he provided his Chinese students with a list of ten topics that might be on the closed-book test, assuming that would help them study more efficiently in an unfamiliar setting. After the exam was administered, Bruce discovered to his horror that he had received a set of papers with virtually identical — that is, nearly word-for-word — answers.

If they had been regular students, Bruce would have suspected cheating. But he soon realized that the students in the Chinese program had simply studied together, agreeing on the best possible answer to each of the ten potential questions — and then memorizing each one. Needless to say, my pal was appalled. It was supposed to be a law school examination, not a memory test. Besides that, he felt pretty guilty about the stunning amount of time his students must have spent perfecting and memorizing all ten answers. And the final exam was looming. What could he do to prevent another fiasco?

"I keep telling them, 'Don't memorize,'" he lamented to me. But it had not done any good. The whole notion of spontaneous composition was, precisely, foreign to them. To the Chinese students, studying apparently meant absolute preparation, with no room for improvisation or surprises. Bruce could not figure out how to get them to concentrate on the concepts without writing scripts.

At first I identified wholeheartedly with Bruce's dilemma. His students were knocking themselves out unnecessarily, while defeating the very purpose of the examinations. They weren't getting much sleep, they weren't really being tested, and they couldn't even be graded individually. Worse, there didn't seem to be an obvious way to bridge the cultural gap. How could Bruce convince his students to be less obsessive, and more spontaneous, about their exams?

But after I thought about it for a while, I began to sympathize with the students' point of view. From their perspective, our law school examination system must have seemed irrational. What is the point of testing a semester's worth of education on the basis of a few hours of rushed writing? Why place such an extreme premium on rapid recall and facile composition, rather than on extensive research and depth of understanding? The Chinese students apparently wanted to be judged on the basis of their studies, rather than on the basis of synaptic speed. They wanted to give their best answers, rather than their quickest ones. No wonder Bruce hadn't been able to convince them to stop memorizing. Given the opportunity, ability, and time, what sane person would fail to prepare exhaustive examination answers?

So it is unsurprising that the Chinese students refused to embrace American law school exams. The real question is why American students put up with them.

There is almost nothing about the typical law school examination that is really designed to test the skills involved in law practice. And many aspects of exams are positively perverse. Take time pressure, for example. By their nature, exams are time-limited, usually to about three or four hours, during which it is necessary to assess the problems, decide on the answers, marshal the material (whether strictly from memory or from an "open book"), and then write what one hopes will be coherent answers. There is no opportunity for reflection, research, reconsideration, or redrafting. You simply dash off your answer and pray you got it right. No competent lawyer would approach a serious problem under comparable conditions (except in an extreme and extraordinary emergency); in fact, that would probably be malpractice.

Yes, a few situations require lawyers to respond promptly to the demands of courts or clients — appellate argument, trial objections, "drop-dead" negotiations, filing last-minute documents, and perhaps drafting the extraordinary deathbed will — but the workaday life of the average lawyer is characterized far more by cogitation, elaboration, extension, and delay than it is by instant answers.

And, of course, the key lawyering skills — the ones that separate highly successful practitioners from mediocrities — are barely taught in most law schools, outside of clinical programs, let alone tested: tenacity, diligence, thoroughness, collaboration, consultation, factual investigation, and, crucially, the willingness to admit error and start over from scratch. Those qualities will actually put you at a disadvantage on law school exams. Far better to rely on flashes of insight and an ability to write on the fly.

The dirty secret (if it is a secret) is that law schools rely on exams primarily because they are easy to grade. The intense time pressure guarantees that the answers will be relatively short and, even more important, that quality will differ significantly among students. Exams do a great job of dividing test-takers into measurable categories, even if those categories measure nothing more than an ability to take tests in an artificial, non-lawyerly setting.

The same thing can be said about the multi-state bar exam, which tests even more information in even less time — although at least the bar examiners have an excuse. They have the daunting task of administering a broad test to thousands of applicants in dozens of states on a single day, with obviously immense security problems. The test has to be quick, and it has to be simple. To their credit, the bar examiners don't purport to evaluate the test-takers on any sort of qualitative continuum. They either pass or fail — a one-point margin is as good as a perfect score — on the basis of acceptable knowledge of the relevant law. And the failures can come back and take the test again.

Law school exams cannot claim the same justifications, but does it really matter? Students don't rebel (after all, they got into law school because they were good at test-taking), faculties are content, and law firms evidently believe that grades mean something. On the other hand, those damn exams send all the wrong messages, emphasizing a sort of counterproductive intellectual stoicism in which you have to come up with the right answer, on your own, or else.

What can that lead to? Perhaps I can sum it up with another story that I heard from another friend, a legal malpractice defense lawyer.

A young lawyer at a small law firm was assigned the task of filing a complaint in a commercial law case. As fate would have it, he blew the statute of limitations by a couple of days. And then he panicked. Rather than admit his error, he created a dummy complaint with a dummy date stamp, and told the client that the case had been filed. He kept the client informed of the "progress" of the phony case for nearly a year, and then reported that, regrettably, it had been dismissed on summary judgment. The client, who was no chump, figured out what had happened and complained to the firm. Needless to say, the young fellow was promptly fired and reported to the disciplinary authorities. This is where my friend came in. He represented the lawyer in the disciplinary proceeding and managed to save him from disbarment, although the poor fool was suspended for three years. But that is not the extent of the disaster. As my friend put it: "Three years later, on the day the suspension ended, the statute of limitations had not yet expired on the underlying case." Relying on his memory, the young lawyer had misunderstood the law, with ruinous consequences.

Of course, he would have learned about his mistake in plenty of time, if only he had gone to someone for advice when he thought he was in trouble. I don't want to blame the kid's moral failings on his legal education, but it doesn't seem to have helped much. No matter where he picked up his self-destructive solipsism, it looks like no one ever taught him how to ask for help. But then, on his law school exams, that would have been cheating.

34

Truth in Citizenship

EVERYONE EVENTUALLY FACES the central contradiction of test-taking. It doesn't matter if you pulled an all night review, it doesn't matter if you thoroughly understand the material, and it doesn't even matter if you know all the right answers. The only thing that really counts is figuring out what the exam-giver wants, and that may be far from obvious. Test-creators have their own agendas, which they do not always fully disclose and sometimes even hide, so the best preparation often involves "psyching out" the test rather than simply learning the subject matter. I had my own particular moment of truth in the sixth grade. And though the disenchanting lesson proved to be extremely useful later in life, I regret to say that it did not come easily.

Mrs. Davis's Social Studies test did not seem very difficult, especially since I'd studied for it rather diligently. I didn't even pause before answering what turned out to be a fateful question: "Why is there an East and West Pakistan?" I just launched into a thorough, although admittedly fairly intricate answer, which I pretty much remember to this day. "In 1947," I explained, "the British agreed to partition colonial India into two independent countries, one for Hindus and one for Muslims. The two areas with the greatest Muslim populations became East and West Pakistan." I was proud of my answer (which was totally accurate at the time, several decades before East Pakistan declared independence as Bangladesh), and I was stunned when the teacher marked it wrong. The correct answer, it turned out, was far simpler, lacking any reference to either religion or geopolitics, to wit: "Because they are separated by India."

My anguished protests were unavailing. "You have to give the answer I'm looking for," said Mrs. Davis, without a hint of irony. "Okay," I thought, "she evidently wants literalism, so that's what I'll give her from now on." My next chance came soon enough, when we were tested on a unit about frozen foods (apparently a noteworthy innovation in 1960). "Can you freeze lettuce?" was the question. Well, that was straightforward enough. Just toss a head of lettuce in the freezer, and a few hours later it will be as hard as a bowling ball. So, yes, you can definitely freeze lettuce, and that is just how I answered the question. As you probably guessed, I was wrong again. This time the teacher was actually asking a much more nuanced — and completely unstated — question, which had eluded me completely. It turns out that she wanted to know whether you can freeze lettuce, and thereafter thaw and eat it? Well, of course not. I didn't even bother to complain.

Sixth grade tests don't have many consequences (even for future law professors), but citizenship tests are another matter entirely, potentially determining the future rights and security of entire families. So in early 2007, I was more than a little alarmed to learn that the United States Citizenship and Immigration Service (USCIS) had announced a new examination format that would "focus on the concepts of democracy and the rights and responsibilities of citizenship." As soon as I read the word "concepts," I knew there was going to be trouble. Concepts call for interpretation, and interpretation can lead to ambiguity, if not always to arbitrariness, if not outright caprice. If they were going to be tested on concepts — rather than simply names, dates, and places — aspiring citizens were going to have to psych out the exam, guessing at the test designer's underlying intent while negotiating the fine line between overly thoughtful and overly literal answers.

A "pilot" version of the test was posted on the USCIS website, so I downloaded the 142 questions, along with the officially approved answers. To the credit of the test-designers, most of the questions allow credit for more than a single answer, although much of the material seemed unnecessarily difficult and pointlessly obscure. There were three questions about the Louisiana Purchase, and another asks for the name of the president during World War I — those are fine things to know, but they aren't exactly essential for informed citizenship. The degree of difficulty can be overcome by diligent study, but the test has deeper defects. Many of the questions are either hopelessly ambiguous, or they accept answers that are flatly wrong, or they exclude answers that are clearly correct. And perhaps worse, some parts of the test have a definite political tilt.

Pilot question number 2 asks, "What is the supreme law of the land?" The only allowable answer is "the Constitution," which is only partially right, and therefore excludes at least two other correct answers. Anyone who has actually read Article VI would know that the "Supreme Law of the Land" includes the "Constitution, and the laws of the United States . . . and all treaties made . . . under the authority of the United States." True, the Constitution could be called the supremest of the supreme, but it's still only one third of the triad. Someone might answer, quite correctly with the other two, and still be marked wrong. Or someone might foolishly decide to take the "concept" concept seriously, by providing a more conceptual answer: "The supreme law of the land is the law that judges in every state shall be bound by, even if the Constitution or laws of that state are to the contrary." That moderately profound answer would presumably be counted wrong—you'll notice that it doesn't specifically mention "the Constitution"—even though it is mostly lifted from the language of Article VI itself.

But wait, there's more. Pilot question number 11 introduces another important ideal, but provides another incorrect answer:

Q: What does freedom of religion mean?
A: You can practice any religion you want, or not practice at all.

Yeah, right. Just tell that to Muslim women who want to keep their faces veiled while passing through airport security, or rattlesnake-handling members of the Church of God with Signs, or polygamists, or peyote eaters, or, well, you get the idea. Religious belief—Jefferson called it "freedom of conscience"—is protected by the First Amendment, but that has never been extended to cover any and all practices. The correct answer, at least according the United States Supreme Court's opinion in *Human Resources Department of Oregon v. Smith*, is that you may believe anything you want, but your religious practices are subject to limitation, or even criminalization, by a "neutral, generally applicable law." But don't write that on your citizenship test, or you might find yourself stateless.

So far, we have looked only at approved answers that were incomplete or imprecise (although that wouldn't be much comfort to test-takers whose more thoughtful answers were marked incorrect), but other questions provide answers that are just plain wrong. Question 122, for example, lists Inuit as "one of the major American Indian tribes in the United States," thus managing to make three mistakes all at once. Although they are native people, the Inuit do not consider themselves Indians, they are not a tribe, and they happen to live in Canada (their Alaskan relatives, who call themselves Yupik or Inupiak, are not mentioned on the USCIS test).

That question might personally annoy only Canadian immigrants, who would probably just grimace at another typical instance of American ignorance about everything north of the border. Another error in the test is far more troublesome. The model answer to Question 76 declares that only United States citizens have the right to apply for federal jobs. But in fact, lawful resident aliens (a category that includes everyone who will be taking the naturalization test) are eligible for employment by many federal agencies, including the Postal Service, and they may also serve in the armed forces. At a time when the military is stretched thin, and when crucial language skills are in short supply, there's no telling how many qualified immigrants will be deterred from enlisting by that bit of misinformation.

Aspiring citizens will inevitably use the pilot test as a study guide, carefully memorizing the approved answers without doubting their accuracy, questioning their relevance, or wondering about the ideological implications. Thus, they will be taught by Question 77 that "everyone living in the U.S. [has the] right to bear arms." The U.S. Supreme Court, however, has never ruled that gun ownership is an individual right, while most federal appellate courts have held that "the right of the people to keep and bear arms" is tied to the institution of "a well regulated militia." Of course, the point here is political not educational. The Bush administration has taken the position that the Second Amendment does confer individual rights, and the USCIS test-drafters have apparently fallen enthusiastically in line. Their expansive interpretation of the Second Amendment would probably surprise most members of the National Rifle Association. The key word is "everyone" (a different question asks about citizens' rights), which would appear to apply even to tourists and illegal aliens, thus putting gun ownership on the same level as freedom of speech and religion.*

Other questions continue that partisan slant. There are two questions about the Federalist Papers, which strongly suggests the drafting handiwork of a member of the conservative Federalist Society. (Who else would care whether immigrants learn to identify "Publius," the pseudonym used by James Madison, Alexander Hamilton, and John Jay?) Another question asks, rather awkwardly, "What does it mean that the U.S. Constitution is a constitution of limited powers?" An approved answer is that "the states have all powers that the federal government does not." That revelation might warm unreconstructed hearts in certain extreme states-rights circles, but it is manifestly untrue according to the Supreme Court's longstanding

---

* As of this writing, the U.S. Supreme Court is considering, but has not yet decided, a case challenging the Washington, D.C., gun-control laws. It is possible that the court will adopt an "individual rights" interpretation of the Second Amendment, but even that would not give "everyone" the right to bear arms, because state restrictions would not be affected by a ruling limited to Washington, D.C.

interpretations of the First and Fourteenth Amendments. The federal government does not have the power to establish a religion, for example, or to abridge freedom of the press, and neither do the states.

Indeed, you could read all 142 questions, and all of the approved answers, without ever encountering such crucial concepts as due process and equal protection of the law, the rights to counsel and to a speedy and public trial, the privilege against self-incrimination, the freedom from unreasonable searches and seizures, protection from cruel and unusual punishment, or the Writ of Habeas Corpus.

And that brings us back to Mrs. Davis who, as you may recall, was adamant that students were allowed to give only "the answers I'm looking for." So it is also with the USCIS. Obsessed as it is with executive power, no arm of the Bush administration would ever look for, much less encourage, answers about procedural rights. Otherwise, immigrants might get the idea that they could challenge, say, arbitrary imprisonment, secret trials, or coerced confessions. Come to think of it, President Bush (not to mention Vice President Dick Cheney and former Attorney General Alberto Gonzalez) probably would have had more than a little trouble with some of the pilot questions about the scope of the Constitution, though that would only inspire them to make up their own answers:

QUESTION 16: Who makes federal laws?
PILOT ANSWER: Congress.
BUSH ANSWER: The President, pursuant to his inherent, unenumerated, and unchallengeable powers as Commander in Chief.

QUESTION 29: Why do we have three branches of government?
PILOT ANSWER: So no branch is too powerful.
BUSH ANSWER: So the President may ignore the other two if he decides to wiretap United States citizens or declare someone an unlawful combatant.

QUESTION 73: What are "inalienable rights"?
PILOT ANSWER: Individual rights that people are born with.
BUSH ANSWER: Rights? What rights? Don't you support our troops?

Given the various foul-ups and evidence of crony-inspired politicization, it's hardly surprising that the USCIS happens to be an arm of the Department of Homeland Security, whose Federal Emergency Management

Agency branch brought us the response to Hurricane Katrina. There's not much left to say but, USCIS, you're doing a heckuva job.

[Postscript: In September 2007, the USCIS posted the final version of the new test, which will be given as of October 1, 2008. While some of the above problems have been corrected, most of them remain.]

35

The Best Policy

"IT SEEMS SURREAL to me," lamented Mary Ann Mason, dean of the graduate school of the University of California at Berkeley. "It is an unnecessary, foolish, tragic incident." You might think she was reacting to a reckless car crash or a wild fraternity prank gone bad, but, in fact, she was talking about a decision by the U.S. Department of Education (DOE) that disqualified thirty Berkeley graduate students from seeking coveted Fulbright grants. While the situation was obviously regrettable, Mason's reaction was overblown, especially since the problem was largely of her own staff's making.

Here are the basic facts:

Applications for the 2003 round of Fulbright-Hays Doctoral Dissertation Research Abroad Fellowship Program had to be mailed by October 20 of that year, evidenced by either a postmark or a "dated shipping label" from a common carrier. The University of California's graduate division had assembled thirty applications on time (they could not be submitted individually) and arranged for a FedEx pickup that would have met the deadline. Unfortunately, the FedEx courier did not arrive by the end of the day, due to what has been characterized as a software error.

At that point, according to the DOE, a simple trip to the post office or a FedEx drop box would have satisfied the mailing requirement. But instead, a university employee e-mailed the DOE, explaining the failed pickup and stating that the package would be sent the next day. There was no immediate reply to the e-mail, and nothing more was done that day. FedEx duly picked up the package the following morning, and apparently agreed to backdate the air bill, incorrectly showing that the applications had been shipped on time.

Eventually, however, DOE officials matched the e-mail to the corresponding grant proposals and determined that they did not meet the deadline, notwithstanding the backdated air bill. After several months of negotiation, including high-level lobbying and a trip to Washington by University Chancellor Robert Berdahl, the DOE held firm. The applications could not be considered because they had not been posted on time. At least sixty other institutions had managed to meet the deadline, and the University of California was not going to get special treatment.

The Education Department's determination to enforce the deadline was debatable, but not irrational. There is always a limited amount of fellowship money available, with many applicants for each possible award. Given the finite resources, every grant provided to a late applicant is necessarily taken away from someone who applied on time.

Lawyers generally understand that some deadlines are absolute, but university administrators apparently do not. Instead of accepting the consequences of their own poor judgment, Berkeley officials lashed out at the DOE, calling the decision outrageous, senseless, stupid, and worse. Most interesting for our purposes, however, was a comment of Mason's, reported in the *New York Times*, that placed the blame on Education Department attorneys:

> The final terrible remark of the lawyers was, "If you hadn't e-mailed Washington, we would have let it go because we wouldn't have known there was a problem," she said. According to Mason, the lawyers' implicit message was "Honesty is not the best policy."

Mason is free to take any lesson she wants from this fiasco, but it is breathtakingly wrong for her to suggest that she and her students were somehow disadvantaged because of their honesty. After all, a graduate division employee (we don't know who) evidently sent in the application packet with a backdated air bill, misrepresenting the actual date of shipping. Nor does it seem that the university ever explicitly corrected the misrepresentation, leaving it instead to the DOE to put two and two together. The *New York Times* reported that the e-mail was "apparently the only evidence that the applications had not been sent on time."

But let's not quibble with Mason's personal definition of honesty, or the recourse to backdated documents. There is something even more fundamentally troubling about her comment. Her obvious claim is that the e-mail's honesty should result in a waiver of the deadline, thus apparently proving it to have been the "best policy." Never mind that it would hurt the chances of hundreds of other students who "honestly" got their applications mailed on time.

Need it really be said? Honesty is the best policy because it is, well, honest — not because it gets you something. Mason and her employees were under an ethical obligation, perhaps even a legal one, to correct the misleading air bill. Her remark suggests a belief that she should have been rewarded for coming clean, but that would reduce truthfulness to the level of opportunism, with dire consequences for education and society.

And that brings us, finally, to the study of legal ethics. Over many years, I have observed any number of law teachers — in professional responsibility, trial advocacy, negotiation, and other courses — tell their students that "lying is counterproductive." Liars, they say, will eventually be caught and disgraced, if not disciplined. At the very least, their reputations will suffer as word gets around, and no one will trust them. The admonition, then, is that lying will hurt your practice. This approach has always seemed questionable to me. I think most lawyers would have to acknowledge that liars (and other assorted cheaters) often succeed and prosper, with no loss of clients or income, nor any other comeuppance. It is impossible to know how many liars have avoided all detection, so there is really no empirical basis for believing that bad actors are always, or even usually, unmasked.

For that reason, perhaps it would be preferable to level with students, telling them that lying can indeed work, at least some of the time. Lying is egregiously wrong, but not because of some shrewd utilitarian calculus. Professional responsibility, after all, involves principles, not expediency, and ethical behavior should be motivated by something more than fear of adverse consequences (or, as Mason intimated, the promise of a possible benefit).

And consider this: If we teach law students to refrain from lying for fear of being caught, what will happen when they find themselves in situations where exposure seems nearly impossible? What then is the motivation to tell the truth? Lawyers today face immense pressure to maximize profits and optimize results. There is always temptation to cut corners or to fib, and too many lawyers have withheld discovery or forged documents. No one ever does that expecting to be caught, and we can only wonder how many have managed to get away with it. There will always be situations in which the advantages of lying seem to outweigh the likely consequences.

Unlike Berkeley's Mason, we need to recognize that truthfulness does not always pay off, no matter how much we wish it would. Of course, we all hope that liars will be nabbed and disciplined, shamed and ostracized. Unfortunately, we cannot guarantee it. Nonetheless (to paraphrase Coach Vince Lombardi), "Honesty isn't the best policy, it's the only policy." Even if you lose your grant.

[Postscript: The Department of Education did not relent, but an alternative solution was implemented. A group working out of the U.S. Department of State agreed to review the applications from Berkeley to identify the most fellowship-worthy students, who were then funded by direct grants from the University of California. In other words, Fulbright lite.]

36

Clinical Commandments

IF THERE WERE an encyclopedia of North Dakota politics, the entry for "gadfly" would probably feature a photograph of Martin Wishnatsky. A New Jersey native who holds a Ph.D. in political science from Harvard University, Wishnatsky arrived in North Dakota in 1991 with an organization called the Lambs of Christ, on a mission to block the entrance of an abortion clinic. He's been there ever since, becoming a high-profile activist willing to go to jail for his anti-abortion work.

Wishnatsky's greatest success, however, came not on the abortion front, but rather in the context of an unusual First Amendment lawsuit against the legal clinic at the University of North Dakota Law School. Wishnatsky claimed that he had been unfairly rejected as a client of the clinic (which is staffed by faculty and law students), and, surprisingly, the U.S. Court of Appeals for the Eighth Circuit backed him up. In a questionable decision issued in January 2006, the appellate court ruled that Wishnatsky had stated a sufficient cause of action for "viewpoint discrimination" — and therein hangs a tale. It started like this.

In 2003 the legal clinic's Civil Rights Project represented five members of an organization called the Red River Freethinkers in a challenge to the placement of a Ten Commandments monument standing outside the city hall in Fargo, North Dakota. The case was tremendously controversial in North Dakota, drawing the wrath of legislators who were upset that the litigation was being financed by a taxpayer-supported legal clinic. Wishnatsky expressed his own outrage in a letter to the editor of the Grand Forks Herald, in which he charged Professor Laura Rovner, the director of the Civil Rights Project, with engaging in "ideological warfare" and called her clients "parlor atheists who delight in attacking the faith of millions."

Rovner was not deterred by the criticism (the state's attorney general would later issue an opinion supporting the clinic's right to bring the case). But Wishnatsky was not deterred either, and he seemed determined to score rhetorical points against the legal clinic and its clients. While the Ten Commandments case was pending (it was dismissed in October 2005, leaving the Fargo monument intact), he sent Rovner a letter seeking help in developing a lawsuit against "Grand Forks County and other relevant parties for having a statue of the Greek goddess Themis on top of the Grand Forks County Courthouse."

Themis is the well-known figure of a blindfolded, toga-clad woman holding the scales of justice. That image, which adorns countless courthouses, does not evoke religious establishment for most people, but Wishnatsky saw it differently.

In language that might have been intended to satirize an American Civil Liberties Union brief, he claimed that "as a Christian, I find such representations of pagan religious figures in public places very disturbing," and indeed, "I feel like a second-class citizen when subject to such governmental displays." He requested the clinic's assistance "on the same basis as that granted to the [plaintiffs] to bring suit against the city of Fargo over the Ten Commandments monument."

After reading his letter, no one could have blamed Rovner for questioning Wishnatsky's motives. But in case there had been any doubt, he underscored his point by sending the letter to the local press and then publishing an op-ed piece in which he suggested that Rovner was "abusing her position . . . to further her own political agenda."

Unfortunately for Rovner, she took the bait. She sent Wishnatsky a letter informing him that due to limited resources, the Civil Rights Project was "unable to accept any new cases at this time." That probably would have ended the ironic pas de deux, but Rovner evidently could not resist going further. Even if they had sufficient resources, she continued, "our independent professional judgment is that your persistent and antagonistic actions . . . would adversely affect our ability to establish an effective attorney-client relationship with you and would consequently impair our ability to [represent] you." Thus, she concluded, "our ethical obligations . . . prohibit us" from accepting the case.

As an inveterate do-it-yourself litigator (with a couple of victories to his credit), Wishnatsky took that as an invitation to sue. In early 2004 he filed a federal civil rights case alleging viewpoint discrimination in violation of the First Amendment. He alleged that Rovner's stated reasons were pretexts, and that she had actually spurned him because of his public criticism of the clinic and the Ten Commandments case.

In fairly short order, the North Dakota district court granted the defense motion for judgment on the pleadings, dismissing the complaint before the development of a factual record. At that point, Wishnatsky enlisted the American Center for Law and Justice — a Washington, D.C., nonprofit law firm founded by the religious broadcaster Pat Robertson — which appealed the case to the Eighth Circuit.

Wishnatsky's appellate counsel raised a single, elegant point: "The government may not categorically refuse services to a person just because that person dared publicly to criticize the governmental provider."

Rovner and the legal clinic, represented by the North Dakota solicitor general, briefed the case quite differently. The dispute was about academic freedom and legal ethics, they argued, not public benefits. Law school clinicians must be free to select cases for educational reasons, and the choice of client "plays an essential role in whether the clinic is able to properly and effectively educate law students." Thus, it was reasonable (and lawful) to reject a disruptive client because his antagonistic speech hurt the clinic's ability to "effectively achieve its goals."

Indeed, Rovner continued to maintain that she was ethically required to decline Wishnatsky's request because his "demeaning and attacking . . . statements" destroyed the trust that is essential to an attorney-client relationship.

The Eighth Circuit ruled in Wishnatsky's favor, reinstating his lawsuit while taking a modest jab at the clinic in the process. According to the appellate court, the clinic's argument amounted to a claim "that it *may* exclude persons from the program solely on the basis of their viewpoint [emphasis in original]." Taken to its logical conclusion, the court observed, that position would allow the publicly funded program to "accept as clients only persons who belong to one political party." Having read the briefs, however, I think that unfairly characterizes the clinic's defense, which was based on Wishnatsky's potential disruptiveness rather than his viewpoint.

But the court was on somewhat firmer ground when it held that the mere fear of disruption could not support "a rule that permits institutions of higher education . . . to discriminate on the basis of viewpoint in the administration of a clinical legal program." For that reason, Wishnatsky had to be given a chance to prove that he had been turned away for speech-related reasons. The Eighth Circuit also rejected Rovner's broader claim, that she was ethically prohibited from representing a client who had attacked her in the press. Instead of turning Wishnatsky away, the court opined, Rovner and the clinic should have considered whether "a fresh start, common purpose, and agreement to bury the hatchet might overcome previous discord."

That was a judicial fantasy, indulging the unrealistic assumption that Wishnatsky was sincerely interested in challenging the Themis statue. The motion for judgment on the pleadings required the court to "accept as true" all of the plaintiff's allegations, but there still ought to have been some sort of reality check. It was painfully obvious that Wishnatsky was trying to make a political point at Rovner's expense, and that no amount of "burying the hatchet" would satisfy him. He acknowledged as much in a phone interview, when I asked if he was truly offended by the statue at the courthouse. "If they [the Ten Commandments plaintiffs] can be offended, then I can be offended," he said, adding that the Freethinkers' case was "conjured up for political purposes," and "in all equity, they should make up a case for me, too."

There was no reason for Rovner to allow the clinical program to be manipulated, especially to the detriment of her existing clients. But I still think she made a mistake — and not just a tactical error — by overstating her claim that Wishnatsky's criticism created an ethical rift.

The legal profession is at its best when we represent unpopular or distasteful clients, including those who have bitterly insulted us. It is true that deep animosity can fatally undermine the attorney-client relationship, but lawyers should be extremely hesitant to pull that particular trigger. In fact, we should do our utmost to overcome such barriers in the case of people with whom we disagree. The question wasn't whether Wishnatsky was antagonistic, but whether he had a viable case.

Academic freedom is an essential value in clinical legal education (I began my career at Northwestern University as a clinical professor in 1975), but there is an important distinction between counseling a potential client and accepting a case. It would be ridiculous to require a publicly funded clinic to represent all comers, but it is not unreasonable to expect every hopeful client to get an objective review. In other words, you don't have to represent everyone who walks through the door, but you do have to keep the door open.

Rovner could have avoided the whole contretemps simply by agreeing to evaluate Wishnatsky's case on the merits. That would have taught her students that First Amendment claims deserve to be taken seriously, even if at first they seem like gimmicks. After all, improbable causes of action can sometimes succeed, so why not take a hard look at Wishnatsky's claim?

A few hours of student research would have revealed that there is no significant contemporary cult of Themis (nor has there been for many centuries), and certainly none that has any likely influence over the Grand Forks County government. That would have been sufficient to reject Wishnatsky's establishment clause claim, while upholding the principle of access to counsel. In fact, Rovner could have used the experience to show her students the difference between a religious display and a work of art and, more importantly, the difference between a legitimate case and a frivolous one. That would have been a great teachable moment — for everybody.

[Postscript: Professor Rovner later relocated to the University of Denver and was therefore dismissed as a defendant in the case. Wishnatsky and the University of North Dakota then reached a non-monetary settlement, agreeing only that the legal clinic would consider future Wishnatsky representation requests strictly on the merits.]

37

Pluto's Plight, and Ours

EVERYONE IS IN favor of honesty, but who decides what is right and true? In court, judges determine the law. In a democracy, political matters are decided by noisy campaigns to shape public opinion, followed by elections in which the candidate with the most votes (usually) wins. Unfortunately, some citizens sincerely believe that scientific issues should also be decided based on vociferous campaigns and popular votes. But majority opinion, no matter how sincere, can never tell us much about scientific truth.

Scientific matters are best determined by researchers who are trained to evaluate empirical data and to declare their findings — regardless of trends in public opinion. This is true whether the subject is as weighty as the origin of species or as seemingly modest as the names of heavenly bodies. The 2006 protest over the decision of the International Astronomical Union (IAU) to reclassify Pluto is just one example of the unseemly tug-of-war between science and politics, with implications that extend both to classrooms and courts.

In response to the decision to demote Pluto from full-fledged planet to dwarf, critics accused the scientists of striking a blow against "the little guy," and perhaps against democracy itself. They often claimed to speak on behalf of schoolchildren, whose anguished letters to the IAU played a large part in bringing the controversy to public attention in the first place. Elementary schoolteachers began to mount a further letter-writing crusade, this time to public officials, using Pluto's loss of status to spur lessons in both composition and civics. After all, if scientists can vote on a description of nature, why shouldn't ordinary people lobby to overrule a decision that they don't like? But the fact is that science is not democratic, and the Pluto petitions sent exactly the wrong message not only about science, but also about democracy and law.

By its very nature, the scientific method requires an endless series of revisions and reevaluations, submitting even the most widely accepted ideas to critical investigation and reconceptualization. Change is inevitable, and it is usually welcomed, if not celebrated. While scientists generally proceed by consensus, new propositions are sometimes subject to a formal vote — but that should never be confused with political voting. Scientists strive to revise their theoretical categories on the basis of new data and improved measurement tools, and although they have their necessary share of human frailties, their professional standards disallow the sort of interest-based voting that is perfectly acceptable in politics and law. Consequently, following a period of rigorous and sometimes passionate debate among physicists, there was ultimately a relatively smooth transition when the new field of quantum physics successfully demonstrated that the old division of matter — into particles and waves — was incorrect. Likewise, paleontologists eventually came to accept the fact that dinosaurs were more closely related to birds than reptiles, notwithstanding their lizard-like morphology. There was a good deal of argument and advocacy along the way, but the ultimate arbiters were the scientists themselves, without any need for public input.

Of course, that is precisely what happened to poor Pluto. New information and refined measurements demonstrated that it simply didn't fit in with the first eight planets, having much more in common with dozens or even hundreds of distant objects in the recently discovered Kuiper Belt. So the scientific vote on Pluto was simply necessary to update the definition of "planet." And that brings us back to the kids. Although they were no doubt motivated by the best intentions, teachers and other adults did children no favors by rallying them behind Pluto's cause. In fact, they risked undermining serious educational goals by suggesting that popular sentiment can, or should, sway scientific conclusions. That sort of thinking leads left-wing deconstructionists to claim that scientific knowledge is merely a "social construct" that serves the political goals of the dominant power structure. Even more dangerously, it leads right-wing votaries of Intelligent Design to believe that the biology curriculum should be determined by school board elections, rather than by, well, biologists.

Although the study of evolution has been essential to the development of lifesaving medical advances, many parents have organized attempts to remove it from their children's education — through elections, petitions, or boycotts — or at least to mute or minimize it. In some locales, large majorities of citizens have protested the centrality of evolution in science classes, although they have usually been thwarted by administrators or courts determined to maintain the separation of religion and science (and thus between church and state), even in the face of overwhelming opposition.

Consider, for example, the Fifth Circuit case of *Freiler v. Tangipahoa Parish Board of Education*, in which a Louisiana school board required that teachers read a "disclaimer from endorsement" at the beginning of every course of study on evolution. The disclaimer would have informed students that teaching the "Scientific Theory of Evolution" was "not intended to influence or dissuade the Biblical version of Creation or any other concept" (capitalization in original). A three-judge panel of the appellate court enjoined use of the disclaimer, and subsequently the full court denied a petition for rehearing. But six judges dissented, joining an opinion by Judge Rhesa Hawkins Barksdale.

Noting that an "estimated 95 percent of the parish students are adherents to the Biblical concept of creation," Judge Barksdale and the dissenters forcefully expressed their distress that the school curriculum presented evolution "as the *sole* explanation for the origin of life and matter," repeatedly italicizing their concern that evolution was the "*only* theory taught" and that students were presented with "*only one concept.*" Because the science curriculum was evidently limited exclusively to science, the dissenters justified the school board's disclaimer in the name of balance. "It neutralizes," explained Judge Barksdale, apparently unconcerned that neutralizing science might not be an appropriate educational goal, especially in a biology class. Ironically demonstrating his own misunderstanding of scientific concepts, Judge Barksdale also suggested that the disclaimer might prompt students to investigate such alternative "nonreligious theories" as the "Big Bang and panspermia," neither of which has anything to do with evolution.

No doubt buoyed by the Barksdale dissent, the school board attempted to take the case to the U.S. Supreme Court. Although certiorari was denied, there was again a dissent, written by Justice Antonin Scalia and joined by Justice Clarence Thomas and Chief Justice William Rehnquist. In a passage that has been called "scientifically irresponsible" and potentially reflecting "a shocking level of scientific illiteracy" (by prominent law prof bloggers Jim Chen and Jonathan Adler, respectively), Justice Scalia lamented earlier decisions that struck down an Arkansas anti-evolution statute and invalidated a mandatory creationism law in Louisiana. Now, in the Tangipahoa Parish case, he complained, "We stand by in silence" while the Fifth Circuit bars a school district "from even suggesting to students that other theories besides evolution — including but not limited to the biblical theory of creation — are worthy of their consideration."

But neither the Fifth Circuit nor any other U.S. court has ever suggested that the biblical account of creation is unworthy of consideration.

The courts have only held that biblical creation involves the study of religion rather than science, and that it cannot be voted into the biology curriculum under another name. Those decisions have not been popular, but they carefully respect the line between science and faith, and therefore the requirements of the establishment clause of the First Amendment. Even ninety-five percent of a district's students should not be sufficient to disclaim (or neutralize) evolution, nor should any majority of schoolchildren be able to restore Pluto to planetdom. In the few school districts with Jewish majorities, would anyone propose that zoology courses should begin with a disclaimer that they do not intend to "dissuade or influence" the biblical story of staves turning into snakes?

Science does not need to be popular in order to be accurate, and voting on science, whether by schoolchildren or school boards, is at best counter-educational. Thus, instead of complaining about Pluto's demotion, teachers would do their students a far greater service by explaining that the scientific method forces us to keep our minds open to new information about the surrounding universe.

And what of Justice Scalia and supporters of the Tangipahoa Parish school board? Perhaps they could learn a lesson from one of the nation's earliest scientists, David Rittenhouse, who was also a mathematician, an inventor, and the first director of the U.S. Mint. One of the first uniquely American inventions was Rittenhouse's orrery — a mechanical device for determining the relative positions of the moon and planets, which he completed in 1770. His fellow colonials took enormous pride in the orrery, with one Pennsylvania newspaper bragging that it was "much more compleat [sic] than anything of the kind ever made in Europe [and that] it must give great pleasure to every lover of his country to see her rising to fame in the sublime science as well as every improvement in the arts." While the device was impressively accurate, it soon proved to be not quite complete, given that it included only the first six planets, ending the then-known solar system with Saturn. Uranus was discovered, however, only slightly more than a decade later, in 1781 (Neptune followed in 1846, and hapless Pluto in 1930). Rittenhouse lived until 1796, but he was never known to complain that advances in astronomy had so quickly rendered his accomplishment slightly obsolete.Nor did he ever seek a referendum — or disclaimer — on the discovery of Uranus.

38

The Bedouin Horse Trade

NOTHING CAN SHAKE your faith in the hypotheses of law and economics like a visit to the Middle East. Of course, the very opposite should be true. The so-called "oriental bazaar" is the prototype of the efficient market where buyers and sellers negotiate continuously, with prices rising and falling in relation to supply and demand, and where the resulting "equilibrium" ultimately allows the market to clear at the end of each day. That model is at the very heart of neoclassical economic theory, as expounded by the contemporary cohort of law and economics scholars. Based on assumptions about the inherent superiority of free markets, they argue resolutely against government regulation, tort liability, anti-discrimination laws, zoning ordinances, and the minimum wage — all of which are said to be unacceptably inefficient. But what if the efficiency assumption turns out to be demonstrably wrong? What if we were to encounter a real bazaar that resolutely fails to clear, where perishable goods remain unsold, and where willing buyers walk away with their figurative hands empty? Could law and economics scholars be persuaded to relent, or at least to trim their claims about the natural efficiency of unrestrained trade? Which brings me to the subject of Petra.

Petra is Jordan's fabled "rose-red city — half as old as Time." The Nabateans, who built Petra during biblical times, located their capital in an almost impregnable mountain stronghold. Even today, it is possible to enter Petra only by passing through the Bab es-Siq, a narrow gorge nearly a mile long and never more than a few meters wide.

What meant security to the ancient Nabateans is now an impediment to tourism. To make access easier, not to mention more romantic, the route of the Bab es-Siq was for many years plied by hundreds of horses-for-hire. For seven Jordanian dinars (abbreviated as 7 JD), a bedouin guide would take you into the site on horseback and meet you later to take you out again. The standard price was fixed, and tickets for the horses were sold at the entry gate.

Tourists could also walk into the site and negotiate for a one-way horse on the way out. The return-only transactions were conducted on a cash basis — no tickets, no fixed prices. Here is where economics failed me. The standard academic model predicts that horse prices should fall throughout the day. As nightfall approaches and the ranks of tourists thin, guides should become increasingly willing to bargain for rides out of the site. This did not turn out to be the case. Indeed, the bottom-line fee for a horse was surprisingly nonnegotiable, sharply contrary to what would appear to be the sellers' rational best interest.

My family of four spent three days at Petra over a New Year's holiday. We walked all the way into the site each morning because we like to walk and because we had been advised (correctly) that the Siq can be better appreciated on foot. Each afternoon, chiefly as an experiment, I attempted to negotiate for horses to take us back through the Siq to the entrance gate. Notwithstanding my superior knowledge of economic modeling, I failed each time. "When are we going to ride the horses, Daddy?" my children asked. "It won't be much longer," I replied, "as soon as the market clears." But it never did.

It was an economic theory-confounding phenomenon. Guides with horses gather at the entrance gate to Petra each morning, making themselves available to arriving tourists. Those who engage horses are walked all the way through the Siq to a large open plaza adjacent to an ancient theater, a trip of approximately a mile and a half that takes around twenty minutes. This plaza is the horse-route terminal, where renters are dropped off on the way in and where they obtain their mounts for the journey out. Of course, no horses linger at the terminal in the morning because the bedouins all gallop back to the site entrance immediately after depositing their incoming riders. American taxi drivers would call this practice "dead heading"; it is the desert equivalent of driving an empty cab to the airport rather than cruising an unpromising neighborhood in an unlikely search for customers.

Things change in the afternoon. As tourists stop arriving and start thinking about going back to their hotels, the horses begin to congregate in the theater plaza. Some of the guides are there to collect return tickets, but most are available for cash hiring. I know this because virtually all of the guides solicit virtually all of the tourists, offering "Horse? Horse?" The scene is chaotic; there is nothing approaching a queue.

This is a market that should clear if economic theory is worth a damn.

Foot-sore tourists should be interested in riding back through the Siq. The bedouin guides should be interested in minimizing their down time. At the right price, many tourists should find riding preferable to walking. For the guides, working should be preferable to standing around. Horse time, after all, is a wasting asset. It cannot be banked or saved for another day. Every "siq-unit" that a horse is unengaged is a unit that is lost forever. Thus, as nightfall approaches and the demand for horses falls, the price for a return siq should become increasingly lower.

But here is how it really worked. The first price quoted for a return siq was invariably 7 JD — exactly the same as for a round trip (about ten bucks at the time). No matter how resolutely I bargained, the price never fell below 4 JD. On each of our three days at Petra we were very nearly the last tourists to leave in the afternoon, with the horses often outnumbering the remaining pedestrians by at least two or three to one. Still, the price never dropped below four dinars.

So we walked. Four of us. Three times. The potential siqs went unsold because we could not arrive at an agreeable price. The result, in the eyes of an economist, was clearly sub-optimal. My family walked instead of riding; the horses idled instead of working. What could be the reason for this "inefficient" loss of value?

Am I a Bad Bargainer?

Economic modeling predicts that the price of a horse should fall with the setting sun to allow the market to clear. One possibility is that the price did fall, but that I was unable to take advantage of it because of poor bargaining skills. Perhaps the bedouin guides saw through my bluff. This explanation fails, though, simply because I was not bluffing. I was completely willing to walk out of the Siq with my family as, indeed, we ended up doing on all three days.

I would have ridden at least once if anyone had met my price, but I was unwilling to overpay for the privilege. It is possible that I failed to convince the bedouins that riding was only of marginal utility to me (poor communication? cross-cultural misunderstanding?), but actions speak louder than words. As the four of us actually proceeded to walk out through the Siq, we were, in the truest sense, bargaining with our feet. Every guide could clearly see four lost siqs receding with our footsteps. According to economic theory, I shouldn't have needed to be a good bargainer, just a good walker.

Was It a Long-Term Strategy?

Another possibility is that the guides were engaged in long-term, strategic bargaining as a form of price support. Withholding goods from the market can result in artificial scarcity, thereby raising prices sufficiently to compensate for lost sales. Perhaps the guides were acting on the assumption that a permanent price floor of 5 JD, at the cost of a few foregone siqs here and there, would serve their interests better than the 3 (actually, a total of 12) dinars that we were offering.

Upon reflection, however, that approach also seems irrational. There comes a time when every missed siq is a deadweight loss to the guide. Early in the day, particularly at the entrance gate, a rational guide might reason that opportunity costs preclude offering discounts to hard-bargaining tourists. That is, the guide who transports me at 3 JD might miss out on the next tourist, who is presumably willing to pay the entire 7 dinars. Because the guides are no doubt experienced at judging the flow of tourists, they should also be able to make efficient decisions as to the relative value of assured, though discounted, employment versus potential work at the full rate.

At the end of the day, though, the calculus must change. On any given day, tourists are a finite commodity. At some point, they all leave and the site closes. As that time arrives, there is no longer any opportunity cost in accepting a half-price rider. Nor should a guide have to worry about selling rides at below cost. The guide's expenses are basically fixed: he has a capital investment in his horse (which depreciates at a fairly steady rate, whether the horse is being ridden or not); the horse eats a constant amount of food; and there are other costs for nighttime stabling, veterinary care, and the like. Significantly, none of these costs is likely to vary significantly according to the number of siqs that the horse is employed each day. I suppose a horse that travels fifteen siqs might eat a few more oats than one that was only engaged twelve times or might be marginally more likely to injure itself, but these costs are so indeterminate and speculative that they would be impossible to assign on a per-siq basis.

As the tourist flow dries up, every foregone siq constitutes a net loss that cannot be recaptured. Again there seems to be no logical reason for a horse to stand idle at the end of the day rather than accept the offer of a market-clearing discount shopper. No single guide stands to profit personally from passing up the sale of a siq; he will always be better off selling rather than standing.

Were the Guides Successful Price-Fixers?

A final, promising explanation is that the guides had succeeded in establishing a cartel that was capable of enforcing minimum prices even at the cost of lost siqs for certain individuals. Although every individual guide has an incentive to cut prices at the end of the day, the community of bedouin guides would benefit collectively from adhering to high fixed prices. The usual solution to this dilemma — which economists call a "collective action" problem — is some sort of effort at price enforcement, either in the form of government intervention or cartelization.

The use of fixed-price tickets at the entrance to the site is obviously an enforcement mechanism. By using, in effect, a single-payer system, the authorities are able to control the price for round-trip excursions. Moreover, the sale of round-trip tickets at the site entrance ensures that most transactions will occur at the beginning of the day, when tourists are plentiful and siqs are at their least perishable. At the same time, the ticket system also functions as a floor by eliminating individualized bargaining. That is an excellent example of a government-sponsored cartel.

No such enforcement system, however, protects the price of return trips. Although tourists holding tickets are entitled to return through the Siq at the fixed price, there are plenty of others who walked into the site. Every such return trip is a cash transaction, subject to individualized negotiation. Indeed, the near-universal attempts to overcharge — by gouging a full 7 JD out of unwitting tourists — demonstrate that the standardized pricing system is inoperative for the return trip.

How could a cartel police dozens — scores? hundreds? — of discrete exchanges, each one consisting of the hand-to-hand transfer of a few dinars? Neither official compulsion nor informal stigmatization could operate in an information void. And in the absence of effective enforcement, the cartel should fail.

First, consider formal, government enforcement. Suppose that it is illegal to sell nonticketed return siqs. Presumably, then, free marketeers, if caught, could be de-licensed, fined, or imprisoned. Given adequate resources, such a regime could surely enforce minimum prices, easily explaining why I was unable to bargain for a discounted siq. I can state with certainty, however, that there was no such setup. I observed dozens of guides freely negotiating cash deals with potential riders; I was constantly offered the opportunity to make a deal myself. If it was illegal to sell non-ticketed siqs, the law was being honored only in the breach and could not possibly have been an effective basis for price enforcement.

Alternatively, it might have been legal to sell return siqs for cash, but only at a fixed price. Given the nature of the freewheeling negotiations, however, this seems extraordinarily unlikely. How could enforcement officials, or anyone else, possibly know the value of the bills being passed from rider to guide? The pressure to offer "secret discounts" was enormous, and the ability to compete for riders by other means was limited. Hence, at least some guides — actually, all guides — should have been tempted to take competitive advantage of the private nature of return transactions.

Finally, there might have been informal enforcement mechanisms. The bedouin guides of Petra appear to form a tight-knit, homogeneous community. Perhaps they have agreed among themselves to adhere to a minimum price structure, and they fear ostracism or stigmatization if they defect. Who would fail to shudder at the taunt, "My dad says your dad sells siqs on the cheap"? ("Does not." "Does so." "Does not.")

In theory, concern over social reprisals could enforce a minimum price. But even an informal mechanism is dependent upon information. Ostracism and stigmatization work only if there is some way to know who needs to be shunned. Again, the highly private, individualized nature of the Siq transactions would seem to rule out the development of the necessary knowledge base. Even a platoon of Siq-police would find it nearly impossible to tell how many wadded bills are being passed from hand to hand. It seems out of the question that guides, busy trying to sell their own siqs, would be able to monitor anyone else's transactions.

In short, the guides appear to face their own prisoner's dilemma. Collectively, their interest is to cooperate by adhering to a high, fixed price. The individual interest of each guide, however, would be best served by defecting, at least at the end of the day. Yet, the structure of their environment provides them with insufficient information to engage in effective price enforcement. Every indicator, therefore, suggests not only that they will defect by lowering their prices, but also that they will compete to defect. Nevertheless, they did not defect. Where was the race to the bottom? Or, as my kids might have put it, "Why won't the market clear, Daddy?"

So What Is the Explanation?

None of the accepted economic models is sufficient to explain why the Petra horse market failed to clear. But theories are one thing and, as we say in the litigation business, facts is facts. The market did not clear. Do we just shrug off this empirical evidence, or might there be an answer that is — gasp! — independent of market assumptions? As Stephen Jay Gould observed in another context, the tyranny of what seems reasonable often impedes knowledge.

So I asked my children why they thought the bedouins refused my offers. "Because you didn't offer enough money, Daddy, and they thought that you didn't respect them." But they still should have preferred the money to just standing around not working. "No, Daddy, they would rather stand around than take less than they thought they were worth."

From a common sense perspective, the answer is painfully obvious. Pride. They were desert horsemen, after all, and they probably were not thrilled about chauffeuring tourists in the first place. There was an amount of money that made the work worthwhile, and they just were not interested in anything less, efficiency be damned. From an economist's perspective, on the other hand, their behavior was irrational. Once engaged in a mercantile trade, once agreeable to schlepping tourists through the site, once willing to bargain over the return fare, what is the logic of refusing to maximize one's return?

But as Holmes put it, "The life of the law has not been logic: it has been experience." The experience of the bedouin has no doubt emphasized the value of pride, not to mention related virtues such as determination and group identification. During nomadic life, it seems likely that pride would be a positive survival feature because it makes one more willing to endure hardship, value each individual, and protect one's family and flock. In other words, the development of stubborn pride should be seen as an evolutionary adaptation to environmental circumstances. Is it possible that the laws of evolution, at least by analogy, might reveal an explanation that the laws of economics have failed to provide?

What I observed at Petra, then, was not the theoretical efficiency of an optimal market. It was the practical equilibrium of an actual market. The bedouin guides had struck a reasonable balance between their tradition of pride and their participation in the tourist-oriented horse trade. They were unwilling to bargain past a certain point, even if that meant earning a little less.

Academic economists have a way of dismissing or discounting inconvenient facts, such as real-life markets that never clear. Those are mere anecdotes, they say, no doubt caused by "externalities" or "information asymmetries" or "market distortions." But those are all excuses. The true test of a theory is whether it actually predicts behavior, and it is no explanation at all to opine that "markets will clear except when they don't." Some unseen hand!

So here is a lesson for academic economists, although I am willing to bet they will find a way to rationalize around it: Efficiency takes us only so far. Equilibrium trumps optimality. Without wisdom, we walk.

39

There Are No Scriveners Here

ACCORDING TO THE Attorneys' Liability Assurance Society (ALAS), malpractice insurer for the nation's largest law firms, the representation of multiple clients in business transactions is one of the leading sources of liability for contemporary American attorneys. In the archetypal situation, a single lawyer or law firm represents (or appears to represent) several different parties who are negotiating a deal among themselves. The lawyer proceeds without providing disclosures or obtaining consents, on the theory that the parties' common goals dispel the possibility of seriously conflicting interests.

This approach is well and good when the deal succeeds and everyone makes money. But some projects collapse, leaving desperate clients wondering why their attorney did not protect them from disaster, or at least warn them of inherent dangers or perfidious partners. These clients do not take kindly to assertions that the lawyer was "counsel for the deal" or perhaps a "mere scrivener." They feel betrayed. They sue for malpractice. And they often win.

It was therefore disheartening to see two prominent law and economics scholars, Jonathan Macey and Geoffrey Miller, endorse the very course of action that has brought so much unnecessary grief to so many lawyers and clients. Developing a model of "efficient" representation, Professors Macey and Miller assert that client consent is unnecessary (because it is inefficient) when a single lawyer represents several negotiating parties whose goals are in "substantial alignment," especially when the attorney is acting as a scrivener. Whatever its theoretical rigor, this conclusion is positively dangerous to practicing lawyers who advise clients in the real world.

Macey and Miller's model of interest-aligned negotiation arises when two or more clients are joining forces in a wealth-maximizing project. That appears to exclude the typical buyer-seller situation, perhaps the most frequent negotiation, where each party is trying to extract as much as possible from the other. It takes little effort to imagine a whole series of negotiations in which the parties care relatively little about joint maximization, except insofar as it increases their own bottom line. Lenders want the highest possible interest and the greatest possible security, while borrowers want the exact opposite. Professional athletes want the highest pay and the most restrictive "no-cut" provisions, though owners want anything but. Contractors want the longest lead time, the most up-front payment, and the fewest performance guarantees, and home-owners want . . . well, you get the point.

It is true, of course, that some negotiating situations — joint ventures, partnerships — seem better to fit Macey and Miller's model of cooperative wealth creation. But there is no way to know what percentage these comprise in the entire negotiating universe, and it does not necessarily follow that such parties' interests are mainly aligned. Macey and Miller recognize that a conflict of interest arises when each party "wants as big a share as possible of the wealth so created," but they subordinate this problem, minimizing the danger it poses to clients, by simply insisting that "substantial alignment" is more significant.

Surely, however, the question of "alignment" will vary on a case-by-case basis. In some negotiations the parties will always rise and fall together, no matter what the precise terms of the agreement. In other negotiations, the parties will be the equivalent of adversaries. And in what is probably the most common situation, the parties will have a host of unrecognized, predicate, or underlying interests that place them well out of perfect alignment, even as they are attempting to increase everyone's wealth. That is why they need lawyers in the first place.

In negotiation, conflicting interests may be submerged or contingent. It is all too easy, in the flush of enthusiasm over foretold riches, for a client to be overly optimistic, naïve, or gullible about the credibility or intentions of a nascent business partner. And this is precisely the situation in which the protection of independent, objective counsel may be most essential.

It is not simply that Macey and Miller are mistaken about the dangers inherent in the context of negotiation. They also contend that a diminished potential for harm may bring a situation below a so-called "consent threshold," thereby removing any need for attorney disclosure or client consent. Thus, if one were to apply their theory, the result would be that attorneys alone would decide whether and how much disclosure (which is to say, protection) clients would receive in the course of negotiation.

Macey and Miller also believe that an attorney can function "essentially as a scrivener, recording in proper legal form an agreement . . . negotiated by the parties on their own." This, they assert, results in "reduced danger of harm to the clients from multiple representation and an increased likelihood that a given case will fall below the consent threshold." But the concept of lawyer-as-amanuensis is chimerical, which will become apparent once we unpack some assumptions.

In fact, the phrase "proper legal form" has no proper legal meaning. Do Macey and Miller expect the lawyer to record the agreement so that it is binding only in principle? Or must the attorney do everything possible to make it unbreakable? Or should it be subject to cancellation on reasonable notice? Even the most sophisticated business negotiators typically agree only on the major items in a deal. After that, they call in the lawyers to work out the details. For any given agreement, there will be dozens, maybe hundreds, of possible "proper legal forms" in which it can be memorialized.

Thus, the notion of "proper legal form" is only the beginning of an inquiry that can have dramatic consequences for the negotiating parties. Will there be reciprocal security interests? Will there be liquidated damages for breach (and if so, can they be adequately distinguished from penalties)? Will there be an acceleration clause, a covenant not to compete, non-waiver of defaults, a buy-sell agreement, a provision for specific performance? Will the mutual covenants be dependant or severable? No matter how thoroughly the parties have agreed, it is the lawyer's role to raise the legal issues they may have neglected or overlooked. And issues that seem purely technical at the outset of a business relationship can easily turn out to be decisive once the deal goes south. "Proper legal form" does not come in a one-size-fits-all format. Rather, it must be tailored to the needs and interests of the parties, which, as we have seen, are almost never congruent even in the most amicable negotiations. There will virtually always be gaps in the parties' agreement. Consequently, the decision to act as a mere scrivener on behalf of multiple clients is a decision to leave the gaps unfilled — to the probable detriment of one client or the other.

This is not to say that a lawyer cannot represent multiple clients in negotiation, or even act as a mere scrivener, but the choice should be the client's, without regard to any theoretical "consent threshold."

Assume for example, that two clients are negotiating a business arrangement, jointly represented by attorney A. There will almost certainly be some differing interests between two clients even if their ultimate goals seem strongly aligned. The rub for the lawyer is that there is no way to know intuitively whether the mutual interests predominate over the differing ones, especially because the eventual course of the business relationship cannot be clearly foreseen.

This leaves the attorney with two options. She can guess or she can ask. If she guesses, she has deprived both clients of her counsel on what might turn out to be a crucial question, substituting her judgment for theirs. So of course, she should ask. In the language of the Model Rules, she should explain the "matter to the extent reasonably necessary to permit [each] client to make informed decisions regarding the representation." Following the lawyer's explanation, the clients can make their own assessments of their goals and interests, each one then deciding whether he or she wishes to proceed with multiple representation. In a word, consent. And thresholds have nothing to do with it.

The essential principle is that the lawyer must place each client in a position to make his or her own informed determination. The attorney's duty is not to refrain from simultaneous representation, but only to make the necessary disclosures (and obtain knowing consent) prior to the simultaneous representation of multiple clients. In that way, each client can decide whether he or she wants to share a lawyer with the other, or whether she would prefer an attorney dedicated solely to her own interests. A lawyer-determined "harm threshold" makes no sense in this analysis, since it is up to the clients to decide how much risk they want to undertake in the first place. In other words, each client must be alerted to the inevitably lurking harms (or potential "cougars," as discussed in earlier essay), not shielded from them.

In the "aligned negotiation" paradigm, a client has no recourse (other than an eventual malpractice lawsuit) if the attorney decides against disclosure and consent. Instead of a conversation, there is only a soliloquy:

> LAWYER: [*Silently*] Hmm? I am representing two parties who are negotiating with each other. Should I advise them of possible conflicts in their underlying needs and predicate interests? Do I need his or her consent before proceeding to represent everyone? Nah! I've concluded that their aligned interests predominate, so I can just go ahead without saying anything.
>
> CLIENT: Were you saying something to me?
>
> LAWYER: [*Aloud*] No, I was just thinking. It was nothing important. Let's get back to work.

Alternatively, let's try to imagine an attorney and client bargaining in good faith over the issue of disclosure and consent. Quite apart from any purely economic model, it seems completely obvious that the client would want information and the lawyer would have scant reason to withhold it:

LAWYER: Since we are just beginning our relationship, let's bargain over whether I should disclose possible conflicts to you and obtain your consent before I represent multiple clients in the same negotiation.

CLIENT: Is there any reason that I wouldn't want disclosure and consent?

LAWYER: Well, it would impose a slightly higher burden on me, and it might slow down the deal while you make up your mind. Depending on what you decide after the disclosures, you could each end up hiring a separate lawyer instead of going ahead with just one.

CLIENT: But that would be my choice, right?

LAWYER: Of course.

CLIENT: Could I figure out the potential conflicts for myself?

LAWYER: You could probably get some of them. But I've had years of training in recognizing how legal terms affect the future of a deal, so it's pretty likely that I would see more than you.

CLIENT: In that case, tell me what I need to know.

LAWYER: Sure.

Indeed, it is impossible even to conceive of a contrary scenario:

LAWYER: I don't think we should really bother with disclosure and consent before you do this deal. It will just slow things down.

CLIENT: What if there is something I need to know?

LAWYER: Umm, well. What you don't know can't hurt you.

In the context of multiple representation in business deals or other negotiations, there is no valid — or even coherent — argument against consent and disclosure. Lawyers have information that clients need and want; that is why the attorneys are retained in the first place. Moreover, much of that information — evaluation of underlying interests, the consequence of various legal provisions, and the impact on privileges — is otherwise unavailable to clients, making it appropriate to place the burden on the lawyer to explain the situation. There will be minimal transaction cost, because the communications will usually be relatively short. (When a disclosure turns out to be lengthy, that must mean there is much to disclose — all the more reason for a client to have the information.)

It is sometimes a good idea for multiple clients to proceed with the same lawyer or law firm when negotiating a business transaction — they can save money, speed the process, and establish a relationship all at the same time. Other times, however, it is a disastrous idea. One of the clients may end up being under-represented, exposed to risk, and perhaps exploited or worse. Rational clients will make different judgments as to their need for independent counsel — the point being that it is the client's decision to make.

PART V

Medical Practice

Introduction

THE BASIC PRINCIPLE of medical ethics was once summarized as "do no harm." Today things are more complex, as physicians wrestle with the overlapping demands of patients, hospitals and health-maintenance organizations, insurance companies, government programs, research sponsors, pharmaceutical companies, and their own self-interests. Unfortunately, medical ethics have not kept pace with the nature of the contemporary health care industry, so it turns out that doctors have a lot to learn from lawyers when it comes to the "Ethics Business," not to mention finding remedies for their own "Mistakes and Cover-Ups."

Lawyers and doctors also face similar, if not comparable, issues of disclosure, determining how much information must be provided to their respective clients and patients. Although the comparison is inexact, it is useful to consider the case of "The Benevolent Otolaryngologist."

Can physicians be persuaded to pay for the legal equivalent of a placebo? "Desperate Doctors, Desperate Measures" asks just how far some doctors will go to persuade themselves that they can stave off malpractice suits.

40

Ethics Business

IF YOU ASKED a random sample of your friends and neighbors, chances are good that virtually all of them would tell you that medical ethics are superior to legal ethics. But at least in a few important regards, they would be seriously wrong.

Consider the case of Dr. Andrew Wiznia, as reported on the front page of the *New York Times*. A highly skilled, exceptionally dedicated pediatric AIDS specialist, he treated hundreds of HIV-positive children at New York's Bronx-Lebanon Hospital Center for many years, achieving notable success and acquiring some substantial government grants along the way. But then Dr. Wiznia announced plans to move his practice to another Bronx hospital, the Jacobi Medical Center, and to take many of his colleagues and patients with him. According to Dr. Wiznia, his relocation would allow him to provide better, more consistent treatment to the children in his care.

The Bronx-Lebanon Hospital Center, however, thought that Dr. Wiznia was practically a thief, using his privileged position and access to information in order to siphon away financing and "steal" patients from his employer. Bronx-Lebanon Hospital filed suit, seeking to enjoin Dr. Wiznia and his associates from treating patients anywhere else for at least six months. Dr. Wiznia countered that the patients did not belong to Bronx-Lebanon and that they should be free to see any doctor, at any hospital, they preferred.

In stark terms, then, that lawsuit exposed the increasingly unsettled ethical gaps between medicine-as-practice and medicine-as-business.

While the Wiznia case was unusual by virtue of its high visibility and vulnerable patients, the fact is that physicians are routinely required — just like television journalists, business executives, and software engineers — to sign "non-compete" agreements as a condition of employment. Also called "restrictive covenants," these provisions protect established physicians and institutions at the expense of newcomers and recent graduates. And, as we shall see, they are always bad for consumers.

Restrictive covenants might once have been little more than a minor inconvenience for apprenticed physicians, but today they raise difficult social issues. Are doctors ultimately free agents, beholden only to the patients whom they heal? Or are hospitals and health-maintenance organizations entitled to protect their investments in facilities and equipment, which may run into millions of dollars, from absconding prima donas, ever in search of the bigger, better deal?

In the long term, the widespread use of non-compete agreements may threaten the doctor-patient relationship in at least three different ways. First, the enforcement of restrictive covenants can reduce the supply of physicians in a community by making it impossible for local doctors to open new offices.

Perhaps more significantly, non-compete agreements obviously serve to limit competition. For example, the doctors at an overpriced or inefficient HMO cannot be lured away by another in the same locale, with the result that one incentive to improve services has been eliminated.

What's more, the existence of restrictive covenants can reduce the collective power of physicians within a particular institution. Since non-compete agreements dramatically increase the consequences of quitting, HMOs and other large employers will have less reason to listen to the suggestions, complaints, or demands of their medical staff.

Let's say that your trusted personal physician just happens to work for an HMO or group practice. Now let's say that she gets fed up with an obdurate bureaucracy and decides to go off on her own. Finally, let's say that your health plan allows you to change providers whenever you wish and that of course you want to follow your doctor. No matter. It is entirely possible that your doctor's contract with her former employer will prevent her from practicing within a radius of, say, five or ten miles for a period ranging from several months to several years.

In other words, she'll have to leave town — and you will, too, if you want to keep seeing her.

Odd as it might seem, in this instance the medical profession would benefit from taking a hard look at legal ethics. Rule 5.6 of the American Bar Association's Model Rules of Professional Conduct explicitly forbids agreements that "restrict the right of a lawyer to practice." This provision, which is in effect in virtually every state, prohibits non-compete agreements, restrictive covenants, and other devices that might be used to prevent a lawyer from leaving one office and working at another.

The purpose of the rule is to "protect the freedom of clients to choose a lawyer." And it works. Numerous courts have held that lawyers have no vested or proprietary interest in their clients, who must always be at liberty to keep, or dump, their attorneys.

If such a provision were equally well established in the medical profession, there would be substantially less doubt that Dr. Wiznia could move his AIDS practice across the Bronx, whatever the consequences to his former hospital. But there is no such rule in medicine. Even if Dr. Wiznia wins this lawsuit, the fact remains that many — these days, perhaps most — doctors are contractually bound to their partners or employers, legally prohibited from setting up shop across the street.

In another front page article, the *New York Times* revealed that major pharmaceutical companies have been paying private physicians as much as $3,000 per head to recruit patients into clinical studies of experimental drugs. In the increasingly lucrative drug industry, the story explained, "patients have become commodities, bought and traded by testing companies and doctors," although the patients themselves are seldom if ever informed that their physicians may receive payment for every subject who joins the study. In fact, many research contracts are considered "corporate secrets," with provisions that actually prohibit doctors from disclosing their participation.

While large-scale clinical studies are essential to the development of new medications, the profit motive creates an unacknowledged conflict of interest between the doctors (who may receive thousands of dollars, as well as other incentives) and their patients (who may suffer side effects, or worse, from the medication). Moreover, many doctors collect such finder's fees without any further involvement in the study itself.

The problem, as Dr. David Shimm explained, is that too many doctors "are enticing and cajoling patients who are in no position to resist their blandishments" to enter what might be inappropriate clinical studies. "What the patients are not seeing," he said, "is that the clinical investigator is really a dual agent with divided loyalties between the patient and the pharmaceutical company."

In one chilling example, a Minnesota psychiatrist was found to have enrolled highly vulnerable patients in drug studies without ensuring that they met eligibility criteria, and he kept them in the studies after their conditions deteriorated. When one man repeatedly refused to participate in a clinical trial, the doctor discharged him from the hospital despite the patient's known risk of suicide. The patient committed suicide only weeks later. Meanwhile, over a ten-year period, the physician collected over $50,000 in lecture and consulting fees from pharmaceutical manufacturers. Although such payments from drug companies, as well as lavish gifts ranging from fancy dinners to resort vacations, have been widely criticized, they are not ordinarily prohibited and they do not automatically constitute professional misconduct.

Once again, legal ethics seem preferable. Rule 1.8(f) prohibits lawyers from accepting compensation from someone other than the client, and Rule 1.5(e) disallows referral fees in the absence of specific written disclosure and consent — and even then it requires that the referring lawyer continue to participate in the representation. Taken together, these rules would foreclose the sort of bounty payments that drug companies have been using in order to muster patients for clinical trials. Likewise, Rule 1.7 requires the disclosure of any "personal interest" that might limit a lawyer's undivided loyalty, while Rule 1.8 prohibits the acquisition of a "pecuniary interest" adverse to clients.

So why do doctors' ethics allow restrictive covenants, finders' fees, and third-party pay-offs, while lawyers' ethics forbid them? It is certainly not because lawyers are more ethical — or empathetic or altruistic — than physicians. Rather, it is because the legal profession could not exist and prosper without extreme deference to client autonomy, with its heavy emphasis on full disclosure and individual choice.

Evict those orphans? Sure, client, anything you say. Beat that murder charge? Whatever it takes to protect your rights. Elaborate tax shelters for the rich? Hey, that's my middle name. For better or for worse, the client is the boss, and it is the attorney's job to facilitate the client's own decisions.

In contrast, the classic professional culture in medicine relies on a model of dependence rather than autonomy. The patient routinely entrusts his or her care to the benevolent physician, who must make the truly crucial decisions. Even the concept of informed consent came late to medical practice, and the early codes of ethics actually prohibited doctors from giving any information to one another's patients, on the theory that "interference" would undermine the healing process. In medicine, the outcome often takes precedence over the process.

Of course, there is much to be said for the "ethic of care." It worked pretty well, so long as most doctors were family practitioners who had long-term relationships with their patients. But in today's commercialized medical marketplace, the potential for exploitation is undeniable, as ever greater financial pressures create pressing incentives to cut corners and cash out.

Health care has now become a huge industry. Yet medical ethics do not seem to have kept pace with the changing environment, no doubt because they were developed to deal with medical issues and have not traditionally been concerned with more worldly matters, such as profit margins and potential conflicts of interest. Thus, doctors (and hospitals) are able to indulge in the useful fiction of the selfless healer, devoted exclusively to each patient's well-being and therefore completely unaffected by monetary concerns. In that noble paradigm, increasingly inaccurate as it may be, there is little risk of conflicted interests, and consequently little need to adopt ethics rules that will prevent them.

For all their many faults, lawyers have always been frank about their place in the world. Law practice is a business. Legal ethics, therefore, were developed largely to facilitate the commercial relationship between attorney and client. And because business requires autonomy, it turns out that "clients" may have substantially more rights than do "patients," especially when it comes to setting the terms of the relationship itself.

Perhaps the distinction can best be summarized by two familiar phrases. Compare "doctor's orders" with "advice of counsel," and consider which is better, and more candid, when it comes to money and turf.

41

Mistakes and Cover-Ups

DR. ATUL GAWANDE — member of the Harvard Medical School faculty, contributing writer for The New Yorker, and best-selling author — regards malpractice cases as worse than useless. They punish doctors, interfere with physician-patient communications, and do nothing to improve care.

Gawande's views are significant because he is a liberal Democrat. He served as a health policy advisor during the Clinton administration, and he still shares a party affiliation with past and current plaintiffs' lawyers such as John Edwards. He favors national health coverage and stem-cell research, and he has little sympathy for big pharmaceutical companies. So malpractice litigation might be the only health-related issue on which he agrees with Republicans, including President Bush, who have called repeatedly for federal legislation to limit malpractice liability. For Bush and his advisors, of course, the issue is intensely political, tied to their general abhorrence of tort liability and their recognition that trial lawyers are a key Democratic contributor base. While Gawande's objectives are far more humane, he mostly adopts the standard positions of the medical profession, which, from a lawyer's perspective, do not begin to tell the whole story.

Gawande's primary objection to malpractice litigation is that it sweeps too broadly, failing to distinguish between dangerous doctors and good doctors who simply make mistakes. Malpractice lawyers do not concentrate on the few truly bad apples or repeat offenders, he believes, because all surgeons can expect to be sued in the course of their careers. It is certainly easy to sympathize with those physicians who find themselves on the receiving end of such lawsuits, many of which are no doubt unnecessary or ill founded. As a social phenomenon, however, the high incidence of malpractice litigation is not shocking.

In 2000, the Institute of Medicine published a report entitled *To Err is Human: Building a Safer Health System* which was intended to provide "a comprehensive approach for reducing medical errors and improving patient safety." The report concluded that "preventable adverse [medical] events are a leading cause of death in the United States," and that "at least 44,000 and perhaps as many as 98,000 Americans die in hospitals each year as a result of medical errors." These numbers would be far higher if the report included serious but non-fatal injuries. The much-cited Harvard Medical Practice Study, for example, concluded that serious adverse events (resulting in prolonged hospitalization or disability) occurred in 3.7 percent of hospitalizations; of these adverse events, over half were preventable and over a quarter were due to negligence.

With numbers like these, it cannot be considered surprising that most surgeons — who are in a high risk field by any standard — might face litigation at least once in their careers. Gawande himself observes that "virtually everyone who cares for hospital patients will make serious mistakes, and even commit acts of negligence, every year." In fact, he continues, "the aberration may be a doctor who makes it through a forty-year career without at least a troubled year or two." He adds, "estimates are that, at any given time, 3 to 5 percent of practicing physicians are actually unfit to see patients."

Whatever the cause, there is obviously plenty of malpractice to go around, although that does not necessarily mean that the current litigation system is the best way to deal with it. Malpractice lawsuits are expensive, time-consuming, and uncertain. They distribute resources badly, with too much money going to attorneys and not enough to victims. Even if litigation works as intended (on any level), its primary objective is compensation, not systemic improvement.

No professor of medicine could look at the current litigation system without longing for a better way to address medical mistakes. Gawande offers the alternative model of the Morbidity and Mortality Conference (M&M conference), where doctors can talk candidly about their errors, if only among themselves. Usually held once a week at most university-affiliated teaching hospitals, the M&M conference allows doctors to "gather behind closed doors to review the mistakes, untoward events, and deaths that occurred on their watch, determine responsibility, and figure out what to do differently next time." Thus, the M&M conference is everything that a malpractice lawsuit is not. Most importantly, it focuses on future improvement rather than past recrimination, thus motivating physicians to expose their errors in order to do better rather than hide them in the hope of avoiding responsibility.

M&M conferences are exceptionally good at helping responsible doctors locate and rectify their problems without fear of liability. That is why forty-nine states have enacted statutory medical peer-review privileges (the sole exception is New Jersey), which protect communications in settings such as M&M conferences. But the M&M conference is no panacea. Gawande himself gives us a chilling account of a dangerous doctor who simply ignored the weekly M&M conferences, and whose colleagues stood by for years while patients were crippled and disfigured. The doctor, whom Gawande calls Hank Goodman, was an orthopedic surgeon whose early career showed great promise. His techniques were up to date, he reveled in his work, he won teaching awards at the hospital, and he performed more procedures than anyone else in his group practice. After several years, however, things began to go wrong. He started to cut corners and ignore patients, making disastrously poor decisions time and again.

If ever there was a doctor who needed urgent, effective peer review, it was Hank Goodman. But that did not happen. Although Goodman's "botched cases became a staple of his department's Morbidity and Mortality conferences," nothing was actually done to prevent him from continuing to operate on unsuspecting patients. There were a few "terribly quiet chats," as Gawande put it, in which Goodman was urged to seek help, but matters simply drifted along for about six years. For all of the crippling damage he was doing, his colleagues refused to confront the truth.

In fact, Goodman even stopped attending the M&M conferences, though who could blame him? Despite increasingly sharp warnings about serious consequences, he continued to skip the M&M conferences until the hospital board put him on probation. Then he continued operating on patients for another year, generating more and more grievous complications, until his hospital privileges were finally suspended.

Gawande sees what he considers to be both dishonorable and honorable reasons for this lax attitude toward dangerous colleagues. The "dishonorable" reason is disengagement. It is easy to do nothing, and much harder to summon the energy and commitment to take stern measures. That is certainly inexcusable when patients' lives are at stake, but Gawande's so-called "honorable" reason is even less satisfying. He says that "no one really has the heart for it." Indeed, "when a skilled, decent, ordinarily conscientious colleague, whom you've known and worked with for years, starts popping Percodans, or becomes preoccupied with personal problems, and neglects the proper care of patients, you want to help, not destroy the doctor's career."

That may not fit everyone's definition of an honorable reason for ignoring life-threatening problems, but it is undoubtedly an accurate description of the reality at most hospitals. It is also the reason that injured patients consult malpractice lawyers, rather than wait for the M&M system to provide a comprehensive solution. Attorneys (and their clients) recognize, if surgeons do not, that it is usually unreasonable to rely on institutions to police themselves — and it may simply be irrational to do so when lives are at stake.

Consider the problem of preventable post-surgical infections, which, according to an estimate from the Centers For Disease Control, may needlessly kill as many as 75,000 Americans annually (other estimates are even higher). One might think that M&M conferences could effectively address this issue, since an astonishingly high percentage of deadly infections appear to be "the result of unsanitary facilities, germ-laden instruments, unwashed hands and other lapses." Sadly, the opposite seems to be true. Even with full knowledge that improved sanitation would reduce mortality, many hospitals and physicians failed to take simple remedial steps. "For years, we've just been quietly bundling the bodies of patients off to the morgue while infection rates get higher and higher," said Dr. Barry Farr, the president of the Society for Healthcare Epidemiology of America.

The Chicago Tribune reported that Bridgeport Hospital, a major trauma center and teaching hospital in Connecticut, experienced an infection rate of twenty-two percent among cardiac surgery patients during the late 1990s. An investigation revealed that "up to half of doctors, primarily surgical residents from Yale University, did not wash their hands before entering the operating room." Other doctors wore their surgical scrubs home and returned to the hospital the next day, without changing their dirty scrubs before entering the operating room. This conduct was clearly observable to others, but it was not corrected — and evidently not even rebuked — as infection rates soared. At one point, in fact, the hospital's doctors voted against testing all patients for infection because it was not "cost effective."

This information came to light, and corrective measures were employed, only after the hospital was sued. After litigation, infection rates were reduced to near zero. This is not to say that lawyers should get all the credit for the improved hospital sanitation, but rather to observe that the hospital (and its surgeons) failed to respond to a life-threatening crisis, M&M conferences notwithstanding, until attorneys made the crisis impossible to ignore.

The other standard complaint about malpractice litigation is that it corrupts the physician-patient relationship. As Gawande put it, "The tort system makes adversaries of patient and physician, and pushes each to offer a heavily slanted version of events. When things go wrong, it's almost impossible for a physician to talk to a patient honestly about mistakes."

Forgive me if I appear cynical, but is it really fair to blame malpractice lawyers for physicians' unwillingness to tell patients about mistakes? Was there ever a golden age, before rampant malpractice litigation, when doctors communicated freely with their patients, openly acknowledging errors and confronting mistakes in the spirit of humble cooperation? I don't think so. And neither does Dr. Jay Katz, who wrote his seminal book, *The Silent World of Doctor and Patient*, in the 1980s, long before the current flood of malpractice cases. If anything, as Katz makes clear, the days before the malpractice explosion were characterized by less communication from doctors, who then routinely refused to acknowledge even the possibility of uncertainty. The great likelihood, I am afraid, is that doctors, being human, are simply reluctant to admit mistakes to their patients, and instead seize upon any available rationalization. Today, the excuse is malpractice liability. In the old days, it was the patients' own welfare — they would not heal as rapidly, it was said, if they lost confidence in their physicians.

In any event, there is considerable evidence that malpractice claims actually decrease when doctors are open and candid about their errors. Enhanced communication is widely seen as reducing malpractice litigation, not inviting it. In 2001, the Joint Commission on Accreditation of Healthcare Organizations adopted a policy requiring hospitals "to provide an 'honest explanation' of medical errors to patients and their families." While patient safety is the primary reason for the new regulation, supporters of the rule further note that candor also tends to reduce malpractice claims. "You save money by doing this," said Dr. Dennis O'Leary, head of the commission, "and the patient's family is appreciative that people were honest."

In this regard, the commission followed the lead of the Veterans Affairs Medical Center in Lexington, Kentucky, which in 1987 adopted a policy of "extreme honesty" in reporting medical errors. Patients are informed immediately about mistakes, and the hospital's office of risk management actually assists patients with filing claims and locating attorneys. "If we're liable, we say so," explained pulmonologist Steve S. Kraman, the hospital's chief of staff. Kraman further noted that "in the vast majority of cases, people don't stay angry when they realize they're being told the truth and are being treated respectfully." The implementation of this policy actually resulted in a substantial decrease in malpractice costs, with the hospital's average payment per case falling to about one sixth of the average for the entire Veterans Administration system.

A study published in the British journal *Lancet* found that as many as 39% of malpractice plaintiffs would not have filed suit if their doctors had sincerely apologized for their errors instead of stonewalling. The authors noted that lawsuits were prompted when patients "were disturbed by the absence of explanations, a lack of honesty, the reluctance to apologise, or being treated as neurotic." A study published in the *Journal of the American Medical Association* likewise reported that at least 24% of malpractice plaintiffs were motivated by perceived cover-ups. In the total sample, 13% of the plaintiffs reported that their physicians "would not listen," 32% said that the doctors had not talked openly, and 48% believed they had been misled. Yet another study similarly found that patients are more likely to sue if they report "feeling rushed, feeling ignored, [and] receiving inadequate explanations or advice."

It is understandable that physicians — and their less altruistic supporters in the Republican Party and the insurance industry — would want malpractice litigation to be limited so that the medical establishment can proceed at its own pace to reduce preventable injuries. Needless to say, there is another way to look at the problem. Perhaps hospitals need to be motivated to enhance patient safety so that malpractice cases will decrease on their own. Heaven knows, there are many things wrong in the world of malpractice litigation. But whether or not doctors are willing to acknowledge it, lawsuits definitely have their place when it comes to preventing medical errors.

42

The Benevolent Otolaryngologist

MY DAUGHTER'S PERSISTENT sinus infection would not clear up, so the doctor gave her a ten-day prescription for amoxicillin. As it happened, our cousin the otolaryngologist was visiting, and he saw the pill bottle on the kitchen counter.

"Boy, I sure wouldn't take this stuff," he said.

"Why not?" I asked. "Doctors had been prescribing it to our family for years."

"Because it has a huge failure rate," he explained. "You could take that entire prescription without doing any good at all."

"So what's the alternative?" It had never occurred to me that a medicine might have a substantial failure rate, evidently known only to the doctors who write the prescriptions.

My cousin rattled off the name of a new, space-age antibiotic that works better and faster than trusty old amoxicillin, explaining that he used it for himself, his family, and his patients. He was obviously disdainful of our family doctor, though he would not allow himself to be openly critical. "Amoxicillin sometimes works," he said, "but there is definitely newer and more reliable stuff available. They call amoxicillin a conservative treatment," he added, "but in my opinion there is no reason to bother with it."

Then he gave me a short course in the meaning of "conservative treatment." Most bacterial infections are self-limiting, meaning that they will clear up on their own in a week or so without any medication or other intervention. An antibiotic might make the problem go away quicker, but overuse of antibiotics carries a significant social cost because they inevitably lose their effectiveness over time. The more a drug is used, the less effective it becomes. Consequently, older drugs have higher failure rates than new ones, sometimes much higher.

Because each prescription chips away a little bit more at the potency of the particular antibiotic, some doctors adhere to a treatment hierarchy in their prescription practices. Minor problems tend to be treated with older drugs — such as the time-worn amoxicillin — since failure is unlikely to lead to serious consequences. Newer, more powerful medications are saved for infections that do not respond to the first course of treatment or for more life- and health-threatening problems. The rationale is that doctors are safeguarding the usefulness of the newer drugs without really risking the health of the patients who get the feeble medication.

Doctors like my cousin do not fully share this rationale, as there are studies that show amoxicillin to accomplish only slightly more than a placebo. Consequently, they prefer to prescribe either the grade-A medication when indicated or else nothing at all. Needless to say, I had no ready way to figure out which philosophy makes for better medicine, but it was fascinating simply to learn that there were in fact two distinct approaches in the first place. But after a little bit of thought, it began to trouble me that my daughter's doctor had made a decision without consulting me — or even informing me that there were alternatives. I would not go so far as to say that I felt betrayed, since I understood her long-term medical objective. But I definitely felt disheartened. It was as though our doctor did not trust me to make the right choice or perhaps valued my daughter's comfort (not her health) less than someone else's. If we were not getting the advanced medication, who was? And finally, I felt powerless. My daughter trusted me, even if the doctor did not, so maybe I should have asked more questions, done more research, or insisted on a more thorough explanation.

I also wondered about our doctor's professionalism. Does the medical profession endorse the tactic of providing a marginally effective treatment when better ones are available? Are patients ever told the truth about what they are getting? And what counts as truth when public health and individual needs are somewhat at odds with each other, and where the patient, and in this case her father, cannot fully appreciate at least some of the many considerations?

Predictably, that got me thinking about lawyers' ethics. Do our rules provide good answers in comparable circumstances? And if they do, would doctors be wise to adopt them?

For attorneys, the problem is often framed as a choice between "paternalism" (or professionalism) and autonomy in the "the allocation of authority between client and lawyer." At what point must the attorney defer to the client's lawful wishes, even if they are ill advised? On what matters may the lawyer exercise exclusive control, with or without the client's input? Those questions are addressed in most jurisdictions by some version of the American Bar Association's Model Rule 1.2, which provides that attorneys must "consult" with their clients concerning the "means" of representation, while reserving the choice of "objectives" exclusively to clients. The distinction, however, is far from precise, especially when the potential requirement of disclosure is considered.

The most difficult questions seldom arise in the representation of rich corporate clients, who pay huge fees and therefore call the shots. Not unlike physicians' families, they get loads of information and the right to make their own decisions free of other considerations. If a client such as General Motors or Microsoft wants its cases handled a certain way, there will be plenty of attorneys eager to comply, even if they might prefer to do things differently. If one law firm declines to follow GM's lawful instruction, there are many others who will gladly abide.

With individual clients, especially if they are poor or unsophisticated, it is a different matter entirely. They are far more dependent on their lawyers and have little independent access to information. Many are unable to change attorneys, either for lack of funds or because counsel was appointed by the court. Thus, the paternalistic lawyer may, if he or she chooses, follow the medical model, exercising nearly full control over the representation and presenting a limited range of choices to the client or sometimes none at all.

For lawyers in these circumstances, the only real restraint is self-restraint, and clients are therefore disempowered. But is that so bad? Why would any decent lawyer ever let a client makes a foolish decision, even for the sake of autonomy? Wouldn't it always be better to "guide" the client's choice, either through subtle encouragement or judicious information rationing? That is where the case of our benevolent (the medical term for paternalistic) otolaryngologist provides a useful foil, because it allows lawyers to think like their most dependent clients. We have all been medical patients at one time or another. We have all reflexively accepted "doctor's orders," based on the familiar assumption that the doctor knows best.

It can therefore be jarring to realize that the doctor is actually making a complex set of value judgments, revealing some information while withholding much more, in order to control the patient's choices. When it turns out that some of a physician's value judgments may be made for the benefit of third parties, it sets the stage for an evaluation of our own relationships with clients.

Returning to the otolaryngologist, my problem was not so much with the nature of the doctor's judgment — which evidently had clear ethical and empirical components — as with the fact that she made it without consulting me. I can accept the idea that responsible practice required our doctor to put public health ahead of my daughter's quick recovery, but that still leaves open the question of whether she should have told me what she was doing. Recall my cousin's explanation that he would prescribe either a currently potent antibiotic or none at all, the first treatment having the virtue of effectiveness and the latter having the virtue of honesty. Instead, my physician opted for a treatment that was both ineffectual and — if not exactly deceptive — clearly lacking in absolute candor.

The conundrum is that lack of candor might be the only way to achieve the public health objective, since most fully informed patients would probably ask for, if not insist upon, the more potent drug (or go elsewhere to obtain it, especially now in the days of Internet pharmacies). If everyone else is getting the newest antibiotic, then it will wear out in relatively short order, whether my daughter takes it or not. One family's ear-aching abstention would have at best a trivial impact on the long-term viability of an antibiotic, unless everyone else were to be equally altruistic. Alas, we can be pretty sure that won't be the case, given that doctors have already over-prescribed amoxicillin into near uselessness. It's a classic tragedy of the commons, but it still makes sense for every informed patient to demand the good stuff.

Thus, my public-health regarding physician rationally chose to give me no choice, an act of general benevolence that was moral and ethical by her own lights. Let's call it mandatory medical altruism enforced by patient ignorance, for the sake of the public good. But I still wonder whether a system of professional ethics should countenance such slight regard for individual choice.

There are comparisons in law. For example, the public good would definitely be enhanced if courts freed fewer drug dealers due to the suppression of evidence. A lawyer could obtain a morally preferable outcome by declining to challenge a bad search, on the theory that a constable's blunder should not have the result of returning a dealer to the streets.

Lawyers do not operate in this manner, of course, but why not? The usual answer is that the "greater good" is actually better served by vigorously challenging unconstitutional police practices, no matter what the consequence for the successful prosecution of a guilty defendant. Accurate as that may be, it is only part of the story. In actual practice, lawyers almost never have the greater good in mind when representing criminals; they just want to win on behalf of their clients, guilty or otherwise. Thus, the case of the benevolent otolaryngologist exposes an apparent professional fault line, with short-sighted lawyers (bound to pursue only clients' narrow interests) on one side, and broad-minded doctors (responsible to a wider community) on the other. But do the rules of legal ethics actually help lawyers stay on task?

To be minimally useful Model Rule 1.2 must provide guidance in two circumstances. First, it must set a standard for ordinary practice. What should be done in the typical situation when the client's "objectives" (which counsel must honor) are obvious and the lawyer's choices are therefore purely "technical and tactical"? A greater challenge is that the rule must confront the extraordinary problem of deep-seated lawyer-client disagreement, outlining what must be done when lawyer and client are at serious odds with one another over an issue that is neither purely technical nor self-obviously an "objective."

Model Rule 1.2 handles the first job well and the second one badly. While appearing to require "consultation" with clients, and sometimes even "deference" to them, its ambiguity ultimately places almost no constraints on lawyer discretion. If applied to our otolaryngologist, for example, an oblique and conclusory statement — "amoxicillin is, in my opinion, the drug of choice" — could be considered consultation, which is all that Rule 1.2 requires.

But if the Model Rules give scant guidance on the consultation mandate, they are even less helpful on the subject of eventual disagreement. Rule 1.2 includes the standard formulation that "a lawyer shall abide by a client's decisions concerning the objectives of representation and . . . shall consult with the client as to the means by which they are to be pursued." The commentary recognizes that on occasion "a lawyer and a client may disagree about the means to be used to accomplish the client's objectives," which would ordinarily lead one to believe that a solution is at hand.

But no such luck. The commentary is limited to a positive description of common practice, with virtually no normative direction at all:

> Clients normally defer to the special knowledge and skill of their lawyer with respect to the means to be used to accomplish their objectives, particularly with respect to technical, legal and tactical matters. Conversely, lawyers usually defer to the client regarding such questions as the expense to be incurred and concern for third persons who might be adversely affected.

Accurate and uncontroversial, but also unhelpful. What happens in abnormal situations where one or the other does not want to defer?

The comment continues: "Because of the varied nature of the matters about which a lawyer and client might disagree and because the actions in question may implicate the interests of a tribunal or other persons, this Rule does not prescribe how such disagreements are to be resolved."

In other words, the most vexing issue is explicitly left unaddressed, apparently because it is too complicated. Consequently, when lawyer and client disagree over a method or tactic, the rule basically pushes the relationship to the brink:

> The lawyer should . . . consult with the client and seek a mutually acceptable resolution of the disagreement. If such efforts are unavailing and the lawyer has a fundamental disagreement with the client, the lawyer may withdraw from the representation. Conversely, the client may resolve the disagreement by discharging the lawyer.

Thus, the client ultimately cannot instruct the attorney concerning means toward objectives. Once the lawyer determines that the disagreement is fundamental, the lawyer may quit or dare the client to exercise the right of discharge.

Once again, the otolaryngologist analogy is instructive, though this time by contrast. We can understand immediately that a physician cannot be ordered by a patient to prescribe a particular drug, antibiotic or not. Otherwise, patients could insist on narcotics, barbiturates, or amphetamines, or other drugs with adverse side effects or contraindications. Faced with a patient's unreasonable demand, the doctor may either resign or inform the patient to seek treatment elsewhere. Thus, a professional ultimatum makes sense in the medical setting.

That makes far less sense for lawyers, however, in large part because legal representation is generally longer term, and less episodic, than medical treatment. Simply put, it is usually much more difficult and expensive to change lawyers than it is to change doctors. As anyone in an HMO knows full well, changing doctors is often quite routine, involving a simple transfer of records and perhaps a new interview and history. Even in cases of serious illness, the standardized nature of medical charts means that the new physician does not need to start over from the beginning.

In contrast, a legal client's case may extend over a period of months or years, with the client paying periodic bills while the lawyer engages in work that the client never sees. The work is usually cumulative, and not easily transferred to new hands. If transferred, much duplication is often necessary, resulting in dramatically multiplied fees. For poor and middle-income clients, therefore, a change of lawyers may be a financial impossibility, or at best create a grave financial burden. A lawyer's threat to quit is seldom accompanied by an offer to disgorge past fees.

A strict reading of Model Rule 1.2 seriously dilutes the notion of client authority, or even meaningful input, concerning the means of representation. Moneyed clients will enjoy considerable control over their lawyers, as always, while marginal clients will be told where to draw the line. In fact, a more candid version of the rule would read something like this: "A lawyer shall consult with affluent clients as to the means by which objectives are to be pursued, and with other clients if the lawyer feels like it."

As much as lawyers idealize client autonomy, it seems that we have embraced the medical model more than we care to admit, conveniently withholding information to make sure that our judgments are not questioned and resorting to "quit or dare" if a client becomes to demanding. Whether you call it benevolence or manipulation, it makes my daughter's doctor look a little more humane.

43

Desperate Doctors, Desperate Measures

INCREASINGLY ALARMED BY the real and imagined inequities of the medical malpractice system, physicians across the country have been looking everywhere for relief. They have lobbied for law reform at both state and federal levels, they have rallied and protested, and some have even gone "on strike." While their efforts have achieved some success — notably in states that have enacted severe damage caps, such as California, Texas, and Indiana — malpractice insurance premiums have continued to rise, prompting repeated announcements that the medical profession is facing an economic crisis.

At least in the short term, no comprehensive remedy is in sight. President George Bush's proposal for federal legislation to limit non-economic damages foundered in the Senate, stalled by a coalition of Democrats and Republicans who were skeptical of the bill's virtues and disinclined to impose federal law in an area that has traditionally been handled by the states. And even if a national damage cap were enacted, it would do nothing to eliminate the so-called frivolous cases that doctors complain about most bitterly.

With so much angst and anger among so many affluent professionals, it was only a matter of time before an astute entrepreneur figured out a way to cash in on the problem. Enter Dr. Jeffrey Segal, a North Carolina neurosurgeon and the founder of an insurance plan called "Medical Justice," which he promotes as a deterrent to malpractice litigation. It is an intriguing idea that just might work. Then again, it might only be a clever marketing scam.

Segal's innovation is based on the astute insight that standard malpractice insurance policies actually encourage litigation. As physicians acquire greater coverage, their pockets grow deeper, and plaintiffs become more likely to bring lawsuits. Worse, plaintiffs' lawyers also become more tenacious, spurred by their belief that insurers can eventually be persuaded (or coerced) into settling some questionable cases. The plaintiffs' lawyers are correct, of course. Insurance companies tend to settle cases on the basis of actuarial models, balancing defense costs against the range of likely outcomes, without overmuch concern for an individual doctor's self-esteem or reputation. Physicians, therefore, find themselves trapped. They are addicted to the very coverage that makes them attractive targets, unable to practice comfortably without malpractice insurance, and therefore compelled to pay whatever the market will bear.

The Medical Justice plan promises to break the cycle. Rather than pay for defense counsel and adverse judgments, Medical Justice covers the costs of counterclaims, offering to pay the "legal expenses to countersue proponents of frivolous suits" and to "obtain redress against hired-gun expert witnesses in their professional societies." By arming doctors to "fight back," rather than merely defend themselves, Medical Justice claims that it can deter lawsuits in the first place, "constrain" the testimony of adverse expert witnesses, and, if necessary, pursue a countersuit on behalf of the insured physician.

But will it work? Will plaintiffs' lawyers — infamous throughout the known universe (or at least among resentful physicians) for their aggressiveness — really be discouraged by the threat of counterclaims? Medical Justice is banking on it. The plan includes sending a "patented" letter on behalf of the policyholder, notifying "plaintiffs and their representatives" that the defendant-doctor has the wherewithal to retaliate in kind. "Medical Justice," the letter says, "pays the legal expenses up to $100,000 to bring counterclaims against any proponent of a nonmeritorious medical malpractice suit."

And if the lawyers can't be intimidated, maybe their expert witnesses can be. Medical Justice has promised to bring professional disciplinary actions against "unscrupulous" experts who have "committed perjury, delivered false testimony, or engaged in fraud or deception." To facilitate all of this, Medical Justice provides its physician-policyholders with a special intake form, requiring patients to state that they will not sue the doctor for frivolous reasons and, even in a legitimate suit, will utilize only board-certified experts. "This sets up [a] potential breach of contract claim," according to Medical Justice's promotional materials.

That must sound pretty good to desperate doctors, especially since it only costs between $600 and $1,800 per year. According to Medical Justice, the "suit rate" for plan members in Florida is less than 2 percent per year, which is far better than an asserted "published baseline of 10–15 percent." That seems like a whole lot of protection for not much money.

Unless it's no protection at all.

The most interesting thing about the Medical Justice plan is that it doesn't really make a commitment to pay for anything. According to the company's basic contract (posted on its website, medicaljustice.com), no benefits are provided "unless the underlying medical malpractice action has been terminated in favor of the Plan Member." If the plaintiff wins, or the matter is settled, or even if the case is simply dropped, it would appear that coverage cannot be used. And even if the physician wins at trial, the plan guarantees only "an analysis of the appropriateness of a case as qualifying as frivolous," following which "the decision as to whether or not to proceed with a counter lawsuit or other action . . . shall be at the sole and exclusive discretion" of Medical Justice. There is no provision for an appeal if coverage is denied, or even a definition of "frivolous case." The other remedies, such as filing disciplinary complaints against lawyers or experts, are also pursued only at the company's "sole discretion."

In other words, the Medical Justice plan has a lot in common with the classic example of an illusory contract: "I promise to paint your house tomorrow if I feel like it."

Perhaps unsurprisingly, it is far from apparent (as of this writing) that Medical Justice has ever actually financed a single countersuit. The "Case Updates" section on its website does not list any countersuits; it only notes cryptically that "Medical Justice is actively involved in over 400 open medical malpractice cases in various states and represents many specialty areas. Medical Justice has been the driving force in getting numerous cases dropped, and has deterred many plaintiffs from filing frivolous suits." Nor do other sections on the site — "Deterrence," "Early Intervention," "Testimonials" — refer to either pending or concluded countersuits.

Some of the posted "Deterrence" examples have a decidedly chain-letter quality, touting stunning and almost immediate results. "A physician in Florida was sued for a missed diagnosis. He was not a member of Medical Justice at the time he was sued." Shortly after the defendant purchased coverage and notified the plaintiff's lawyer, however, the opposing expert changed his opinion and "the case was dropped completely!" An enthusiastic testimonial reads, "I was named in a meritless suit in September, 2003. I joined Medical Justice in August, 2005. The case was dropped within days. The system works." Maybe so, but it would at least be helpful to know the actual ratio of warning letters to dismissed cases.

In a 2003 telephone interview, I asked the general manager of Medical Justice, Dr. Graeme Hampton, about the absence of countersuits. He told me that the company had in fact initiated professional disciplinary proceedings against two expert witnesses. Both of these actions, he pointed out, were actually outside policy coverage, since the underlying cases had been settled or dropped. Nonetheless, Medical Justice pursued the disciplinary complaints because the physician-experts were deemed particularly irresponsible. And also for publicity, he explained, that would show that the policies work. Four years later, however, only two such "Prosecutions" were mentioned on the website, and it is impossible to tell whether they are the same ones noted by Hampton.

Despite the paucity of information on the Medical Justice website, the company's CEO and general counsel published an op-ed in the *Wall Street Journal* in July of 2007 again touting their success at deterring malpractice litigation — and again providing no details of either successful disciplinary complaints or countersuits. They did, however, make a number of other highly doubtful statistical claims. For example, they began by with the rather stunning exaggeration that at "any given moment in the U.S., approximately 60,000 medical malpractice suits are being tried." They supplied no source for that figure, but based on a 2005 study by the National Center for State Courts, it is unlikely that more than 4,000 medical malpractice cases have ever been brought to trial in a single year, let alone at the same moment. It is possible that they only meant that 60,000 such cases are pending at any given time (although that is an odd mistake for an organization's "general counsel" to make). But even so, that rather starkly undermines their subsequent claim that the "average doctor is sued at a rate of 8%–12% per year," compared to a rate of only 2% for Medical Justice members. Yes, 60,000 is roughly 10% of the total number of physicians in the United States, but most cases last for two years or longer; moreover, relatively few "problem doctors" account for a disproportionate number of malpractice filings. Thus, even by its own figures, Medical Justice overstated the typical doctor's lawsuit rate by a factor of two or three. That is no incidental error, since Medical Justice's whole marketing pitch is based on achieving a lower "lawsuit rate" for members than non-members. But it may well be that there is not much difference at all once you actually look at comparable statistics.

In any event, the success of Medical Justice policies relies on their possible *in terrorem* effect. In order to work, they must strike fear in the hearts of potential adversaries — preferably in advance. Lawyers, however, are notoriously immune to such warnings, in large part because few attorneys intentionally bring frivolous cases (and also, of course, because they have malpractice carriers of their own).

Expert witnesses, though, are considerably more vulnerable. Physicians in particular are acutely sensitive to matters of reputation and status. It might well be that professional societies can exert some control over freewheeling witnesses, inspired by complaints from Medical Justice. Of course, the targeted doctors are unlikely to take it lying down. They will retain counsel to defend the charges, and many of them will challenge disciplinary measures in court. All of this will be financed, no doubt, by still more malpractice insurance.

Ultimately, there is an inescapable irony to the Medical Justice plan. Where once there might have been a single malpractice case, resolved for better or worse, we are now looking at the prospect of multiple threats, countersuits, disciplinary actions, and injunctions — not to mention appeals — creating welcomed work for hungry litigators.

To paraphrase Justice Louis Brandeis, it appears that the remedy for bad litigation — even in a doctor's world — is more litigation.

Afterword

AS WE HAVE seen throughout this book, honesty is the necessary premise for virtually all of law practice, and yet truth is elusive and frequently hard to achieve. Other legitimate values — such as confidentiality and advocacy — often prevent absolute candor, while human frailties — denial, self-regard, bias, preconception — inevitably interfere with our understanding or recognition of rigorous truth. Still, we soldier on, usually doing our best within the inherent limitations of both the legal system and our cognitive capabilities. Perhaps the most important lesson is that we must ever be alert to the influences that impede our perceptions and dull our judgment. Consider the effect that partisanship can have on the appreciation of truth.

On March 6, 2007, I. Lewis "Scooter" Libby, former chief of staff for Vice President Dick Cheney, was convicted in federal court on four counts of perjury and obstruction of justice, the jury having found him guilty of lying to a grand jury during the investigation of a CIA leak case. Judge Reggie Walton sentenced Libby to thirty months in prison and denied his request to remain free on bail pending appeal (soon afterward, the appellate court also refused Libby's request to remain free during the appeal). On July 7, 2007, President George W. Bush commuted Libby's prison sentence, while leaving the conviction (as well as a $250,000 fine) intact. Said the president,

> "[A] jury of citizens weighed all the evidence and listened to all the testimony and found Mr. Libby guilty of perjury. . . . I respect the jury's verdict. But I have concluded that the prison sentence given to Mr. Libby is excessive. Therefore, I am commuting the portion of Mr. Libby's sentence that required him to spend thirty months in prison."

While President Bush at least acknowledged the seriousness of the perjury and obstruction of justice convictions — "[I]f a person does not tell the truth . . . he must be held accountable" — many of Libby's other supporters believed that the commutation was too little, too late. Instead, they insisted that Libby should have been granted a full pardon on the ground that he had not really committed any crime at all, given that no one had ever been indicted for the various leaks to the press. In the words of Robert Novak, the columnist who started the entire controversy by identifying Valerie Plame Wilson as a CIA operative, "I don't see how you can have obstruction of justice when there is no underlying crime." Other prominent conservatives, including Fox News commentator Fred Barnes and *Weekly Standard* editor Bill Kristol, made similar claims, as did presidential candidate and former senator Fred Thompson.

That was an odd argument from people who supported the impeachment of President Clinton based on his false statements to a grand jury in a case where there was "no underlying crime." Paula Jones, it should be recalled, sued Bill Clinton for sexual harassment, which is serious, of course, but not criminal. After Clinton lied in his deposition — falsely denying his relationship to Monica Lewinsky — independent counsel Kenneth Starr launched an investigation and eventually called Clinton before a grand jury, where the president repeated his false testimony. But the only subject matter of the investigation was whether Clinton had lied about Lewinsky in the first place, and then covered it up. In other words, the whole Starr inquiry was never about anything beyond perjury and obstruction of justice, without even the possibility of uncovering a substantive "underlying crime." In fact, Jones's sexual harassment complaint was ultimately dismissed on summary judgment, so there may not even have been an underlying tort (although Clinton later paid $700,000 to settle the case).

Nonetheless, conservatives such as Novak, Barnes, and Kristol asserted that Clinton's falsehoods amounted "high crimes and misdemeanors," and the Republican-controlled House of Representatives agreed, voting two articles of impeachment, one alleging that he gave "perjurious, false and misleading testimony" to Starr's grand jury, and the other alleging that he attempted to "delay, impede, cover up, and conceal the existence of evidence" in the Jones case. Although the Senate did not convict Clinton on either count, which would have required a two-thirds majority, fifty Republican senators (including Fred Thompson, on the obstruction of justice count) voted to remove the president from office.

Within the relatively short span of eight years, we have seen important office holders and journalists first argue that perjury about a non-crime warrants impeachment of the president, and later that it does not even justify a day in jail. Now, one might conclude that Novak and company have a cavalier attitude toward truth, or that they are simply hypocrites or rank political opportunists, but I think the reality is more complex. If pressed, the pro-impeachment conservatives would surely articulate a series of distinctions between Clinton's situation and Libby's, and they would mostly be sincere. Clinton, for example, was forced to admit his false statements (though not without temporizing), while Libby remained silent (presumably maintaining his innocence). Clinton's affair with a young intern was morally blameworthy, while Libby's disclosures to Tim Russert turned out to be redundant (Richard Armitage having already outed Plame to Novak). There are probably many more such distinctions between the two cases, but it is far from clear that any of them actually makes a meaningful difference. Is there any rational way to fault Bill Clinton and yet exonerate Scooter Libby?

It is hardly surprising that liberals and conservatives will arrive at different answers to that question — not because one side is more honest or has greater purchase on the truth, but rather because our interpretation of facts (and hence, our very conception of truth itself) is so heavily determined by our preexisting allegiances and values. No one is immune to such influences, which are frequently unrecognized or unacknowledged. Many liberals, for example, were willing to overlook Clinton's exploitation of a twenty-four-year-old volunteer, while simultaneously lobbying for stricter laws against creating a "hostile work environment."

As it turns out, there are almost (although not quite) always two sides to every story, and there may be many more viable positions in every dispute. People constantly disagree. They disagree about events, principles, motives, needs, and consequences. And yet, almost no one — from Bulldog (discussed in the preface) to Robert Novak (see above) — ever deliberately tells an outright lie. Instead, they tell 'em as they see 'em, with or without realizing that their perceptions are shaped by their own experiences, preferences, and goals. For better or worse, the legal system must be open to all sides, allowing every position to be completely explored and every story to be fully aired. That is why we have lawyers and courts. Although the judicial system may sometimes appear to disregard or discount the truth, it is most often simply accommodating the contending and contradictory viewpoints that are inherent in a free enterprise economy and an open, democratic society. No one said it would be easy.

Notes and Sources

While most of the essays in this book have appeared previously — either in *The American Lawyer* or elsewhere — several are completely new and almost all of the others have been significantly updated and expanded.

Preface

My first op-ed was "Policing Police Who Terrorize," *Chicago Tribune*, August 31, 1995.

1. Sex, Lies, and Depositions

Bill Clinton's autobiography is *My Life* (Knopf 2005). Judge Wright's contempt ruling is reported in *Jones v. Clinton*, 36 F.Supp.2d 1118 (April 12, 1999). This essay is expanded and adapted from "The Clinton Miscalculus: If The President Had Trusted His Lawyer, History Might Be Different," *The American Lawyer*, November 2004.

2. My Lawyer Made Me Do It

Quotations from the Boston Archdiocese spokeswoman were reported in Robin Washington, Eric Convey, and Tom Mashberg, "Victims' Advocates Rip Church Over Deposition of Therapist," *Boston Herald*, January 17, 2003. This essay is adapted from "My Lawyer Made Me Do It," *The American Lawyer*, May 2003.

3. Morally Gray

Shirley Gaspar's case against Wal-Mart was first reported in "Clerk Sues Wal-Mart After Firing Over Film," *Omaha World Herald*, October 30, 1999. This essay is adapted from "What's An Employee To Do?" *The National Law Journal*, March 19, 2001.

4. McKinney's Bluff

The circumstances surrounding Cynthia McKinney's bluff were widely reported in March and April 2006; for details, including quotations, see "McKinney Blames Altercation on Racism, *Associated Press*, April 1, 2006. This essay is updated, expanded, and adapted from "McKinney vs. Capitol Police: Who'll Blink First," *Chicago Tribune*, April 5, 2006.

5. The Truth about Torts

The story of Mr. and Mrs. Dumbfounded appeared in Dear Abby's syndicated column for October 23, 1997. The Firestone Tire fiasco occurred in the autumn of 2000; see Lauren Comander and Melita Marie Garza, "They Should Have Done Something When They Knew: Firestone Tire Failure Victims Ask Why Recall Came Too Late," *Chicago Tribune*, Septermber 3, 2000. For details about Linda McDougal's unnecessary mastectomy, see "Victims of Medical Error Testify on Capitol Hill," *Minneapolis Star-Tribune*, January 24, 2003. The Institute of Medicine report is *To Err Is Human* (2000). The problems — and litigation-motivated solutions — at a Connecticut hospital were reported in Michael Berens, "Infection Epidemic Carves Deadly Path," *Chicago Tribune*, July 21, 2002. This essay is expanded and adapted from "A Lesson for Mr. and Mrs. Dumbfounded," *The Chicago Tribune*, December 1, 1997; "'Greedy Lawyers' Are Often The Public's Allies," *Newsday*, October 4, 2000; and "Medical Malpractice at a Discount," *Chicago Tribune*, January 22, 2003.

6. A Missing Witness

The best account of the Martha Stewart trial is Jeffrey Toobin, "A Bad Thing: Why did Martha Stewart Lose?" *The New Yorker*, March 22, 2004. The Homeric quotation is from *The Iliad* (Pagles trans. Penguin Classics 1991). This essay is adapted from "Oyez, O Muse," *The American Lawyer*, June 2004.

7. Freedom Stories

George Lakoff's pithy book is *Don't Think of An Elephant: Know Your Values and Frame the Debate!* (Chelsea Green 2004). This essay is adapted from "A Chicago Story," *The American Lawyer*, November 2005.

8. The Importance of Being Honest

All quotations from the Oscar Wilde trial are taken from Merlin Holland, *The Real Trial of Oscar Wilde* (Harper Perennial 2004). This essay is adapted from "The Importance of Being Honest," 8 *The Green Bag 2d* 163 (2005).

9. False Flats

The story of John Gellene is taken from Milton Regan, *Eat What You Kill: The Fall of a Wall Street Lawyer* (University of Michigan 2005). This essay is adapted from "False Flats," 19 *Georgetown Journal of Legal Ethics* 275 (2006).

10. Who Deserves the Truth?

The Colorado Supreme Court upheld Mark Pautler's punishment in *Matter of Pautler*, 47 P.3d 1175 (2002). Quotations from Pautler are found in Sarah

Huntley, "Prosecutor Admits He Lied," *Rocky Mountain News*, March 8, 2001. This essay is updated and adapted from "A Prosecutor's Complex Dual Role," *The National Law Journal*, June 25, 2001.

11. When Honesty Isn't Enough

The Illinois Appellate Court upheld Joe Dowd's fee petition in *Corcoran v. Northeast Illinois Regional Commuter Railroad Corp.*, 345 Ill.App.3d 449 (2003). This essay is expanded and adapted from "Dispiriting the Law," *The American Lawyer*, August 2004

12. Hypocrisy on the Left

Lynne Stewart's pre-sentencing statement to the court can be found on her website, lynnestewart.org. This essay is expanded and adapted from "Stewart's Sanctimony," *The American Lawyer*, January 2007.

13. Requiem for a Faithful Lawyer

This essay is adapted from "Faith, Hope, and Lawyering," *The American Lawyer*, May 2005.

14. Evolution of Myth

The best account of the Scopes trial, including quotations from Darrow's cross examination of Bryan, is Edward J. Larson, Summer for the Gods: The Scopes Trial and America's Continuing Debate Over Science and Religion (Basic Books 2006). Inherit the Wind, by Jerome Lawrence and Robert E. Lee, debuted on Broadway in 1955 and became a Hollywood film in 1960. It has been performed many times subsequently, on television and in theaters, including a Broadway revival in 2007. This essay is adapted from "Godly vs. Secular," The American Lawyer, September 2005.

15. Hidden Interests

This essay is adapted from "Malpractice Alert: No Conflict, but a Conflict of Interest," *Business Law Today*, January–February 1997.

16. When Conventional Wisdom Goes Wrong

Professor Leipold's study was published as "Why Are Federal Judges So Acquittal Prone" 83 Wash. U. L.Q. 151 (2005). Regarding Judge Weinstein's decision in the "Mafia Cops" case, see John Marzulli, "Judge Rubs Out Mob Cop Verdict: Overturns Convictions Due to Time Technicality," *New York Daily News*, July 1, 2006. This essay is adapted from "Why Judges Acquit," *The American Lawyer*, September 2006.

17. Sensory Deception

This essay is adapted from "Marshal Law," The American Lawyer, October 2004.

18. How Lawyers (Ought to) Think

Many of the definitions of cognition errors have been taken from Jerome Groopman, *How Doctors Think* (Houghton Mifflin 2007), and Richard Horton, "What's Wrong with Doctors," *New York Review of Books*, May 31, 2007. The relevant Federal Rules of Evidence are 403 (exclusion for prejudicial impact), 404 (character evidence), and 702 (expert testimony).

19. Truth in Humor

This essay is adapted from "In Facetiis Verititas: How Improv Comedy Can Help Lawyers Get Some Chops," 7 *Texas Review of Entertainment and Sports Law* 1 (2006), coauthored by Thomas Hankinson. Del Close's book, coauthored with Charna Halpern and Kim Johnson, is *Truth in Comedy: The Manual of Improvisation* (Meriwether 1994). Quotations of Viola Spolin are from her book, *Improvisation for the Theater* (Northwestern University Press 1999). Mick Napier's book is *Improvise: Scene from the Inside Out* (Heineman Press 2004).

20. Confronting Cougars

Dave Smith's book is Don't Get Eaten: The Dangers of Animals that Charge or Attack (Mountaineer Books 2003). There is also a companion volume by Buck Tilton, Don't Get Bitten: The Dangers of Things that Bite or Sting (Mountaineer Books 2003). This essay is adapted from "Cougar Spotting," The American Lawyer, March 2006.

21. Life Imitates Baseball

Chief Justice Roberts's entire opening statement to the Senate Judiciary Committee was printed in the *New York Times*, "Court in Transition: I Come Before the Committee with No Agenda; I Have No Platform," September 13, 2005. The official rules of Major League Baseball can be accessed at mlb.com. This essay is adapted from "Making the Call," *The American Lawyer*, January 2006.

22. The Elusive Transparency of Ethics

For the Supreme Court's recusal acrobatics in *Credit Suisse v. Billing*, see Tony Mauro's "Recusal Report" in *Legal Times* for March 22, 2007. Concerning Justice Breyer's ethics consultation in the *Booker* case, see Tony Mauro, "Breyer Consulted Ethics Expert over Sentencing Case Recusal," *Legal Times*, January 17, 2005. The Code of Conduct for United States Judges (lower federal courts, excluding the Supreme Court) can be viewed at uscourts.gov/guide/vol2/ch1.html.

This essay is updated and expanded from "Ethical Culture," *The American Lawyer*, July 2005.

23. Ducks in a Row

Justice Scalia's nonrecusal opinion is *Cheney v. District Court*, 541 U.S. 913 (2004). His initial comments to the press were reported by David Savage in "Trip With Cheney Puts Ethics Spotlight on Scalia: Friends Hunt Ducks Together, Even as the Justice Is Set to Hear the Vice President's Case," *Los Angeles Times*, January 17, 2004. The social science study on recusals and stalemates is Ryan Black and Lee Epstein, "Recusals and the 'Problem' of an Equally Divided Supreme Court," 7 *J. App. Prac. & Process* 75 (2005). Scalia's earlier discussion of amendments to the federal disqualification statute, 28 U.S.C. 455, was in *Liteky v. United States*, 510, U.S. 540 (1994).

24. An Honest Day's Pay

The chief justices' annual *Reports on the Federal Judiciary* can be viewed at supremecourtus.gov/publicinfo/year-end/year-endreports.html. President Bush's call for a pay increase is included in the Weekly Compilation of Presidential Documents, which can be found at findarticles.com/p/articles/mi_m2889/is_1_39/ai_97629608. This essay is updated and expanded from "Judging Pay," *The American Lawyer*, March 2003.

25. Confirmation Mud

John Aschcroft's comments about Justice Ronnie White were reported in Anthony Lewis, "What Ashcroft Did," *New York Times*, January 27, 2001. For the story of Charles Pickering's nomination, rejection, and eventual recess appointment, see Neil A. Lewis, "Bush Seats Judge after Long Fight, Bypassing Senate," *New York Times*, January 17, 2004. Alberto Gonzalez's rebuke of Priscilla Owen was in *In Re Jane Doe*, 19 43 *Tex. Sup. Ct. J.* 910 (2000). An attempt to tie Owen to Enron can be read in John Nichols, "Karl Rove's Legal Tricks: Packing the Judiciary with Right-Wingers," *The Nation*, July 22, 2002. Justice Alito's comment on his recusal practice is reported in Peter Baker and Charles Babington, "Alito, White House Woo Moderates," *Washington Post*, November 2, 2005. This essay is expanded and adapted from "The Judge and The Cross Burner," *Baltimore Sun*, February 28, 2002; "Sniping Fails to Study Judge's Merits," *Atlanta Journal-Constitution*, August 28, 2002; "Judicial Temperament," *Baltimore Sun*, November 28, 2005 (with David McGowan); and "The Alito Confirmation; How Democrats Lost the Political Battle," *San Diego Union Tribune*, February 1, 2006.

26. A Spouse Speaks

Virginia Thomas's op-ed was "To Judge Pickering: They Can't Take Away Your Honor," *Wall Street Journal*, March 14, 2002. For Rutherford B. Hayes's unflattering nickname, see James Bendat, *Democracy's Big Day: The Inauguration of Our President* (iUniverse 2004). Peter Berkowitz's comment appeared in "Tribe vs. Truth," *The Weekly Standard*, February 4, 2002. This essay is adapted from "Political Activities of Supreme Court Spouses," 18 *Virginia Journal of Law and Politics* 635 (2002).

27. Veiled Justice

The transcript of Ginnah Mohammad's appearance before Judge Paruk can be viewed at volokh.com/archives/archive_2006_12_10-2006_12_16.shtml# 1166121763. Concerning the difficulty of evaluating truthfulness based on facial expressions, see Mike Caro's Book of Poker Tells (Cardoza 2003) and Joe Navarro's Read 'Em and Reap (Collins 2006). This essay is expanded and updated from "Veiled Truth," The American Lawyer, March 2007.

28. Bullying from the Bench

Judge Kent's acerbic opinion is *Bradshaw v. Unity Marine Corporation*, 147 F. Supp. 2d 668 (S.D. Texas 2001). Kent's "patently insipid" and "obnoxiously ancient" tirade was in *Labor Force, Inc. v. Jacintoport Corp. & James McPherson*, (No. G-01-058; June 7, 2001), viewable at greenbag.org/kent_scanned.pdf. This essay is adapted from "Bullying from The Bench," 5 *The Green Bag 2d* 11 (2001).

29. Thought Control

The Indiana Supreme Court initially suspended Michael Wilkins in *Matter of Wilkins*, 777 N.E.2d 714 (2002), and reduced the sanction (while maintaining the finding of misconduct) in *Matter of Wilkins II*, 782 N.E.2d 985 (2003). Justice Scalia's harsh comments about Justice O'Connor were in *Webster v. Reproductive Health Services*, 492 U.S. 490 (1989); his stinging words for Justice Stevens were in *Zuni Public School District No. 89 v. Department of Education* __ U.S. __ (April 17, 2007); his sharp critique of Chief Justice Roberts was in *Hein v. Freedom From Religion Foundation*, __ U.S. __ (June 25, 2007). This essay is updated and expanded from "Which Hurt Their Dignity More, A Lawyer's Rude Comment or the Judges' Harsh Response?" *Legal Times*, December 2, 2002.

30. Platonic Censures

The Seventh Circuit's rigid deposition decision is *Redwood v. Dobson* __ F. 3d __ (February 7, 2007). The video of Joe Jamail's infamous deposition has been removed from YouTube. This essay is expanded and adapted from "Above It All," *The American Lawyer*, May 2007.

31. Stupid Judge Tricks

Judge Gary Davis's financial manipulations are reported in *In re Davis*, 946 P.2d 1033, 1036 (Nev. 1997). The story of Judge Ralph Baldwin's beery jury fête is found in *In re Baldwin,* No. 98-2695-F-69 (Washington Commission on Judicial Conduct, June 5, 1998). Judge Richard Jones's threats and profanities are unexpurgated in *In re* Jones, 581 N.W.2d 876, 884 (Neb. 1998). Judge Howard "Buster" Spencer's offensive conduct is reported in *Mississippi Comm'n on Judicial Performance v. Spencer,* 725 So. 2d 183 (Miss. 1998). Judge Gregory Caskey's injudicious e-mail is found *in Public Admonishment of Caskey* (California Commission on Judicial Performance, July 6, 1998). Judge Sharah Harris's ill-advised liaison is detailed in *In re* Harris, 713 So. 2d 1138, 1138–39 (La. 1998). This essay is adapted from "Stupid Judge Tricks," 41 *South Texas Law Review* 1301 (2000).

32. Baring It All

The Adrianna Dominguez video was first reported in Veronika Belenkaya, "It's Juris-Imprudence: Holy Torts! Law Student in Erotic Vid," *New York Daily News,* April 10, 2007. For details of the Trustafarian story, see Marisa Lagos, "Boalt Student Posted Fake Threat to Hastings," *San Francisco Chronicle,* April 21, 2007. Dean Edley's announcement of disciplinary proceedings can be viewed at transnationallawblog.typepad.com/transnational_law_blog/2007/04/a_letter_from_u.html. My op-ed supporting Matthew Hale's bar admission is "Equal Justice for a Prairie State Bigot," *Washington Post,* February 24, 1999. The Illinois Supreme Court denied his petition in *In re Hale* 723 N.E.2d 206 (1999). This essay is expanded and adapted from "Bare Facts," *The American Lawyer,* July 2007.

33. False Positive

This essay is adapted from "Artificial Intelligence," *The American Lawyer,* March 2005.

34. Truth in Citizenship

The final version of the new naturalization test is posted on the USCIS website, uscis.gov. This essay is expanded and adapted from "I Made the Government Admit It Was Wrong," *Salon,* February 21, 2007; and "The Citizenship Test: New, Improved, and Wrong," *Salon,* January 2, 2007.

35. The Best Policy

Dean Mary Ann Mason's comments are in Dean E. Murphy, "Missed Pickup Means a Missed Opportunity for 30 Seeking a Fellowship," *New York Times,* February 5, 2004. This essay is adapted from "Virtue Is Its Own Reward," *The American Lawyer,* April 2004.

36. Clinical Commandments

The Eighth Circuit case is *Wishnatsky v. Rovner,* 433 F.3d 608 (2006). For details on Wishnatsky's request for legal assistance, see Stephen J. Lee, "Fargo Activist Wants UND Law School Help Removing Greek Goddess from GF County

Courthouse," *Grand Forks Herald,* October 31, 2003; and Stephen J. Lee, "Justice for All? Christian Activist Says an Eye for an Eye, and Goddess Themis Should Fall," *Grand Forks Herald,* December 2, 2004. This essay is updated and adapted from "Thou Shalt Not . . ." *The American Lawyer,* July 2006.

37. Pluto's Plight, and Ours

Judge Barksdale's dissenting opinion is *Freiler v. Tangipahoa Parish Board of Education,* 201 F. 3d 602 (5 Cir. 2000). Justice Scalia's dissent from denial of certiorari is *Tangipahoa Parish Board of Education v. Freiler,* 530 U.S. 1251 (2000). The description of Rittenhouse's orrery appeared in the Pennsylvania Journal and Weekly Advertiser, April 26, 1770, and can be seen (along with much else on the orrery) at: library.upenn.edu/exhibits/pennhistory/orrery/orrery.html. This essay is adapted from "People for Pluto," *The American Lawyer,* November 2000.

38. The Bedouin Horse Trade

The description of the ancient city is from the nineteenth-century poem *Petra,* by John W. Burgon. The full couplet reads: "Match me such marvel, save in Eastern clime / A rose-red city — half as old as Time!" John W. Burgon, *Petra,* in *Poems* (1885). This essay is adapted from "Notes on the Bedouin Horse Trade, or Why Won't the Market Clear, Daddy?" 74 *Texas Law Review* 1039 (1996).

39. There Are No Scriveners Here

Macey and Miller propounded their efficiency model of conflict disclosure (or rather, nondisclosure) in Jonathan R. Macey and Geoffrey P. Miller, "An Economic Analysis of Conflict of Interest Regulation," 82 *Iowa L. Rev.* 965 (1997). The ALAS's concern about loss prevention and multiple representation is reflected in Brian Redding, "The Law Firm of the Future: An Ethics and Malpractice Perspective," 70 *Temple L. Rev.* 1253 (1997). This essay is adapted from "There Are No Scriveners Here," 84 *Iowa Law Review* 341 (1999).

40. Ethics Business

Dr. Wiznia's relocation difficulties are reported in Randy Kennedy, "Doctor's Effort to Move Practice Leaves Patients in a Tug of War," *New York Times,* April 8, 1999. Regarding the problem of undisclosed compensation (and other conflicts of interest) for recruiting participants in clinical trials, see Kurt Eichenwald and Gina Kolata, "Drug Trials Hide Conflicts for Doctors," *New York Times,* May 16, 1999; and Gardiner Harris and Janet Roberts, "After Sanctions, Doctors Get Drug Company Pay," *New York Times,* June 3, 2007. This essay is updated and expanded from "Medical Practice in Need of a Treatment," *The Orlando Sentinel,* May 30, 1999; and "Ethics on the Sick List," *The National Law Journal,* July 19, 1999.

41. Mistakes and Cover-Ups

Atul Gawande's discussion of medical malpractice litigation is taken from his book, *Complications: A Surgeon's Notes on an Uncertain Science* (Metropolitan Books 2003). The Institute of Medicine report is *To Err Is Human* (2000). The infection control problems at Bridgeport Hospital (and elsewhere, including the quotation from Dr. Barry Farr) were reported in Michael Berens, "Infection Epidemic Carves Deadly Path," *Chicago Tribune*, July 21, 2002. Jay Katz's landmark book is *The Silent World of Doctor and Patient* (Free Press 1984). The Joint Commission on Accreditation of Healthcare Organizations policy statement on admitting errors was reported in *American Health Line*, January 2, 2001. Concerning the cost-reducing impact of admitting mistakes, see Janet Wells, "Hospitals Must Disclose Doctor Errors," *San Francisco Chronicle*, December 24, 2000; Mark Crane, "What to Say if You Made a Mistake," *Medical Economics*, August 20, 2000; Charles Vincent and Magi Young, "Why Do People Sue Doctors? A Study of Patients and Relatives Taking Legal Action," *Lancet*, June 25, 1994; and Gerald Hickson, Ellen Wright Clayton, Penny B. Githens, and Frank A. Sloan, "Factors That Prompted Families to File Medical Malpractice Claims Following Perinatal Injuries," 267 *JAMA* 1359 (1992). This essay was adapted from "Like a Surgeon," 88 *Cornell Law Review* 1178 (2003).

42. The Benevolent Otolaryngologist

This essay was adapted from "Division of Authority between Attorney and Client: The Case of the Benevolent Otolaryngologist," 2003 *University of Illinois Law Review* 1275, coauthored by with Robert Burns.

43. Desperate Doctors, Desperate Measures

Documents can be found on the Medical Justice website, medicaljustice.com. The 2007 op-ed is by Jeffrey Segal and Michael Sacopulos, "Do-It-Yourself Tort Reform," *Wall Street Journal*, July 12, 2007. More accurate data concerning the frequency of malpractice litigation is found in National Center for State Courts, "An Empirical Overview of Civil Trial Litigation" (2005). This essay was updated and expanded from "Reversible Suits," *The American Lawyer*, December 2003.

Afterword

For President Bush's full statement upon commuting Scooter Libby's sentence, see "The President's Statement," *New York Times* on July 3, 2007. Robert Novak's comment on Libby was reported in Deborah Solomon, "The Plame Game," *New York Times Magazine*, July 15, 2007. The complete text of the Clinton Articles of Impeachment can be found at cnn.com/ALLPOLITICS/resources/1998/lewinsky/articles.of.impeachment/.

Index

NBC News, 95
Neal, William "Cody," 65–67
Neptune, 206
Newsday, xii
Newton, Nell, 181
New York Bar Committee on Character, 180, 182
New York Code of Professional Responsibility, 183
New York Daily News, 180, 183
New York Times, 165, 195, 224, 226
New Yorker, 38, 229
Niger, 41
Northwestern University, 201
Novak, Robert, 248, 249

O'Connor, John, 147
O'Connor, Sandra Day, 142, 146, 165
Office of the Solicitor General, 170
O'Leary, Dennis, 233
Owen, Priscilla, 141, 142
Oxford University, 45

Paruk, Paul J., 150–152
Patient-therapist relationship, 21
Paul, Josh, 119, 121
Pautler, Mark, 65–67
Pay: of federal judges, 134, 137–138; at law firms, 135, 137; of law school deans and professors, 137; of United States' Supreme Court Justices, 134
Peay, Austin, 80
Petra, Jordan, 207–209, 213
Pharmaceutical companies, 34
Physician-patient relationship, 232
Pickering, Charles, 139–140, 145, 148
Pierzynski, A. J., 119–121
Plato, 170
Pluto, 203, 204, 206
Post-surgical infections, 232
Protagorus, 2

Radford University, 95
Rahman, Omar Abdul, 73–76
Read 'Em and Reap, 152
Red River Freethinkers, 198, 201
Redwood, Erik, 167, 168
Redwood v. Dobson, 167, 171
Rehnquist, William, xii, 134, 135, 136, 142, 205

Reinsdorf, Jerry, 121
Resignation of federal judges, 135–136
Restrictive covenants, 224–225
Rittenhouse, David, 206
Roberts, John, 6, 117, 123–124, 125, 126, 142, 165; and 2007 Report on the Federal Judiciary, 134, 137; and testimony before United States Senate Judiciary Committee, 119–120
Robertson, Pat, 200
Roe v. Wade, 123
Ross, Bart, 77
Rovner, Ilana, 170
Rovner, Laura, 198–202
"Runaway" juries, 33, 101
Russert, Tim, 249

Safety Forum, 32
San Francisco Chronicle, xii
Saturday Night Live, 109
Saturn, 206
Scalia, Antonin, xiii, 99, 123, 124, 165, 205, 206; and ethical issues raised by duck hunting trip with Dick Cheney, 127–133; and recusal from cases, 131; and recusal motion filed by Sierra Club, 132–133
Schumer, Charles, 143
Schwarzenegger, Arnold, 40
Scopes, John, 80–81
Scrushy, Richard, 87
Second Amendment, 191
Securities and Exchange Commission, 36–37
Segal, Jeffrey, 242
Shimm, David, 226
Sierra Club, 117, 127; and recusal motion regarding Justice Antonin Scalia, 128–132
Silent World of Doctor and Patient, 233
Simpson, O. J., 87
Smith, Dave, 111
Social Darwinism, 81
Society for Healthcare Epidemiology of America, 232
Sodomy, illegality in nineteenth-century England of, 44
South Street Fund, 61
Spencer, Howard "Buster," 173
Spicer, Wells, 91
"Spilled coffee" case, 33
Spolin, Viola, 104–105, 106, 107
St. James Theater, 46

About the Author

STEVEN LUBET is the Williams Memorial Professor of Law at Northwestern University, where he directs the Fred Bartlit Center for Trial Strategy. He is the author of *Lawyers' Poker: 52 Lessons that Lawyers Can Learn from Card Players* (Oxford University Press, 2006), *Murder in Tombstone: The Forgotten Trial of Wyatt Earp* (Yale University Press, 2005), and *Nothing but the Truth: Why Lawyers Don't, Can't, and Shouldn't Have to Tell the Whole Truth* (New York University Press, 2001). He is also the author of a coursebook, *Modern Trial Advocacy*, now in its third edition (Nita, 2004).